Every Day But Sunday

Jennie F. Copeland

Every Day
But
Sunday

The Romantic Age of New England Industry

Illustrated

Boston, Massachusets

First Edition - 1936
Designed and Printed by
Stephen Day Press

Second Edition - 1956
Printed by The Mansfield Press

Third Edition - 1998
The Mansfield Historical Society and Heritage Books

Fourth Edition - 2005

ISBN: 0-9759737-1-1
PUBLISHED BY BLUE MUSTANG PRESS
www.bluemustangpress.com
Boston, Massachusets

Printed in the United States of America

DEDICATED

TO

THE TOWN OF MANSFIELD

AND

THE PEOPLE IN IT

Miss Jennie Freeman Copeland

That her works as beloved author and historian, loyal townsman and devout churchman, may live forever in the high esteem in which she was held throughout a rich and useful life.

Born in Mansfield April 14, 1879
Died in Mansfield September 28, 1956

Foreword

Today's Mansfield residents have become accustomed to living in a typically modern and active suburb at the dawn of the 21st century. However, Jennie Copeland's *Every Day But Sunday* takes the reader back to a different era in Mansfield. Originally published in 1936, this local classic provides a look at "Our Town" as it was in the industrial age of the 19th century. Miss Copeland's book provides a detailed and readable account of Mansfield's diverse industries, which included bog iron, coal mining, machine shops and foundries. She also tells of the many goods produced in the town, such as tacks and nails, straw bonnets, baskets, cranberries, cutlery, and jewelry. An entire chapter is dedicated to the importance of the railroad, which today's reader will consider an interesting link to the Mansfield we know now.

Every Day But Sunday is not merely about Mansfield's industry in days of old. It also provides fascinating descriptions of daily small-town life in another era. Miss Copeland portrays facets of life that were vital in Mansfield at the time, like choral societies, brass bands, lectures, military companies, horse racing, and torchlight parades.

Jennie Copeland's portrait of "Our Town" is an accurate and romantic look at Mansfield in the industrial age. Mansfield is fortunate to have had the prolific Jennie Copeland call the town her home for 77 years. Born in Mansfield in 1879, Jennie Copeland was locally educated and attended Mount Holyoke College. Throughout her long and productive life she never lost her passion for researching the history of the town she loved. In addition to *Every Day But Sunday,* Miss Copeland authored a series of well-known articles titled *Mansfield in Other Days*. Originally published in the *Mansfield News* during the 1920's and 1930's, the series of essays offered a look at a wide range of topics from the town's past. Jennie Copeland was also the founder and first president of the Mansfield Historical Society, and donated her home at 53 Rumford Avenue as a permanent headquarters for the society upon her death in 1956.

Today's reader will feel the affection that Jennie Copeland had for her hometown of Mansfield, Massachusetts. Now in its fourth printing, *Every Day But Sunday* remains a romantic and enjoyable portrait of the small industrial town that Mansfield once was. It is with great pleasure Mansfield Historical Society presents this fourth edition printing of *Every Day But Sunday*. It is our hope that you will find this publication a most pleasurable reading experience. Mansfield has undergone remarkable change since it was the "Our Town" described by Jennie Copeland in the pages that follow, but time has not diminished the relevance and enjoyment of the story that is told.

Andrew Todesco
Secretary
Mansfield Historical Society
April 2005

CONTENTS

ILLUSTRATIONS

CHAPTER ONE

Beginnings and Bog Iron

THIS is a true story of work and play in a small New England town. It is both the story of Yankee individualism, and a record of the romantic beginnings and early development of industry in America. The narrative centers in one town, which is called Our Town. It might as well be your town, for its story is typical of that which might be told of many New England communities in the nineteenth century.

In reality it is Mansfield, Massachusetts, a town in the uppermost part of the County of Bristol, leaning against Norfolk County. Its northern edge had always been a boundary line: first between the Wampanoag and Massachusetts Indians, then the demarcation of the towns of Plymouth and Dorchester, or, in other words, of the Plymouth and Massachusetts Bay Colonies.

When the selectmen perambulate the bounds they walk with the town fathers of Foxboro on the north, on the east with the selectmen of Easton, on the south with Nortonians, and on the west with men of Attleboro.

The town is nearly a parallelogram, longest from east to west. It covers twelve thousand, nine hundred and thirteen acres, on which no hill is visible. Three small rivers running from the north, furnished nineteenth century water power. Its inhabitants at the beginning of the eighteenth century were Englishmen, who came either from the environs of Boston, or from Taunton, which once included Our Town.

You may never have heard of Mansfield. On the surface it is so dull that nobody has ever bothered to write its history. The Indians and white men found nothing in it over which to fight, nor did it attract British soldiers. Washington never came this

1

way to find a bed.   No belle of Our Town ever danced with
Lafayette.   No poet or scientist was born here.   No capitalist
made his millions here.   No nationally known crime has occurred within its borders.

There are yellowed documents, however, which disclose
exciting facts beneath the surface of this ordinary town; and
stories of its past have been kept alive by word of mouth.   Together these reveal the pulsating life of a plain people—the
kind God made so plentiful, because, as the philosopher has
said, God seemed to like that kind.

The early settlers were so occupied with clearing their land
for homesteads that they had little interest in establishing any
outside industry.   They, however, received encouragement to
start a grist mill.   In 1684, when there were at the most but two
settlers here, the proprietors of the Taunton North Purchase
voted them "between twenty and thirty acres in some convenient place for a mill."   Nothing further was done about this
until March, 1714, when twelve acres were granted to John
Hall and Josiah Pratt, "provided they set up a grist mill and
have it going so as to make meal on or before the first day of
May in the year 1717, and there keep a mill in good repair, fit
to make meal from time to time forever."   John and Josiah appear to have been in no hurry, and the time was extended
two years.   By April, 1719, the mill was going.   Once started, it
ground its meal for years, and even after it ceased, a handful of
grist was ground yearly as tribute for the grant, until the mill
fell or was torn down.

As the settlement grew, other small grist mills came into existence.   Men raised a little more beef, or corn, or cured more
hides than they could use themselves, and sold the surplus.

The first industry in the community, systematically carried
on and involving capital and labor, was the traffic in bog iron.
This form of iron was found in low places where it had washed

over the sand and rocks and had precipitated into solid formation as the water evaporated. Bog iron yielded 25% to 50% iron ore to the depth of two feet in the ponds. With tongs, one man could gather two tons a day. In the low places of the forests it was easily dug. Shallow trenches seen in the woods today show where the work was done. A new crop was produced in about twenty years. Bog iron contained phosphorus and impurities which greatly impaired its qualities for producing strong iron. On the other hand, the phosphorus gave an excellent surface with clean edges and lines. Because it was easily accessible and easily converted into usable iron it was highly prized by the colonists who were able to dig it. They used it to manufacture cooking utensils, farm implements, and firearms.

Bar iron was used as a medium of exchange during periods of scarcity of money. While Andros was governor of Massachusetts it was as valuable as gold.

One old letter reads: "So pray pay to Joseph Crosman one hundred of iron as money." Mr. Crosman's pockets must have bulged. Likewise the minister and the school master received their pay in iron. It was also used to buy an ox. Rev. Samuel Danforth, the fourth minister of Taunton, paid his "servant mayd" with iron.

The discovery of bog iron in considerable quantities in Our Town played no small part in the settlement in the east section. The mention of iron ore on the land there appears in many of the oldest deeds. One writer has declared that the prosperity of America was founded in iron and pork.

The iron industry here was started by the Leonards. From the time the first iron works were set up on the Saugus River in Lynn, in 1643, when Henry and James Leonard came over from Pontypool, Wales, to work in them, the name of Leonard has been associated with iron. James Leonard, on the discovery of iron ore in Taunton, was invited to move there, and did so in 1652. Within a quarter of a century his sons were taking up claims and buying iron ore land in the surrounding country and making agreements whereby they had a right to dig ore on any man's land by paying the owner "one shilling a tun for every tun of iron ore they shall dig."

By 1700 one of James Leonard's grandsons, Major George Leonard, had become a very wealthy man and owned a large forge in one part of Norton and much ore-bearing land in another part of Norton that later was set off as Our Town. He died in 1715, leaving no full grown child.

His widow, Anna Leonard, was a woman of unusual courage and ability. She had borne her husband ten children, and several months after his death a posthumus child came into the world. Nothing daunted by the situation in which she found herself, she continued to run the forge. As the years went by she bought land wherever iron ore was to be found. Her son, Ephraim, was ten years old at the time of his father's death. By the time he was twenty-one she had annexed many acres to the property that his father had willed to him in the Norton North Precinct (Our Town) and built him a house and a forge. Here began the first real industry of Our Town.

Ephraim Leonard became the most important man of the town. He gathered the ore from a radius of more than a mile, north and south. An old map of Foxboro shows "Linard's mine" over the line in that town. He bought ore from his neighbors, he held town offices, he was influential in the church, he became a colonel in the Colonial Wars, he was appointed judge in 1747 and held the office until the Revolutionary War. He hobnobbed with gentility of Boston, among them Governor Hutchinson. Had Ephraim Leonard lived two hundred and fifty years later he would have been termed a capitalist.

At the time that he did live there was no banking system in the province and very little hard money available. The government issued paper money for a short time, but in 1740 withdrew it from circulation. Therefore a Land Bank, a private institution, was originated in Boston as a means of issuing paper currency, called bills of credit. Any man needing money was urged to become a partner and secure his share by mortgaging his land. Eventually the scheme drew into its clutches eight hundred and sixty-three partners, four hundred of whom belonged in Boston, with the rest, mostly plebeian owners of small estates, scattered within a hundred miles of the provincial capital. Each member was to pay three per cent on the money and one fifth on the principal, yearly. The payment might be in bills or in products and manufactories, at such rates as the directors might set from time to time. Consequently, the project was given the name of Manufactory Scheme and the private individuals at the head of it, Directors of the Manufacturing Company.

The tender of commodities as payment was not new. Twenty years before, the men of Our Town paid their taxes in "Shingles, Clabords, pine-boards, Rey, Indin Corn, wheat, oats, beaf, pork, butter and chese." To such a list was now added "mechanable hemp, flax, cordage, bar iron, linen, tanned leather, flaxseed, bees' wax, bayberry wax, nails, tallow," and similar things.

Ephraim Leonard's brother, Judge Leonard, the leading man of Norton, was one of the seven directors of the Manufacturing Company, and Ephraim was a partner. Such was the respect given the financial standing of the Leonards that doubtless their influence led John Caswell and his brother, Jedidiah, to become partners of the new scheme.

John Caswell's share was thirty pounds on the principal and four shillings, three pense as interest and costs. To cover this he seems to have mortgaged fifty-five acres. This transaction took place in June, 1740. The very next month, Governor Belcher issued a proclamation cautioning the people not to receive or pass notes of the company. This, or something else, frightened John Caswell. In September he sold his share to the directors for seventy-five pounds, "in bills of credit called manufacturer's bills." This, however, as proved later, did not relieve him from all his troubles.

In spite of the fact that the governor of the province repeatedly issued warnings and caused the directors of the scheme to be removed from any official position they might be holding in the province (George Leonard was deprived of his place as Judge of the Court of Common Pleas), and even dissolved the Legislature which upheld the Land Bank, the system continued to hold favor.

Finally, in March, 1741, England took a hand. Parliament declared that the Act 6 of George I, Chapter 18, (1720) prohibiting bills of credit by private corporations in England, "did, does, and shall extend to her colonies and plantations in America." This fell like a thunder bolt upon the bank. The bank was thereby dissolved and the holders of its bills were given the right of action against every director or partner for the recovery of their money. Some of the partners were for defying the law. The directors were wise enough to throw themselves upon the mercy of the General Court.

The matter was not easily smoothed out. People in no way connected with the Land Bank very much resented the interference of England. Mobs threatened to invade Boston. They continued to honor manufactory bills, and even as late as Nov. 23, 1741, Our Town "voted, that the maneyfactery-bills shall pay ye town's charge this year."

George Leonard, as one of the directors, suffered heavily. Seventeen years after he had issued a declaration that he had burned all bills as they came in, had destroyed the plates and had not struck off any bills since the act of Parliament, and after he had paid all assessments, even seven hundred and forty-three pounds, eight shillings and seven pence of lawful money claimed by James Otis, of Boston, he was petitioning the General Court for the redemption of the bills, as the Court had promised. Part of the estate of Samuel Adams of Boston, another director, was advertised to be sold at public auction on August 24, 1758, to satisfy the bank creditors. A week from that date, however, his son and heir, Samuel Adams, the Revolutionary patriot to be, stopped the proceedings by protesting that it was illegal.

The small land holders, who had been partners, suffered even more. Many lost their entire property. Although John Caswell of Our Town apparently stepped out of it early, in September, 1764, he issued a "warrant of distress" to the General Court stating that his petitions had not been satisfied.

How much Ephraim Leonard suffered as a partner of the Land Bank does not appear. His military and civic offices receive more attention in existing records. Both he and John Caswell won honors in the French and Indian Wars, one as colonel and the other as lieutenant.

Alas! Colonel Leonard's glory led but to the grave. His forge at his death was given up. There was no kinsman left to run it. Though the colonel had four, possibly five wives, he had but one child, a son, who developed into a brilliant lawyer, but who unfortunately, through his acquaintance with Governor Hutchinson and others in Boston, and possibly influenced by his uncle George's unhappy Land Bank connection, became an ardent Tory and was driven from America, never to return, and his property confiscated by the State. The aged Leonard's last days were spent alone, except for his faithful slaves. No more were Leonards connected with the iron industry in Our Town, though through several generations iron ores on the land were reserved for Ephraim Leonard's heirs. His brother, George, having survived his Land Bank troubles, had all that he could do conducting his forge, or bloomery, in Norton, and running for Congress (he was a member of the first, third and fourth Congresses of the United States) without taking over the forge in Our Town after the death of Ephraim.

Even before Ephraim Leonard's death another forge had been started in Our Town. With iron in such abundance competition was to be expected. Already there was a forge over the line in Stoughtonham, and another in Easton. That second forge in Our Town was built in 1765, by ten men in various walks of life; two of them were styled "gentlemen," one was a bricklayer, one a physician, and the others, yeomen. They selected a spot on the Canoe River, a mile north of Ephraim Leonard's, near the Stoughtonham line, and agreed to build the forge, to equip it fully with tools, to build a "Cole" barn, a dwelling house, a dam on the river, and whatever bridges, gates, and dykes should be necessary. Their legal agreement covered every contingency that might arise. Dr. Sweeting was chosen clerk and apparently along with his medical practice was to superintend the building and stocking of the furnace. Most of the land had come from Dr. Sweeting. He reserved for his own use the water not needed for the furnace, and if the company should fail, the land was to go back to him. Samuel Wild, one of the so-called "gentlemen," was to build the forge at his own cost and also bear one eight of the other expenses. Without doubt he was the largest stockholder. The others had quarter, eighth and sixteenth parts.

The company was short lived. Like many a later business enterprise the men put in their money, got the buildings up and equipped, and then something went wrong. In this case it seems to have been the fault of "Gentleman" Samuel Wild, who had promised so much. In a year and six months he was sued by bricklayer Waley Sullard for forty-three pounds, nineteen shillings, and two pence damage, besides the cost of the case. This amount was Wild's right in the furnace. Shortly the company was dissolved, and several of the men started furnaces in other towns. So far as is known this furnace lay idle several years.

The Revolutionary War brought a need for firearms. Here was a comparatively new plant well situated near the Stoughtonham furnace that was making guns for the continental soldiers. In some way French merchants in Boston heard of it and arrived on the scene.

Pierre Aldolph, Pierre Joseph Lion, and Alexander Dauby, all "of old France," according to the deed, bought fifty acres of land, the dwelling house, and the "Mansfield Furnace" with all its rights and privileges. This was in 1779, at the time of inflated currency. They paid two thousand pounds. The same month, Pierre Adolph with Francois Dalet, another French merchant of Boston, bought adjoining land. Adolph and Dauby moved here, but Dalet had so little interest in the venture that sixteen months later he sold to another Frenchman. Such was the instability of currency that the fifteen acres for which Dalet had paid 3000 pounds in September, 1779, sold in January, 1781, for 8,250 pounds.

From now on for a few years there was business activity among the Frenchmen. Not content with owning the Mansfield Furnace, they bought the Stoughtonham Furnace over the line and enlarged the company to six members. One of the new partners was a Frenchman, named Barbathean, owner of the La Mahandiere sugar plantation on the island of Guadeloupe, in the West Indies. He, it seems, owed Franesque Moufle Goss, another owner of the Mansfield Furnace, 60,000 Tournois Livres, and settled this debt by giving Goss as security his sixth part share in the Mansfield and Stoughtonham furnaces. Gradually one after another of the Frenchmen withdrew until only Dauby and Aldolph were left. Aldolph had more or less trouble with law suits and by 1785 his only remaining possessions were a house, a garden, and twelve acres of land. These he sold and then moved away, leaving Alexander Dauby the only Frenchman in town. Soon after Dauby's arrival he had married a local girl, who bore him eight children. With her he remained to die and be buried among her people.

A half century passed before industry brought in other foreigners, and a century before there were more than a few individuals with a foreign tongue in Our Town. The waters of the Canoe River never again furnished power for iron casting. From 1750 on, bog iron was found less and less in the swamps and forests until it practically disappeared. This caused rolling mills to secure pig iron. Not for more than fifty years was another furnace started anywhere in Our Town.

CHAPTER TWO

Tacks and Nails

THE TURN of the century found Our Town without a manufacturing plant of any kind. There may have been half a dozen mills where meal was ground or lumber sawed. Each was probably a one man, or at most, a family affair, where neighbors brought their corn, rye, and logs, and paid for the work, quite likely, with beef, pork, hides, homespun cloth, homemade shoes, or handmade nails.

Nails became increasingly important as material for barter. In nearly every farmhouse there was a corner where nails and tacks were hammered out by hand. Men spent their evenings and stormy days in such work. The process was long and tedious, and for many years the entire operation was handwork. Later came the cutting machine to cut the rods. Even after that, the heads and points had to be hammered by hand. By working hard, a man could produce two thousand tacks a day. Many of the farmers bartered their nails at Solomon Pratt's store for West India goods, which were chiefly rum, molasses, and spices. Pratt took the nails over the road to Providence and brought back raw cotton for his mills. That, however, is aside from this story.

The labor of nail making was greatly reduced when, in 1790, Jacob Perkins of Newburyport, Massachusetts, invented a slitting and heading machine. Mr. Perkins had served his apprenticeship with a goldsmith, and in 1789 he had made dies for the copper coinage of Massachusetts. From 1790 to 1800 thirty-four patents were granted for machines used in the process of making nails, and by 1828 there were one hundred and twenty-one such patents. The use of machinery greatly increased the manufacture of tacks and nails, and by

1810 nail rods comprised twenty-five per cent of the total output of iron in this country.

Certainly the tack and nail manufacture was the coming industry in 1800, and Simeon White of Our Town got into it. He was a middle-aged man, who had served in the Revolutionary War. He had a son, Simeon, who also was interested in the business. There is a family tradition that Simeon White was the first manufacturer of tacks on a large scale in this country.

For some years after the establishment of Simeon White's nail and tack factory, farmers continued to finish nails in their homes. Many of them got the cut rods from Simeon Snow, who had a cutting mill on the Canoe River where Ephraim Leonard had his forge, or from John Williams, who had a cutting mill on the Wading River in the west part. After heading and pointing the nails by hand they bartered them as formerly at Pratt's store. Other farmers did business with the Newton Iron Works Company in Newton. One of the principal men of that company was Robert Fuller, who had grown up in Our Town. When Robert was a boy his mother had married Micah Allen of Our Town and had come here to live. Robert, though in early manhood he left town and became prosperous in Newton, never lost his interest here.

An old paper left by one of our farmers shows that farmers were regularly carrying on transactions with the Newton Iron Works, through Robert Fuller, during 1814-1817. An item for Jan. 15, 1814, which is typical of them all, reads:

	Bot. of Newton Iron Works	
9 Bundles Nail Rods	4—2—00 @ 30	27—00
Reffuse Rods	0—3—00 @ 27	3—37
Nail Bands	0—3—00 @ 30	2—99
To 1 pattent Silk Hat		6—50
		————
		39—86

Cd
By 1 Cask 10 Wrought Nails 278 @ 12   33—36
By 1 Keg 8 Wrought Nails   42 @ 15   6—30
By Cash in full   20
                                         ———
                                         39—86

Simeon White and Micah Allen were both ardent Baptists and, lacking a Baptist meetinghouse in Our Town, they both traveled to Foxboro to meeting. Considering that denominational relation, it is quite probable that Simeon White's son should have done business with Micah Allen's step-son in Newton and bought his nail rods there, though we have no proof.

By 1814 Simeon White Jr. was deeply interested in the business, if not the sole proprietor. He had married, been a soldier in the War of 1812, and had settled down. From now on, the Simeon we speak of is the younger man.

Simeon White built two fair sized mills, a green one on the left hand side of the road, and a red one on the right. The red mill was operated by water power, while the green one had, in addition, an engine and boiler which could be used when the water power gave out. In these two mills he made a high grade of tacks and nails for the shoe trade. Later, carpet tacks were manufactured.

Simeon had ten children, seven of whom were boys. All of his boys, with the exception of the oldest and the youngest, were at sometime connected with the business. Charles, the oldest was a farmer; Gardner, the youngest, went west, perhaps attracted by the California gold. He did not remain long in California, but went to Carson City, Nevada, where for many years he was the postmaster.

Not only did Mr. White's sons work in the mill, but also his neighbors' sons, and in later years, his granddaughters and other girls, "papered" the tacks; that is, they attended to the boxing and packing.

Some of the tacks and shoe nails were undoubtedly used in the local trade, for there were a number of shoemakers in town, but most of the merchandise was shipped to Boston. Before the days of the railroad it was put in a great covered wagon that looked, judging from an old drawing, like a prairie schooner, and the load was drawn to Boston by four bob-tailed horses. Tack plate was brought back. In later years the same wagon took the goods to the train at East Foxboro. In 1845, the Whites were making seventy-five tons of tacks and nails. Ten years later their business amounted to one hundred and fifty tons, valued at $21,000.

Besides iron nails, part of the Whites' products were zinc nails, made from zinc brought from the Norton Copper Works.

Simeon White was looked upon as one of our wealthiest men. An inventory of his estate reveals that at the time of his death he was worth $11,044, which shows the value of a dollar, and what constituted wealth in Our Town, in 1844. The importance of Simeon White and his sons is shown by the fact that the section where they lived was known as Whiteville, and still bears that name long after the last White has left.

The business, which Simeon White's sons continued after their father's death, prospered until the epoch of big combines began. The biggest of these in the tack industry was the Field Tack Company of Taunton. This firm was started, in 1827, by Albert Field, when he was thirty-one years old. It has been said that he learned the tack business of the Whites, but that is hearsay. At any rate, he started in Taunton with two machines and one room. He enlarged and kept on enlarging his business. With his own guimp tacks he drove out of the American market the English clout nails. When his sons grew up he took them into the business and it became A. Field & Sons Nail and Tack Works. In 1860, it became the Taunton Tack Company, operated by A. Field and Sons, and was doing a $370,000 business. In 1891 it became part of the Atlas Tack Co. of Taunton.

Such was the company with which the Whites had to compete. It was about the time that Mr. Field's firm took the name of Taunton Tack Company, in the 1860's, that Mr. Field approached the Whites, suggesting a merger. The Whites headed by Franklin, who was perhaps somewhat headstrong, refused to combine. Today we know what it means to hold out against a trust. They did not, until they tried to buy tack plate and found that the tack combination had so cornered the market that they could get no plate, or at least not at a price that was not prohibitive. There was no alternative; the Whites had to give up business in 1868. They simply stopped work. In after years one could see through the windows the tacks lying where they were cut, and boxes partly filled.

A little while before the Whites were forced to close their shop there was another tack business started. In fact, in 1865, there were two others listed. The only one of these two that we know about was the one at the south end of the town on the Rumford River, near the site of the first gristmill. The man who started this tack factory was Marcus Tolley Tollero Cicero Richmond Rounds, simply Marcus R. Rounds for business purposes. One of the Whites of Whiteville came to work for him. Mr. Rounds gave up tack making at the same time, and for the same reason, that the Whites did.

Even while making tacks, the Whites used their mills for other kinds of work. At the red mill they used the power for sawing wood. All the men in the neighborhood brought their wood to be sawed, especially on a holiday, when they had a regular sawing-bee. In the green mill birch hoops were made.

An even more surprising line was carried on at the green mill. One would hardly expect to find sausage making in a tack mill, but such was the case. At the proper time of year the farmers brought their meat to be ground and run through the sausage filler into the skins, or bags.

After the debacle of the tack industry the green mill was used from time to time for other purposes. For a good many years William Moorehouse made awls there. At one time Simeon White's grandson used it to make horn jewelry. But never, after 1868, were any tacks or nails made in Our Town.

CHAPTER THREE

Cotton Factories

OUR TOWN was not slow to start manufacturing cotton after the strained commercial relations with England, following the *Embargo Act* of 1807, and the *Non-Intercourse* Act of 1809, limited the importation of cotton thread and cotton cloth. In 1810, the Mansfield Cotton Manufacturing Company was formed. That was just twenty years after the first cotton mill, in which perfected machinery was used, had been built by Samuel Slater in Pawtucket, R. I. Several mills were soon built around Pawtucket, and Samuel Slater was financially and actively interested in many of them.

It was but natural, with a real demand for manufactured cotton and with the successful Slater mills so near at hand, that ambitious men should turn their money into building cotton factories. Taunton men built one in 1806; Attleboro had a mill in 1809. These were included in the seventeen cotton mills listed around Providence. By 1810, there were fifty-four cotton mills of the Slater type in Massachusetts.

In was in that year that fifteen men, one half of them local people, formed a company with a capital of $16,000, divided into thirty-two shares of $500 each. The mill was built in the center of the town on the Rumford River. David Gilbert, who had owned the land, and Solomon Pratt, who for twelve years had been running the only store in town, and who had been trading in nails and other products brought in by the farmers; each took eight shares. Most of the others took two shares each. The method of financing was patterned after what was called the Providence System, which differed from what was known as the Lowell System in that a few stockholders held all the shares. Under the Lowell System the merchants did not sink a great deal of their own money, but distributed the stocks widely, a few small shares to a person.

In many other ways there was a sharp cleavage between the process and practices of Lowell and those carried on around Providence. Lowell had developed some American machinery, and debarred Providence from using it. The Providence group, having started with Arkwright machines built by Mr. Slater after models that he mentally brought over from England (actual models would never have been allowed to leave England), clung tenaciously to British methods. Lowell built fewer and larger mills. Providence mills were smaller and more numerous. The Providence output stood for quality; the output of Lowell for quantity.

The Mansfield Cotton Manufacturing Company built a mill 60 x 32 feet, two stories high, with a gambrel roof. Eight dormer windows on each side made the attic available for extra space. They began with two spinning frames and a spinning mule.

The business was spinning, twisting, and manufacturing cotton yarn. The operation of the machinery was simple, and most of the work was done by women and children. Five sevenths to six sevenths of the cotton mill operations everywhere were done that way. The pay was small. The average wage paid to cotton mill workers, and we suppose that included the men, women, and children, from 1820 to 1830, was forty-four cents a day. In the decade from 1830 to 1840, it had increased to ninety cents, and from 1850 to 1860, it had become $1.03. A day was twelve to fourteen hours, according to the season. In the winter, it was eleven to twelve hours with no time out for breakfast. At other times of the year, thirty minutes were allowed for breakfast and thirty to thirty-five minutes for dinner. Mealtimes were considered a part of the operative's day.

In 1842, a petition, bearing three thousand names from Fall

River, Mansfield, New Bedford, Attleboro, and Newburyport, was sent to the legislature asking for labor laws and their enforcement. That same year another petition was sent from Fall River regarding fewer hours for children. A law had been passed in 1836 requiring that children under fifteen years should receive three months' schooling before being allowed to work. This, according to Horace Mann's report, in 1840, did not meet with great favor, and was not generally obeyed. Reasons given for this disfavor and disobedience were the Puritan dislike of idleness and a regard for other people's morals. Operators contended that "the morals of the operatives will necessarily suffer if longer absent from the wholesome discipline of factory life, and leaving them to their liberty."

As a result of the Fall River petition an act was passed in February, 1842, making it the duty of the school committee in each town in the state to prosecute all breaches of the Act regarding child labor passed in 1836, and also making it illegal to employ a child under twelve years of age more than ten hours in any one day. A fine of fifty dollars was set for each offence.

It was not until the late 1840's that there was any sign of reduction of labor hours for adults.

Notwithstanding the long hours and small pay, there never was any difficulty in getting labor. Women hailed the cotton factories as liberators from economic slavery.

Boarding houses were almost a part of every mill. And at every mill where the Providence System prevailed, at least part of the pay was in commodities at the company store, which was equipped along with the mill. The Mansfield Manufacturing Company voted, in May, 1811, to "carry on a business of merchandize in both West India and Dry Goods."

Besides building the mill, a store, and a boarding house the Mansfield Cotton Manufacturing Company erected an additional small building 25 x 18, half a story high, for storing cotton. In the main factory building a place was set off for a bed, so that, as a precaution against fire, there would be someone in the building to go from room to room, every night at ten o'clock.

Five years after the company was formed, a dividend of one hundred dollars on each share was declared. In gold? Ah, no. It was to be paid, either in cotton goods at wholesale prices, or in dry goods out of the company store, as the owners of the shares desired, "within one year, as the agent of the company may find it convenient."

There appears to have been a Mansfield Dye Company, which did the dyeing for the cotton company. As this was years before the introduction of aniline dyes, the colors must have been produced from purely vegetable extracts.

On the third of February, 1819, it was voted that the directors of the Company purchase of the Mansfield Dye Company their real estate in Mansfield, if it could be obtained at a reasonable price. If not, to prepare materials and build a dye house. Just how they got their dye house does not appear, but they got one, for:

In 1821, the company, at one of its business meetings, which, according to vote, were held in the factory boarding house, "voted to lease Dye House and apparattus for Colouring yarns 13 months from the first day of March next, the Saw Mill, Dwelling House, which Seth Smith now occupies, and the Blacksmith shop for one year from the first day of April next for the sum of $125 to any person of respectability who shall engage to pay said company said sum in one year from said 1st day of April, the person who improves said premises is to have the benefit of the Dyer and the Dye stuffs now on hand in said Dye House."

By 1822, the financial affairs of the company were in bad shape. Early in January of that year they voted to sell all the real estate and machinery of the company for $8000. That included the factory, tools, blacksmith shop, and dye house. Six weeks later, they thought better and reconsidered the vote. Then they decided to run the mill and voted that the proprietors bind themselves to each other to pay their proportion of debts.

A little over a year later, Captain Seth Talbot of Dighton paid $150 to exonerate himself from possible debts of the company. Captain Seth knew what he was about.

The next year, 1823, the company decided that weaving would be more remunerative than spinning and voted to exchange two spinning frames, two or three cards, a twisting machine, a roller engine, a cutting machine, and a fluting engine for a loom and apparatus for weaving. They also voted to borrow one thousand dollars.

One year later the stockholders were assessed $250 a share.

The change from spinning to weaving seemed to have proved a good thing, for, in 1828, the company voted to buy more looms and apparatus, and to put them in as soon as possible.

As we look over their records we find two kinds of agents at the mill; one, who was superintendent of the operatives, and another, who was responsible for the purchase of everything from the many "broom corn brooms" and bobbin baskets required in the mill to pantaloons and velvet belts for the store. Moreover, the second agent conducted the company store, the boarding house, and in some cases hired the help.

Some items from the account books of the agents of the Mansfield Cotton Manufacturing Company show the diversity of their activities, and give an insight into the lives of the workers in 1822-23. We find that the two Dunham brothers, young men in their twenties, sold everything from codfish at four pence a pound to half a piece of "crape" at $5.13. A pair of shoes were $1.00, some even as high as $1.33, boots were

$3.00, a man's hat $2.50, a vest .75, sugar 13 cents a pound, 14 pounds of "flower" .67, potatoes 20 cents a bushel, a skein of thread 8 cents.

The Dunhams record a contract made with Asa Pond. By the agreement Pond was to *Bord the help that C. and A. Dunham shall hire to worke for them and Bord the men for Eight shillings per week and the girls for one Dollar per week. The said pond Doth have one half the house where Jonathan Cobb now lives and garden that belongs to that part. The said pond doth agree to have all the provisions of C. and A. Dunham at cash prices that he shall want fore one yeare from April the 1st 1822.*

Other agreements were entered into, viz.:

Between C. and A. Dunham on the one part and Obidiah Eldridge on the other part. Dundam and Comp doth agree to pay the said Eldridge thirteen dollars per month and Do agree to pay the Children of Sd. Eldridge thirty Six shillings to Commence the first of April 1822."

Mamd of agreement Between C. and A. Dunham and John Briggs. We do agree to pay the said Briggs thirteen Dollars and seventy five cents per month and said Briggs doth agree to work fore said Dunhams the space of twenty four months to commence the furst of April 1822."

Mamd of an agreement between Amasa Pratt and C. and A. Dunham we do agree to pay said Pratt Eighteen Dollars per month for one year and give him Training days and town meeting days gratis.

The said Pratt doth agree to work in the Blacksmith Shop the space of one yeare for Eighteen Dollars per month and find his tools with those in the shop. This made at Mansfield this first day of April in the year of 1822.

We pause over the Bickner girls. On June 23, 1822, Margaret was paid $10.92 cash, and credited $10.67 for thirty-two days' work. Eliza was given credit for $10.92 for thirty-two and three quarters days' work. There must have been a death in the family the next month, for each takes out of her credit $5.13 for half a piece of "crape." Perhaps they inherited something; the next month they are reckless and each invests in a twenty-five cent velvet belt and a pair of gloves. Margaret's gloves cost forty-two cents. Eliza gets along with twenty-four cent ones. The next balancing of the Bickner's account came on Sept. 24. Eliza was then credited with $14.57 for work from June 21 to Sept. 1, forty-three and three quarters days. Out of that was taken $7.30 to pay her board. Margaret's account was about the same. The next month Eliza had on account a pair of lamps at fifty cents and Margaret got twenty-five cents worth of oil. Apparently a dollar a week board did not include lights. Eliza got reckless again and took a yard and a half of ribbon, at thirty-seven cents a yard, on credit.

The Bickner girls made more money than Mrs. Johnson; for fifteen and one half days' work she was credited with only three dollars and seventy-five cents.

Another family of interest is Nancy Freeman and what appears to be her son, Philo. Philo seems to have worked, though the book does not say how much he received. Nevertheless, Nancy had to buy him his hat and vest, get his shoes tapped and pay his board. Moreover, she had to get credit for cash for that spendthrift son (we hope Philo was not her husband) to the amount of thirteen cents one time and twenty-six cents another. Nancy herself liked to spend. All on one account she got a piece of "crape" for five dollars, a pair of shoes for a dollar and another pair for a dollar and a quarter (perhaps for Philo), a velvet belt, a handkerchief, a pair of "hows" at fifty-eight cents, and worsted "hose" at seventy-five cents, a "bonet" at a dollar and a half, four yards of "cambrick," six yards of "calaco," and seven yards of "Bumbast." After all that she had to have cash for Margaret Bickner. Probably Nancy had borrowed it of Margaret and this was to pay her back. At another time Nancy got "9 sheets of riting paper."

That old book gives some surprising revelations of the good old days. George Freeman had to have a quart of rum when he went to Providence, and Dexter Whiting was paid for half a day's work on Sunday.

And where did the Dunhams get their provisions to sell? Well, Mrs. Cobb sold them butter at sixteen cents a pound, and also cheese. William Copeland sold "Orzey and Charles Dunham 29½ pounds of salt poark for $3.60." Fanny Bates was paid one dollar and eighty-three cents for cutting and making pantaloons.

There was much more in the book, but who cares if they did pay a dollar for "fetching 2 bales of cotton from Providence," or buy for Peter Coffin eighteen bales of cotton to spin?

Luther Cobb was the agent to run the mill in 1823 and here follows his contract:

Mansfield, Jany 2, 1823.

It is this day agreed between the Mansfield Cotton Mg. Company and Luther Cobb that the said Luther run the Company's Cotton Mill until the first day of April next, the said Company to keep said Luther constantly supplyed with good Cotton, the waste on the Cotton limited at twelve per cent and said Luther is to spin such numbers of yarn as the agent of Co. shall direct from No. 7 to No. 17 both inclusive and deliver the same to said agent whenever requested, and the said company to hereby agree to pay said Luther seven and a half mills per skein for making, doing up in square bunches and papering said yarn, said company to find paper and twine. Said Luther is to keep the Mill neat and clean at all times, and every part of the work is to be done in a neat and workmanlike manner and said Cobb is to take proper care of the Machinery in said Mill and to use it in a skillful manner and if said Ma-

chinery should be injured by his carelessness or neglect or any of his workmen he shall be answerable for reasonable damages. And it is further agreed between said parties that said Luther improve the Dwelling House where Johnthan Cobb now lives and the Dwelling House where Capt. O. Eldridge now lives untill the first day of April next for which he is to pay said Company Thirty four Dollars. The said Company aforesaid to have as many cotton bags as is necessary to Bale their yarn in.

(signed) *Elk. Bates for said Co.*
Luther Cobb

Witness Obadiah Eldridge

The Mansfield Cotton Manufacturing Company continued for years, the stockholders changing from time to time until, by 1841, Solomon Pratt, the "Cotton King" of Our Town held all the shares. From then until the time of his death, in 1848, Mr. Pratt ran the business alone. After his death his sons ran it for a short time, then sold to Charles Morse of Easton, who bought the property for $5,500. Mr. Morse continued the manufacture of thread under the old firm name. In 1859, Mr. Morse died and after that very little cotton business was carried on at that mill. It soon became a jewelry shop.

Four months after the Mansfield Cotton Manufacturing Company was formed in 1810, another group of men got together and formed another company. The site they chose was where Ephraim Leonard, years before, had had his forge, and near the nail-cutting mill of Simeon Snow. Most of the men interested lived nearby. The others, with one exception, lived not far away, in Norton, or Easton. The one exception was Solomon Pratt, at the center, who had shares in the newly formed Mansfield Cotton Manufacturing Company.

This second company bought land and a water privilege "sufficient to drive eight hundred spindles and all the water necessary to carry the same for the purpose of spinning cotton and woolen yarn." The company was called the Union Cotton and Wool Manufacturing Company. At this time cotton mills were springing up everywhere, but comparatively few factories in eastern Massachusetts and Rhode Island were spinning wool.

In the eighteen twenties, when the Mansfield Cotton Manufacturing Company was having its difficulties, the Union Company was having hard times. Shareholders withdrew; there were mortgages, and what not. Finally, in 1831, there was a complete change. Boston men, headed by Elbridge Gerry, as president, became the principal owners.

Mr. Gerry in all probability was the son of Governor Elbridge Gerry, who had died in the office of Vice-President of the United States, in 1814, and from whose redistricting plan in Massachusetts, the term Gerrymandering had arisen. Governor Gerry's widow, Mrs. Ann Gerry, was doubtless the same "Ann Gerry, widow," who owned land and buildings in Our Town in 1831. That being the case, we like to think that she came here to live and that her unmarried son, Elbridge Gerry, president of the Union Factory Company, spent some of his time with her. The Gerrys would have given distinction to any community. Mrs. Ann Gerry before her marriage had moved in the best New York society, and as wife of a Massachusetts governor and vice-president of the United States, enjoyed acquaintance with the best people of Boston and Washington. The diary of Elbridge Gerry Jr. gives a delightful picture of his travels by horseback from Boston to Pittsburgh, into Virginia, and to Washington where he was frequently entertained by Dolly Madison at the White House.

While Elbridge Gerry was president of the company, in 1836, the partners, still spinning cotton and wool, changed the firm name, and it was incorporated as the East Mansfield Manufacturing Company. Elbridge Gerry was a little later succeeded by his brother, James T. Gerry of Boston, as president of the company.

Again, in 1844, there was another change of ownership, perhaps by mortgage sale. At this time David Hartwell came to run the mill. As there is no record of a sale to him, we may conclude that he leased it. For years it was known as Hartwell's mill and the school in that district was named for him.

Living in East Mansfield with David Hartwell was his brother, Frank Hartwell, remembered as a phrenologist, going about feeling of people's heads, and informing them of their characteristics. David Hartwell's children consisted of one boy, John, and four girls, some if not all of them, born in Our Town.

Of the daughters, Kate remained and married here; the others went to Washington. Kate's husband was Howard Perkins, one of the mill owners before Mr. Hartwell came.

Mary Hartwell had a romance before she left here. While she was teaching school her lover, Edward Seele, a lawyer, was critically ill and sent for her. By his death bed she was married to him. Later she married Henry Bennett of Fall River. Their married life was spent in Washington, at one time living in the house formerly owned by General Grant.

Emma Hartwell also had a love affair here. That, however, was broken off before she went to Washington. At the National Capital she held an important position for forty years with the Treasury Department.

Helen Hartwell, at birth registered as Ellen, followed the others to Washington, where she became an artist of note. Her art education was perfected in Paris under the direction of William Adolph Bougeureau. One of her paintings received a gold medal in Washington, and was in the Cocoran Gallery in that city, and now hangs in Mansfield's Library.

All of the daughters of David Hartwell, as well as himself and his wife, are buried in Our Town.

Mr. Hartwell probably ran the mill for twenty years, then came another change. This time Smith Gray of Walpole, M. D.

Ross of Boston, John Pearce of Roxbury, and Howard Perkins bought three acres of land, the factory, two houses, and the water privilege for $3400. Three years later these men sold the same property for $6750 to Stephen Sibley of Chelsea. Mr. Sibley never came here to live, but continued to run the mill, now concerned solely with the manufacture of thread, until it burned in 1868.

Nobody knows the cause of the fire at the mill. One forenoon, when everybody was at work, there was an explosion in the cotton in the room where Lyman Francis was at work at the picking machine. Although terribly burned about the hands and face by the flames that immediately flared up in the cotton, he rushed to the floor above and helped the girls and women out of the burning building. Somebody hurried to the schoolhouse across the street and the school bell rang out the alarm. It was too late, the bomb, or whatever it was that had caused the explosion, had done its work. The mill was never rebuilt.

One year after the Mansfield Cotton Manufacturing Company built their mill, and ten months after the company was formed in the east part, the Rumford Manufacturing Company was formed to build a mill at the south end of the town on the Rumford River. Eleven men made up this company, chief among whom was Solomon Pratt, already mentioned as a principal owner in the other two companies. With the exception of two, all the men of the company belonged in Our Town. One of the heaviest owners, Phinehas Gline, formerly of Westmoreland, New Hampshire, had not lived here long. Phinehas was a wanderer. At the age of twenty-four he had arrived here, calling himself a "trader," and had bought a forty acre farm. That was in 1811. Two years later, when the cotton company was forming, he took five shares. More cautious men took three, and many ventured but one.

On the property which the company bought there was an

old gristmill, perhaps the very one that John Hall and Josiah Pratt had built one hundred years before, when they were granted the land by the proprietors of the Taunton North Purchase. At any rate this was the site. There were also on the twenty-two acres of land acquired, two dwelling houses and a blacksmith shop. The price was $3062.

During the first years, thread was doubtless the only product. Very few mills made cloth in the beginning. The thread, after being spun at the mill, was put out into homes to be woven into cloth. Women in their homes also picked over cotton waste at five cents a pound.

In the 1830's, cloth was made at this mill, but much happened before that.

Everything seemed to go well for a time, though there was some sale and exchange of shares. Gline added to his stock, sold his house and bought another nearer the mill. He doubtless was the agent of the factory. The next thing we know, Gline had sold his shares in the company and was in Plattsburg, N. Y. All was not well at the mill. That was in 1820, just about the time things were going wrong at the other mills in town.

We might expect that a third mill going wrong would be more than Solomon Pratt could stand. On the contrary, he finally got the whole of this Rumford River Cotton Company into his own hands.

In 1830, the mill burned, and with the mill all the machinery and six thousand dollars worth of stock, all uninsured. The dauntless Pratt immediately rebuilt and filled the new factory with looms and other machinery from Taunton. It was said that the year that the building was completed he made enough to pay for both building and equipment.

Mr. Pratt carried on the business here until the time of his death. It was then sold to Marcus Rounds for the manufacture of tacks, and after Mr. Rounds' time was used for making coffin trimmings, jewelry, and later screw drivers and glass.

While Mr. Rounds had the mill it burned and was rebuilt. In 1917, it again burned.

During the cotton mill days the women in this neighborhood were so quarrelsome among themselves that the locality was nicknamed "Sodom," and the name has held to this day.

Solomon Pratt must have had some idea of his limitations, for, in 1814, when the Mansfield North Manufacturing Company was formed, he kept out of it. Except for two men from Providence, most of the shareholders lived in the vicinity of the factory, which was on the Canoe River at the northern border of the town, where the Mansfield Furnace had been at the time of the Revolutionary War.

The shareholders,—we almost said men, which would not do at all, for lo, "Fanny Copeland, single woman," was a shareholder among the rest,—had their difficulties. They laid their troubles to the agent, Arunah Copeland, Fanny's brother. In ten articles they set forth why he had proved unworthy of the trust imposed on him.

To begin with he was negligent and inattentive in getting their weaving done when they had a ton of yarn on hand. Then he neglected to settle with a man in Taunton until sued, and thereby the company "lost above 30 dollars."

He did not arrive at the company's store "to do their business until about 10 o'clock in the winter and 8 o'clock A.M. in the Summer, generally."

He charged up "almost every day when he did no business of any consequence for the company."

He was "not firm and substantial in his bargains," and thus left room for dispute.

He bought "thirty hundred Georgia unland cotton, which took more water to card."

Added to these there were four complaints about the way he kept his books. He had to go.

Not only did Arunah lose his job, but the matter was taken

to the circuit court and there, March, 1818, the rest of the shareholders recovered judgment against him for $230.20. Added to that were costs of suit fees, etc., making the whole amount to $245.78. The property of the poor man was seized and he left town.

Right away the company went to pieces. Solomon Pratt had kept out of it entirely, except that he and his brother-in-law, Elkanah Bates, acted as appraisers of the property. It was sold at auction to the lowest bidder.

Through a century the factory passed from one to another, and during that time in it were manufactured satinette, cotton batting, bicarbonate of soda, even ebony piano keys. Finally, in 1919, the Water Department of the town bought the property for protection to its water supply, and tore down the old building.

In 1814, there were, as we have shown, four cotton mills in Our Town; two in the east part on the Canoe River, and two in the central part on the Rumford River. Within a few years, two more were built, in the west part on the Wading River.

The first of the West Mansfield factories was built by Robert Skinner, a year or more before his death, in 1816. After he died it was carried on by his sons, Herbert and Welcome. Part of the mill was let for wool carding. This was more or less a family affair, with shares in the hands of brothers and sisters until 1837, when they sold to three Hale brothers from Providence, one of whom was brother-in-law to the Skinners.

In 1842, the Hales sold to three Smith brothers of Providence. Included in the sale was the machinery, such as shafting, one picker, one self-acting mule, five spinning frames, one clips speeder, three brakes, one drawing frame, one spooler, one warper, one cloth press, eighteen looms, four hundred pounds of cotton, twelve pounds of cotton yarn, and four hundred yards of cotton cloth. For this they paid two thousand dollars down and gave a mortgage for eight hundred.

Up to 1865, the factory was known as the Hale Mill. By that time it was in the hands of one of the Smith brothers, who that year gave it to his son, Charles M. Smith. A month after Charles received it, he sold to James M. Sayles, another Providence man, for $8000.

This mill was run longer than any other cotton mill in Our Town. More or less work was done there until 1871, when the mill was burned. A gristmill, which also served as a sawmill, was later built on the site.

When Robert Skinner built his mill, John Williams, less than a mile up the river, was successfully running two mills; one for cutting nails, and the other for sawing lumber and grinding meal. In 1820, or perhaps a little earlier, Mr. Williams sold the nail shop and that part of the water privilege to his sons, Marcus, Rufus, and John. There the young men put up a cotton factory. Having no experience in setting up machinery, they hired David White of Easton to come here to do that for them. Mr. White made his patterns from wood and, after casting the parts in brass, set up the machinery in brass and got the mill going.

The Williams brothers at their factory employed about forty hands making cotton cloth and thread, which was carried over the road to Providence. The factory was run by some member of the Williams family until 1850, when the main building was burned. Neither the company store, nor the picker house was destroyed and those were afterwards converted into residences. The factory site was later used for a knife factory.

Having called attention to the attitude toward education and mill work for children that existed everywhere in the eighteen twenties and thirties, it is interesting to pause over the Williams family. As in every other mill, small children worked fourteen hours a day in their factory, but the Williams family had some regard for schooling. Rufus was bereft early of his wife and two infant children. A few years later, in 1826, he died and by his will left one thousand dollars to the school district where he was born and brought up. The money was to support the summer school (there were then two terms a year) and was to include "all scholars living in the vicinity of the Williams Mills on the west side of the river as far as the house owned by David White." This was the Quaker neighborhood and the Williams family were Quakers. Mr. Williams stipulated that the school be taught by a female. "It is my desire that the school mistress be a woman of such exemplary, sober, moral conduct as to teach the scholars good manners without hat or knee service and that the agent appointed to procure a teacher do not first enquire the cheapness, but the ability and worth of the person."

Marcus Williams had five children. One died in early womanhood. Of the others, the only son became a practicing physician in Maine, as did two of the girls; that is, one practiced in Maine and the other elsewhere; the fourth daughter studied law, but died before she could be admitted to the bar. Rather remarkable for girls in those days.

Adeline, especially, carved a place for herself in the world. She was born in 1835. When she was twenty-five she began the study of medicine in the New England Female Medical College in Boston. Of course no men's college would then admit women to any of its courses. Consequently this small institution was started for the few women who chose to become pioneers among women in the medical profession. Miss Williams remained two years, then, in 1863, under Unitarian auspices, she went to North Carolina to teach in a school for free negroes. After more than a year of teaching in the south she returned to her medical studies, this time in New York city, where she completed her course and graduated from the Medical College for Women. She commenced her work as a homeopathic physician in her native town. One who knew her then, said, "She was a plaguy good looking girl." She stayed here several years, then moved to Minnesota, where her influence in the work of women in her profession was marked. After ten years she longed for the east and returned to Boston for a year. Next she toured Europe for a year with the original Fiske Jubilee Singers. On her return from across the water she again went to Minnesota. Once more, in February, 1880, she returned east. This time she settled in Worcester, where she practiced until her health gave out. Her last days were spent in Augusta, Maine, presumably with her sister, Nancy. She died in Augusta in 1890.

In 1832, when there were six cotton mills running in Our Town, a seventh was built here. This was the sole property of Solomon Pratt and his brother-in-law, Elkanah Bates. They built on the Rumford River, on which river at that time Solomon Pratt already had two mills that he was financing practically alone.

What sort of man was this Solomon Pratt? He is said to have been tall and commanding in appearance and dictatorial in conversation. One of his contemporaries said of him that if he were to walk down Broadway in New York city, people would turn to look at him. Mr. Pratt had his thumb on all the business in the center. He ran the only store in town before the mill stores were built. He collected straw braid and straw bonnets and paid for them in goods; likewise he gathered in handmade nails. These commodities he carted to Providence where they were sent by schooner to New York. On the return trip from Providence the wagons brought back raw cotton for the mills and goods for his store. He was the local magistrate, and town banker. In short, Squire Pratt was the whole thing.

For their new venture Pratt and Bates had to build a large pond as well as a mill, mill houses, and a large factory boarding house, which was later dubbed by the frightened Irish families who moved from there on account of supernatural noises, "Castle Thunder." In the mill, the company made cotton cloth for fifteen years with apparent success. In 1847, Mr. Bates died and Mr. Pratt died the next year. Mr. Pratt's heirs tried to run the mill, but in 1850, the mill burned. With so much cotton waste around, it was the inevitable end of most cotton factories.

The fire of the Pratt and Bates factory was on the morning of town meeting day, a typical March one, with a high wind, but notwithstanding, circumstances were favorable. With all the male population assembled a few rods distant, certainly more immediate help was available than could possibly have been gathered under any other conditions. The schoolmaster of district No. 5 dismissed school and took the older boys to help fight the fire. With nothing but buckets to work with it was impossible to save the mill. The fire fighters confined their efforts to saving the nearby buildings, the small house opposite, and the large house just referred to as Castle Thunder. Carpets were secured from somewhere and spread upon the roofs. Those were kept soaked with water. Thus the fire was confined to the factory, which was burned flat.

The next year Robert McMoran and Robert Fulton bought the property and built a knife shop.

In none of the seven cotton factories was a great deal of money made. Even Mr. Pratt, who seemed to have such a fine grasp of the business, left very little money at his death.

Elkanah Bates had been a little more careful with his money. What is more, his son, Benjamin, gained valuable knowledge in the Pratt and Bates factory and went from here to Lewiston, Maine, where he was most successful as a mill owner. His gift of $75,000 to a small Maine College caused the institution to change its name to Bates College. At least that much good came from the cotton mills of Our Town.

CHAPTER FOUR

The Romance of the Straw Bonnet

WOMAN'S PRIDE and woman's ingenuity laid the foundation for one of the great industries of this country. The making of straw headgear in America was probably the only business of the women, for the women, and by the women in the early nineteenth century. Men may complain that women have invaded their realm of business, but in this case it was man who entered woman's sphere and shared in her profit and glory.

Somebody made the first bonnet, but who? Read the *"Essay on the Manufacture of Straw Bonnets,"* printed in Providence, Rhode Island, in 1825, and you will feel sure that it was Mrs. Naomi Whipple, wife of Captain John Whipple. Mrs. Whipple as was customary, assisted her husband in his business and was in the habit of receiving a consignment of English straw bonnets from a Providence importer. In 1797 she conceived the idea of making a bonnet. With the help of a neighbor, she unraveled a piece of braid to see how it was done and produced the desired result. She showed other women and soon was employing them to make bonnets, which she not only supplied to her customers, but shipped to New York, where they sold with the imported articles.

·The summer of 1799 saw Providence young ladies going away to boarding school wearing new straw bonnets of their own manufacture. One of these was Sally Richmond, who went to the Wrentham Academy. Sally taught the ladies with whom she boarded the process of braiding straw. The Wrentham women passed the knowledge on to the women in Franklin, the next town. Before many years both towns had entered to a considerable extent into the straw business, doing the work in the homes.

For thirty years Providence believed that Mrs. Whipple was the pioneer woman in straw work. Then a rival came on the scene. Mrs. Betsy Metcalf Baker, at that time seventy years of age, said that it was all a mistake, that she herself, and not Mrs. Whipple, was the one who had made the first bonnet. At the age of twelve she had lived in Providence and almost daily as she passed the Whipple shop gazed longingly upon the straw bonnets displayed in the window. The only way was for her to attain one was to make it. She experimented and succeeded. It was she, she said, who taught Sally Richmond.

The people of Westboro, Massachusetts, put in still another claim. They tell of Betty Fay, the charming daughter of one of the town's leading men. Betty, a leader in an aristocratic circle, resolved, not only to have the finest hope chest, but a dower of hard money. She decided to make bonnets to sell to her friends and to send the surplus to Boston. Staid matrons were shocked; they considered it beneath her social position to engage in the business, yet Betty persisted. When the youngest son of the Whitney family asked her to marry him she told him that her business took all her time and that he would have to wait. He waited three years, then, early in February, 1765, Eli Whitney and Elizabeth Fay were married, and in time became the parents of Eli Whitney, the inventor.

Framingham has its story about the first straw bonnet.

In those days, when cross country communication was lacking, it was possible that bonnets made in Westboro, or Framingham, were not known in Providence.

Within a year or so of the time that Sally Richmond of Providence taught the Wrentham women to braid and sew straw, Betsey Makepeace of Norton went there visiting and learned the art. On her return home she taught her friends. By 1802 the straw business was started in Norton. The making of straw bonnets was never a leading industry there, but a portion of the money that endowed Wheaton Seminary was earned by Laban Wheaton in that manner.

The woman to start the business in Foxboro was Eunice Everett. Foxboro in time became the leading straw town in the country. In 1865, that town was doing a $2,000,000 business that made the name of Foxboro known all over the world wherever women wore hats.

Providence, having given the industry a good start, seemed to drop out of the picture. During the first seventy-five years of the nineteenth century the straw business was located in a few towns southwest of Boston. In the northern part of Massachusetts palm-leaf hats were made. The only place we hear of straw work outside of Massachusetts at that time is Cleveland, Ohio, and it was taken there by a woman from Mansfield, Massachusetts.

In 1817, Jane Pratt Dunham with her husband started west. As they approached the little hamlet that later became Cleveland, they saw a large field of rye. Stopping at a nearby farmhouse, Mr. Dunham told the owner that Mrs. Dunham knew how to braid rye straw, and that there was money in the rye field. Mrs. Dunham, it happened, was the niece of Solomon Pratt, who in Mansfield was making money collecting braid, putting it out to be made into bonnets, and selling the bonnets. She showed the women how to braid, and soon the Dunhams started the business of collecting braid and later making hats. Before long they bought a farm of their own on what is now Euclid Avenue and Mr. Dunham became an innkeeper. After several years, he replaced his log home with a large frame building. The building, long used as a country tavern, is now an art center. It was, however, in the straw business, as we understand it, that he made his money.

In Massachusetts, during the first twenty years of the nineteenth century, the straw business grew rapidly, then began to decline. The chief reason for this was over-production. Bonnets had been sent all over New England and to New York, where they were shipped to the Middle Atlantic and Southern states, until practically every woman had a bonnet. Then rich women again bought imported leghorns, so that they might be distinguished from the wives of less successful men. There seemed no help for the business until the bonnets wore out, or the styles changed.

According to the essay of 1825, to which reference has already been made, this new enterprise among women produced undesirable results. Girls began to feel their independence. Instead of assisting with the house work, spinning and weaving, and doing lighter farm work, they spent their time braiding and sewing straw. They began to disdain the product of the hand loom and were ashamed to be seen spinning. Many girls were growing up in ignorance of knitting and weaving.

The writer of the essay goes on to tell of the bad effect of this new work on the health of the girls. Long hours in a sitting posture without exercise brought on many ills. The girls themselves felt the lack of exercise and to obviate this, and to give them an occasion to wear their new clothes, balls and dancing schools sprang up. To those they wore their thinner dresses instead of homespuns and contracted colds and consumption.

This braiding business affected the men, also. They hated to see the women lose their dependence. Moreover, if the girls were always braiding, the only way for the men to be with them was to braid too, and that had a tendency to make the men effeminate.

Dr. Stanley of Attleboro, Mass., held a similar opinion of the evils of the new industry for girls, and preached on the "Vanity of Straw Bonnets." He said that it fostered a dissolution of character, a sinful luxury, avarice, extravagance, loss of gentility, neglect of duty, a growing passion for balls, and a carelessness as to health and studies. Truly, the young people of that day presented a serious problem.

This pious preacher overlooked the fact that in 1804, by their industry and enterprise, the ladies of the first parish of Wrentham purchased an "elegant organ" by their contribution of straw bonnets, which were sold in Maine. (The agent who disposed of the bonnets in Maine is said to have made "a pretty good spec" above his commission.) In another town the women gave of their braiding until there was one thousand dollars for missionary work among the Indians.

Economists feared that unless the straw bonnet business was stopped there would be a depletion of rye and a famine would follow.

In spite of all those dire predictions, the braiding of straw became a regular industry in practically every home in the towns in southeastern Massachusetts near the Rhode Island line. Most farmers grew rye straw. About the middle of June, before it ripened, the women gathered the best of it into bundles. This they soaked in hot soapy water and left on the grass to dry. When thoroughly dry the straw was cut at the joints into eight to twelve inch sections and made into bundles. The bundles were again put into hot soap suds. Then came the bleaching. In the bottom of a barrel, which had been made air tight, was placed a pan of live coals over which sulphur was sprinkled. Suspended over the sulphur fumes was the wet straw. For the very earliest braid, the straw was used whole, but soon the women devised a small instrument to split the straw. The next process was braiding.

All the women braided; so did the children. By the time the children were ten years old their "stint" was ten yards a day in some families, in others, five yards on school days and fifteen, on days at home; most people had a special homemade rule by which to measure. Aunt Peddie Reed had a more original way of measuring, when she was a girl. She sat by an upstairs window and let her work fall out. When it reached the ground her day's work was done. When one became proficient she could work by touch, and so braid by the light of the open fire, by candle light, or even by the light of the moon. Two girls of Our Town sat up one entire night and braided by the light of the moon, "just for the fun of it."

No. 7, four strands, was the most common braid and in the early days the rate of pay for making that was from two, to two and a half cents a yard. For the very fine braid, from three to four cents were paid. By 1852, braid brought from five to fourteen cents a yard. In the earliest days the pay was usually in commodities, rather than cash. It was to the local store like Solomon Pratt's in Our Town, or to some store within driving distance, that the braid was taken. The storekeeper then put the braid out to other women to make into bonnets. The same women seldom both braided and sewed, as some were more expert in one process than the other.

It was not long before men began to seize the opportunity of increasing and enlarging the industry. Solomon Pratt was the man in Our Town who gathered in the straw and paid for it in goods from his store. He began this about 1820, when he was so active in the cotton industry. Like other straw agents, he opened up regular routes and sent out men on circuits, covering thirty miles around, to gather up braid, distribute it, and bring in the made bonnets. Routes overlapped, but that made no difference. Foxboro agents came to Mansfield and went to Norton, Easton and Taunton. Mansfield agents went to Norton, Easton, Taunton ,and miles beyond.

The position of a bonnet merchant was held next in honor to the professions. Indeed, the idea of gentility was so inseparably connected with the business that many entered into it for the position, and, because of lack of preparation or experience, failed financially. Our Town. however, was fortunate in having a man of business ability undertake it. The story was vouched for by one of Solomon Pratt's agents that at one time Mr. Pratt accumulated enough straw for 15,000 bonnets, and that there was a profit of two dollars on each bonnet.

Agents of Mr. Pratt's time, and later, began their trips just after Thanksgiving and made their calls at intervals of two weeks until May or June. Some of these trips consumed the whole two weeks. From house to house they went, collecting the skeins of braid, fifty to one hundred yards to a skein. To other women they carried the braid, thread, sheets of cloth numbers, and blocks on which to shape the bonnets.

The first blocks were literally whittled out of wood. As women then did not demand "one-of-a-kind" bonnets, one block might last a whole season, or even longer. Only as the style changed was the block changed. Small shops were set up for making bonnet blocks. Our Town never had a shop set apart for that distinct purpose, but the neighboring town of Foxboro had at least two. Later, plaster of Paris blocks were introduced and were made in the bonnet factories by men who were still called whittlers.

Some of the earliest agents, who went out with the blocks and straw, went on foot with great packs on their backs; more went on horseback with a pair of bags, or panniers, thrown over the horse.

Even in those far off days there was a conflict of Capital and Labor. An old poem, of 1848, tells the story.

> A maiden by the window sat—
>   'Twas late in the afternoon—
> The straw-man was passing through the gate
>   He had just gone out of the room.
>
> A pile of Florence was by the door
>   And a pattern bonnet near,
> Some tickets and thread lay on the floor
>   And a plaster block in the chair.

The next three stanzas, which we omit, tell how sad the maiden was.

> And so they've cut our wages down
>   A three-pence on a piece;
> And now they are riding round the town
>   As merry as they please.
>
> They think it is but three small pence
>   They've taken from our pay;
> But a three-pence equals four red cents
>   And that's eight cents a day.
>
> Eight cents a day is forty-eight,
>   And four half cents is fifty.
> There's half a dollar vanished straight
>   To make the straw-man thrifty.

Three more stanzas of lament and then:

> There are just as many stitches to take,
>   And many yards to sew;
> My fingers as many bonnets must make
>   But to another the money will go!
>
> I still must eat and drink the same,
>   And rest my weary eyes;
> It costs as much to clothe my frame,
>   But another will have the supplies.

The reader is spared the harrowing details of the last sixteen lines.

Though Solomon Pratt was the first straw goods merchant in Our Town, John Rogers was the real father of the straw bonnet industry, or perhaps we had better say that the mother of the industry was Eliza Ann Rogers, his wife, who abetted him and ever urged him on. Before his marriage, in 1833, he had been a likable, easy-going young man, without a great deal of ready cash in his pocket at any one time. Full of energy and vim herself, Mrs. Rogers directed her husband's capabilities into business lines.

In 1836, Mr. Rogers began his straw business in a small way in a single room of a private residence. The work of braiding and sewing was all done in the homes until about 1848, when he began having a few women come to sew for him in the front room of his own house. The bulk of the sewing was still done outside. Busy homemakers could really accomplish much sewing at intervals during the day and evenings. Little girls were initiated into the art of bonnet making by being taught to sew the crowns. Boys, and girls too young to sew, filled cushions full of threaded needles. A cent a hundred was good pay in homes where that service had a cash value.

From the star, Mr. Rogers' business kept increasing. His early market was New Bedford and Providence, later he shipped to New York. Before 1850 he had outgrown his front-room quarters and about that time built a factory directly back of his house, where he employed many girls and some men. In the 1880's that building was greatly enlarged, and more men and girls were employed.

The "girls" of the straw shop ranged from sedate (?) little maidens of eleven or twelve to grandmothers of eighty and over. Mrs. Hannah Ingraham was nearly four-score years before she quit, and Mrs. Louisiana Stewart worked until she was over eighty, or as long as she could totter across the street from her house. Mrs. Stewart it was who contended that they were all girls just as long as they worked there. For some that meant working for thirty, forty, and even for forty-five years. The girls were from many of the best families in town.

By no means did all the girls belong in town. A very large proportion of them came from Maine. The Maine girls boarded here during the winter and returned to their homes in the spring. For a while they carried out that plan, until one after another met some man of Our Town who disapproved of the homeward journey and suggested Our Town as a permanent abode. The home folks in Maine must have thought that the straw shop had a matrimonial bureau connected with it.

The building never boasted a punch clock and the girls came and went as they pleased. Some of them came at surprisingly early hours. Mrs. Hannah Ingraham wanted to leave early, that is five-o'clock in the afternoon, and came at five in the morning, in order to get in a good day's work. Doors were seldom locked. Little Abbie Deane across the street used to run in at daybreak. Sometimes she would find herself alone and sometimes there were others there early to work with her.

Girls of eleven and twelve worked during school vacations, and vacations were longer then than now. The pay of the girls was not excessive—two fifths of a cent for wiring a hat, and for both lining and wiring, one whole cent. Mrs. Rogers kept the count and looked after the pay. The girls thought that she doted on fractions. They hated fractions and, not wishing to be bothered, managed to make the work come out so that it would be even cents. Small as two fifths of a cent may seem, those little girls often earned fifty dollars in a season and out of that bought their clothes. That was in the 1860's.

Though they were wage earners they were still children and sometimes fooled and giggled. Mrs. Rogers, in her soft-soled shoes, would steal up to them and reprove them. She, however, allowed them to talk and tell stories. One girl in particular told stories so well that the others took turns wiring a hat for her that she might give her whole attention to recounting some thrilling tale that she had read in the *"New York Ledger."*

The desire to hear stories and the love of fun was not confined to the children. Emma Brintnall, the boss of the sewing room, after she had given out the straw, used to sit down and read novels aloud while the girls worked. At times the young minister, the Rev. Jacob Ide of the Congregational Church, came in and read to the girls. When no one was reading there was a constant chatter. The straw shop was a grand place to gather news.

Working on straw seemed to foster attributes that made desirable wives. Statistics of the marriages are a proof. Moreover, somebody felt so deeply on the subject that he wrote a poem of one hundred and sixty lines entitled "The Straw Shop Girl."

> If ever in strains poetic
> > I sing the praises of woman,
> To show how the angelic
> > Is blended with the human,
> I'll never go for a sample
> > To the city's giddy whirl,
> But step into the Straw Shop,
> > And take a sewing girl.

.   .   .   .

> From quiet homes of comfort
> > From all along the strand
> They come, with souls determined
> > To earn what'er they can,
> And get a pile of money
> > Before they get a man.

> From early morn 'til twilight
> > And often later still,
> Through Spring and Autumn changes,
> > And Winter drear and chill,
> They line and crimp, and pucker,
> > Ticket, wire, and trim,
> And try to keep up courage
> > Though the pay is rather slim;

They ache, and sweat, and shiver
    Shiver, cough, and ache,
And it costs so much for bees wax,
    A thread will often break,
Alexis, Kirkwood, Wayelet,
    Cecil and Saratoga,
Rough and Ready, and Shoo Fly,
    The styles I can't name over,
And it takes more brains to make them
    Than most of them will cover.

O! the dread initiations
    Of strangers in the shop,
And the idle criticisms
    The careless ones will drop:
She is not very pretty!
    How stiff she walks, I'm sure!
I hope she dresses funny!
    Her father must be poor!
But these are only trifles,
    To give amusement merely,
When all get well acquainted
    They love each other dearly.

Such petty tribulations
    Are soon forgotten, quite,
But not the heartless comments
    Outsiders circulate.
I've heard the poor mechanic,
    And often silly fops,
Speak sneeringly of women
    Because they work in shops.
Yet, in all our cities
    One cannot fail to see
Men occupying places
    Where women ought to be.
If men are really better,
    What is the difference, pray?

Both work in shops together
    Because they need the pay.
No shame, nor yet dishonor,
    Can rise from one's condition,
But rather in the manner
    Men slight their occupation.

.   .   .   .

The Straw Girl goes to meeting
    On a pleasant Sunday night
Takes the seat that's offered,
    Supposing all is right;
She looks uncommon pretty
    Is richly dressed, perhaps,
And excites the admiration
    Of all the nice young chaps;
They wink at one another,
    Put on a foreign air,
And if she blushes deeply,
    Turn half around and stare;
A lady just behind her,
    In gorgeous crinoline,
Thinks she looks as she feels,
    A thing almost divine;
Who's that in front, I wonder?
    The proud lips scornful curl—
No one of any consequence,
    Only a Straw Shop Girl!
And when the meeting's over,
    The young gents throng the door
In solid lines of battle,
    At least four ranks or more.
From sidewalk down to sidewalk
    In beautiful array;
With slurs for every gentleman
    More fortunate than they,

They give the sweetest glances,
    The mustache an extra twirl,
In hopes to make an impression
    And pick up a Straw Shop Girl.
But she isn't so easily captured
    As many may suppose;
Don't always judge a gentleman,
    By his mustache or his clothes,
She may accept your company
    Go with you to the ball,
And when you think you've got her,
    You haven't after all.
Not that she's coquettish
    Or wants to fool a man,
Only plays off a little
    As women always can;
Only a little policy
    They have to simply prove
Whether a fellow is honest
    And how much he's in love.

Love is a wonderful passion,
    It makes or mars us all;
By love we walk with angels,
    By love the angels fall.
And when I pass the Straw Shop,
    In sun or moonlight gleams,
If ever I should discover
    The angel of my dreams,
And both are much delighted
    Each other there to see,
But to hitch for life together
    We cannot quite agree;
I know, in my sober musings,
    Away from the giddy whirl,
My soul will be the better
    For loving a Straw Shop Girl.

There were dull days in the business. Some weeks there were hours when the girls had to wait for material. They were prepared for just such emergencies. Mrs. Peddie Reed always had her patchwork by her, some had crocheting, and others needlework. All sorts of ideas and patterns in fancywork were exchanged, also suggestions, for homemade Christmas presents. No wonder lifelong friendships were formed in the straw shop.

When the building was new and Mr. Rogers was active in the affairs of town and church, the building served more than one purpose. A room on the top floor was used as a meeting place for the order of Masons, then newly organized in Our Town. In later years, after the Masons had moved to more spacious quarters, this room, a place of mystery with its peculiar arrangement, became a dumping place, and was called the Mason's Attic.

The main floor was sometimes converted into a place for entertainment by the ladies of the Congregational Church, or a Christmas tree for the Sunday school of the same church.

On occasions in later years there were feasts in the straw shop. These came at no set time and with no regularity. Such a dinner might take place in any month of the straw shop season, when business was not too driving, yet not every year. It seems to have been a spontaneous affair, and exclusive. When the girls in the wiring hall had a party, the girls in the sewing room, or the machine room were kept out, unless it was to look in on the decorations. It was the same way when the reeling room girls had their party. Each room was a little sisterhood by itself, when it came to social affairs.

One can imagine the talk and preparation that preceded a room dinner. The place was most elaborately decorated with festoons of colored paper streamers, flags, or bunting. The table was cleared of all work and over it spread a fine cloth. Best dishes were brought from home. A bouquet of flowers and dishes of fruit garnished the festive board, and such food! It made one's mouth water to hear about it. A complete turkey dinner, with none of the fixings omitted. They even had candy at the end. When all was in readiness, just before they ate, they usually had a photographer come in to take a picture of the bountiful table and another picture of the girls seated ready to eat. Those old pictures show happy groups of motherly women with a little young blood mixed in. Prominent in the pictures there was always one man, Elwin Carpenter, superintendent of the girls, and promoter of the dinner. The girls, of course, wore the fashionable dress of the time. Every one of them had discarded her practical working apron and had put on a big, white, starched apron, such as any well-dressed woman in Our Town wore in her home, when she sat down in the afternoon.

Even during working hours a little fun was sandwiched in. April Fool's Day was one of the red letter days on their calendar. Such antics! None who worked there at the time will forget Eva Hardon with a box on her back, assuming the role of hand-organ man, followed by the monkey, Emma Gardner, a tiny woman, deformed in body, but not in spirit. In and out among the workers they went, amid roars of laughter.

Sometimes, when business was a little dull, the younger people went on rambles. Once a large group celebrated May Day by a morning walk. Led by William Graves, the young superintendent, they started out all on a morning fair, the lads and the lasses of Rogers' Bonnet Shop. Mr. Graves' fancy brought them to the unromantic East Foxboro railway station. There, on the station platform, they had a May Day dance, minus the maypole. In the midst of the frolic the Boston train pulled in, and at the wild suggestion of "let's go," they climbed aboard.

Sometimes little things that the girls did casually had quite unexpected results. One morning during the Spanish-American War, just after Hobson's victory, a quartet was singing patriotic songs as they worked. John W. Rogers, one of the owners, happened in. He waited until the song was finished and then gave three cheers. Someone produced a small flag and stuck it in a spool to keep it upright. Thereupon the thought was born that the Straw Shop should have a big flag. Funds were collected, a flag was bought, and a flagpole erected. When all was in readiness the entire force assembled in the yard for the flag raising with the proper ceremony.

All these stories may give the impression that the girls did little hard, or regular work. They did work hard, and in the best days of the business, say in the eighties and nineties, earned at piece work as much as six dollars a day in the height of the season. Six dollars then had a good purchasing power. Even in the days of braiding and sewing in the homes the women worked steadily and produced results. Many a woman with her housework, and three or four small children to look after, earned a hundred dollars in the winter sewing straw at sixty-two and a half cents a bonnet. Think of making thirty-six hats of fine straw in eight days. It was done, though it meant sitting up until midnight. One woman in Wrentham earned two farms sewing straw.

The many stories told about the girls does not mean that the men in the business were unimportant, or uninteresting. Men designed the headgear, made the bonnet blocks, bleached the straw and the finished hats, did the sizing, dyed the braid, pressed the hats or bonnets, inspected them, packed them, and shipped them.

To enumerate the steps takes little time, but often the process was complicated. For example, straw and hats, after being bleached had to be dried. To do this the product was placed on racks in the yard back of the shop. What straw could not be spread there was hung over the fences along the street.

Imagine a sudden windstorm! For a few minutes men and boys had a busy time chasing rolling hats and flying braid.

Now the sizing. Starch was the earliest sizing used. Later that was replaced with glue. The sizing man seemed to ooze glue; it dripped from his finger tips, it was all over his clothes, it stuck to his watch, his glasses were smeared with it.

When the bonnets had received the proper amount of sizing they were sent to the pin-blockers in the attic. Sometime, after bonnets gave way to hats, pin-blocking was given up, and hats were blocked in the basement (Hell's Kitchen) on electrically heated forms.

Out of the blocking room into the press room went the women's headgear. When bonnets were in style the work was done by machinery by handflatters. Later hydraulic presses were introduced and the handflatters became pressmen. Curt Brown pressed, by one method or the other, for fifty years. He was an expert and was paid accordingly, ten hours a day, at twenty-five cents an hour.

When sewing machines were introduced, about 1880, a machinist was hired to look after the machines.

About the time the new addition was put on the shop, in the early eighties, the firm introduced a new department for making felt hats. This gave the men all the year round work; straw, from about Thanksgiving time until late spring, and felt in the summer and early fall. The felt cones, made elsewhere, were brought here to be shaped.

The story is told that at one time Mr. Rogers went to Fall River to see a man, named Marshall, who was in the cone business. Mr. Marshall was not very gracious when he showed the samples, until Mr. Rogers gave him an initial order for fifteen thousand dozen. Twice that season Mr. Rogers' firm duplicated that order.

It is said that one year the men in the firm (this was after John Rogers had died and when his son John W., and a partner ran the business) each cleared fifty thousand dollars from straw and felt goods.

The hats made in our town had a wonderful reputation. It has been said that none better were made anywhere in the world. Some of those made of the finest imported braid brought from twelve to eighteen dollars apiece from milliners. The factory price for the best velvet hats was ninety-six dollars a dozen.

Mrs. Jennie Rogers loved to tell the story of the hat that her husband, John W. Rogers, bought her in Boston. She asked him for a chip hat just after he had shipped the last one. Mr. Rogers was an indulgent husband and said she should have one though they would have to go to Boston to get it. They went to an exclusive store and were shown just what she wanted. The price seemed rather excessive and Mr. Rogers remarked on it. The saleswoman assured him that it was an imported hat and therefore costly. Mr. Rogers turned back the inside band and discovered his own number. He said nothing, but paid exactly ten times what he had sold it for at wholesale. The saleswoman was right; he had sold two hundred thousand such hats for the Paris trade and some of them had been returned to this country—"imported."

In the early days, when work in the shop lasted only during the winter and early spring months some men found occupation by going out on the road with bonnets to sell. Many of these were seconds from the shop, or bonnets that were slightly out of style, and were disposed of in the back country places by selling them from house to house, Yankee peddler fashion. The first John Rogers himself used to make such trips down on Cape Cod. In 1840 Lloyd Allen and Avery Dunham went into Maine. These were contrasting characters; Lloyd Allen, short, round and pink-cheeked; Avery Dunham, tall and spare. Avery it was who probably did the most talking and joking; Lloyd was the keen observer and gave the most accurate report of the trip when they got back.

Sam Tolman, a handflatter, and incidentally a practical joker, was perhaps the truest Yankee peddler. In the spring, he started off on foot with two big boxes, 3 x 2½ x 2, one under each arm. The bonnets of that period were so small and light that he could carry a supply to last a couple of weeks. If the stock did not hold out, he used the last as samples and took orders. One of his most profitable fields was Martha's Vineyard. There the women had little chance to learn what was being worn on the mainland, and less opportunity to buy when they did hear the style news. In this way Tolman's visits were a real boon, for he always told them just what women were wearing and how to wear it. One year, when the bonnets were flat and the size of small saucers, he told the island women that it was the fashion that year for a woman to wear two, one on the front of the head and one on back over the bob, or in the speech of today, bun. Consequently, every customer bought two. How he laughed over it when he got back to Our Town!

There was another story he told with much glee. On this occasion he was coming up from Cape Cod. At night he stopped, as was his custom, at a farmhouse, and asked if he might have lodging with meals. He proffered a bonnet in payment.

"I don't want your bonnet," the woman said emphatically, though she allowed him to come in for the night.

In the morning he told her that he wished to pay her. He opened his pocketbook and took out a handful of paper script, the currency of the time. Out of the five-, ten-, and twenty-five-cent bills, he selected a fifty-cent bill. Upon his return home he told of the transaction and burst out laughing when he came to the bill episode.

"I'd been trying to get rid of that for a year, but they said it was counterfeit. I can't go to her house again. She don't want my bonnets and I don't believe she wants my money."

We do not have to go away from the shop to find something to laugh about. There was the handy man about the shop, who did odd jobs when the men were at work and after they had gone home. He was not paid high wages and was allowed to keep his own time sheet, which was seldom questioned, until one day he handed in, "One day, 25 hours." Asked how he could get twenty-five hours in one day, he replied,

"Why, I worked the noon hour."

Then there was "Doc" ————, the dye-house helper, who maintained that his father, over in Ireland, had been able to cure rheumatism, and that he had the same power. Elwin Carpenter took him up. The bargain was on. Elwin Carpenter was to be given a dog, if he secured a patient, and the patient was to pay five dollars, if cured. Mr. Carpenter brought in an old man from West Mansfield, and summoned the "doctor" from the dye-house.

"Sure, Oi'll cure him. Wait till I get me a pair of new socks."

With difficulty they got the old man upstairs. The doctor laid the patient face down on the floor and after putting on the new socks began running up and down the man's back. When the man was allowed to get up he thought that maybe he did feel a little better and managed to hobble away, with instructions to come back for further treatment, but he never came. The "doctor" became anxious for his money and went to West Mansfield to see his patient. He came home as poor as he went.

"Begorra," he complained, "Ye niver tould me he'd fallen off a roof and had a broken back."

In the meantime Carpenter had received the dog, the dog had chewed up the clothes on Mrs. Carpenter's clothes-line and had run away, never to be seen again.

About 1867, another straw shop was started in Our Town by Charles H. Mowry, a straw worker from Upton, Massachusetts.   Mr. Mowry used the building, which was formerly the Union Store and hall, at the north end of the town, perhaps a mile from the Rogers' shop.   He hired half a dozen girls to sew, wire, and line the hats.   The pressing and dyeing he did himself.   At the Rogers' factory Charles Mowry had a brother George, variously known as "Little Mowry" and "Stub Mowry," because he had to have a platform on which to stand to reach his bleaching tub.   After bleaching all day for Rogers, "Little Mowry" spent his evening bleaching for his brother. After a time, George left Rogers and the two brothers went into partnership.   They then took on a few more girls.

The girls here had a good time, just as they did at the other shop.   "Just like going to a party every day," said one of the girls on the way to work.   The shop was situated next to a side track in the railroad yard.   Some of the girls carried on flirtations with the trainmen.   Now and then the girls had a pie from Mrs. Mowry's Aunt Avildia's kitchen on the floor below the workroom,   Not that Aunt Avildia voluntarily sent up the pies, but one of the boys used to wheedle her into giving them one, when he went down stairs for water on baking days.   The young people had keen noses and timed their water trips by the smell.

The hats that the Mowrys made were sold mostly in Boston, but if any woman in town wanted a hat she could get it there and Mrs. Mowry would trim it in the latest style.

Very soon after the brothers formed a partnership they developed another line, which in time became the most important.   This was bleaching, pressing, and dyeing hats and bonnets for out-of-town firms.   New hats were thus treated, and old hats reblocked and pressed.   The re-pressing was done by hand flats.   For the new hats they had a machine, called a bumper, for pressing.

After the Mowry brothers had been at work about ten years, their building burned. That ended their straw business.

As for the latter end of the Rogers' business: John Rogers ran it until 1865, or 1866, then retired, leaving the plant in the hands of his son, John W. Rogers. After a time J. Frank Comey of Foxboro came into the company and the firm became Comey and Company. Mr. Rogers ran the Mansfield factory, and Mr. Comey the New York office. Both men grew old in the business. Mr. Rogers had no children; Mr. Comey's children were not interested. The day came when neither man wanted the responsibility of continuing the business. Mr. Comey withdrew first, in 1914. Mr. Rogers carried on for five years alone, then, in 1919, sold out to the Marian Hat Works.

The Marian Hat Works was a reliable firm and the men were agreeable to work for, but the spirit and the atmosphere of the old Rogers' shop had gone. For some reason the company did not continue long. A new tenant for the building did not appear and the shell stood empty for awhile. In April, 1925, there was a fire that did enough damage to render the shop worthless. In June the remains were pulled down and the last vestige of hope for the revival of the straw business in Our Town, died.

This was a blow from which Our Town has not fully recovered. Many a home in Our Town in the previous generation owed its foundation to the straw shop.

Today, the straw business of the United States has forsaken the country towns and the big shops, where hats were turned out in quantities; it is found in back rooms in city buildings. The output of the small concerns is variety, rather than mass.

Here and there may be found, in Massachusetts, the remnant of an old-time shop, but the Knowlton factory in West Upton, founded in 1832, is the only one of the big straw factories still doing business.

GRAND RUSH!!

TO G. W. & C. H. MOWRY'S,

WASHINGTON SQUARE,   MANSFIELD.

ALL READY FOR THE

SPRING CAMPAIGN!

New Goods in all Lines; Cheaper than ever!

CHAPTER FIVE

The Railroad

WHEN a good horse could travel ten or twelve miles an hour and a stage could go from Boston to New York in three days, why spend great amounts of money to lay rails and try the doubtful and dangerous experiment of running a steam-drawn coach over them? So thought many of the people of Our Town when they heard that such a railroad was to be put through here. The new device had been tried out in New York state, and on the first trip, in 1831, the clothing of some of the passengers had caught fire from the flying sparks of the engine.

Stage drivers and tavern keepers resented the "tarnation thing," as old Noah Fillebrown called it. Judge Laban Wheaton, founder of Wheaton Seminary, vigorously opposed the plan of the builders of the Taunton Branch to run from Mansfield through Norton Center, because he believed that it would decrease the value of property there, and through his influence the road ran to the east of the village.

The original plan for the road from Boston to Providence, through Our Town, was to have tracks supported by stone sills, capped by granite stringers, with iron bars, or straps bolted to them, and to have the road operated by horse power. It was estimated that a single horse could draw a load of eight tons, including the weight of the carriage, at the rate of three miles per hour, working seven hours a day, or working three hours a day could draw a carriage with twenty-five passengers nine miles per hour.

The charter for this road was granted June 22, 1831, and the road from Boston to Providence was completed July 28, 1835. Service was begun six weeks before that, but as the viaduct at

Canton Junction was not done, passengers were carried around that in teams.

One would expect that the building of the railroad through the town would have brought forth complications that would have started town meeting debates, but never once is it mentioned in the records. During the period when the road was being built and opened, the voters legislated in regard to schools, the poor, and the restraint of swine running at large. Instead of getting excited in meeting over the railroad, they were all stirred up over the finding of the body of a baby in Otis Sweet's mill pond. When we look for some mention of the opening of the road we find the guess as to who the mother of the babe might be.

The work of construction brought new men to town and gave work to some already here. The actual labor of building the roadbed was done largely by Irishmen. The railroad and coal mine brought quite an Irish colony to Our Town.

One of the requirements prescribed by the Board of Directors of each of the newly formed railroad companies of Massachusetts was that the men building the roads should be temperate. The contractors were told not to give the men spirituous liquors, but to substitute tea, coffee, and cold water. That apparently did not meet the favor of the Irishmen. They struck for a daily allowance of grog and for higher wages.

This strike was by no means a peaceful one. The workmen armed themselves with clubs and attacked most anybody they met. The contractors were their special objective and these men were rescued with difficulty. The workmen who were reluctant about striking were also in peril of their lives. The mob threatened to demolish one or two buildings where they thought some of the workmen were hiding. Along the route there was a reign of terror as the strikers marched from below Attleboro to Sharon, adding to their forces all along the way, until they had more than three hundred rioters. The high sheriffs of Bristol and Norfolk Counties were called out, and they, realizing that the mob was beyond their control, summoned the Stoughton Grenadiers and the Washington rifle corps of Attleboro. The presence of military force along the railroad prevented further disturbance. The leaders of the riot were arrested. Nine men were taken to the Dedham jail and six to Attleboro. The six who were taken to Attleboro were lodged under military guard at the Wilmouth Hotel and taken before the district court in the morning. There they were bound over to the June session of the Court of Common Pleas in Taunton.

The six men, when they appeared in Taunton, were charged with having made "great noise, tumult and disturbance for the space of twenty-four hours," with assault on one William Stall, whom they "did beat, wound and ill treat," and also, they "did make an assault, beat, wound and bruise and ill treat" one Jacob Stever. Furthermore, "they did hinder and obstruck divers good and peaceable citizens of the Commonwealth in the pursuit of their usual and lawful occupation, to the great terror of the people." The jury found them all guilty and sent them to the House of Correction at New Bedford, two to hard labor for three months and the cost of prosecution ($90.20), another for one month of hard labor. The other three got off with ten days' labor.

Nobody knows whether the strikers got their daily grog and increase in their pay.

Shortly after the work was started on the Boston and Providence road, a charter was obtained and work begun on the road known as the Taunton Branch, between Mansfield and Taunton. Here, somehow, the workmen managed to evade the directors' ruling on drink. Many of the workers boarded at the Four Corners in a house owned by Micah Allen, across the road from Mr. Allen's own home, and the men made such a disturbance at their drunken carousals that Mr. Allen went over with an ax and stove in their barrels of liquor.

Drunk or sober, the men got the Taunton Branch road done, twelve miles of the straightest road in Massachusetts. It was opened on August 8, 1836.

An old book, written in 1849, concerning Massachusetts, says of the Boston and Providence Railroad: "It is on a continuous line from Maine to New Orleans. The most important branch of the road in Massachusetts is that from Mansfield, twenty-four miles from Boston, which passes to Taunton, Fall River and New Bedford, completed in 1840." That was the opinion of 1849. In 1929 the New Haven Company deemed the branch from Mansfield to Taunton worthy only of a single gasoline car run twice a day each way! Three years later even that was abandoned and one of the two tracks removed, leaving the other to be used by occasional freight trains.

Our Town was much in the limelight in early railroad building days. In 1846 still another railroad charter was granted to run into Mansfield—this one from Mansfield to Foxboro, Wrentham, Bellingham, to the line of Cumberland, Rhode Island, fifteen miles. That never materialized.

A road from Mansfield northward, passing through Foxboro to Framingham, was officially opened May 1, 1870. In the *"Dedham Gazette,"* dated September 25, 1869, we glimpse the first train as it passed over the road from Foxboro to Mansfield.

"Distinguished Arrival. Quite a sensation was caused in this town (Foxboro) on Saturday evening last by the appearance of the first train over the Mansfield and Framingham Railroad, under the conductorship of Mr. Fred Paine of Mansfield. It was simply a construction train, but nevertheless the citizens assembled in large numbers to welcome its arrival. The Foxboro Brass Band was in attendance and performed its part in the impromptu ceremonies with the skill and good taste for which it is noted. Cheers were given for the road, and for its President, E. P. Carpenter, Esq., of Foxboro. President Carpenter, who was on board, responded in a neat and appropriate speech. The bell rang, the whistle screamed, the band played, and the train, freighted with as many of the crowd, male and female, as could possibly be stowed on board, started on its return to Mansfield. After a pleasant ride, despite the accommodations, and a short stop at Mansfield, Conductor Paine attached a couple of passenger cars to the locomotive, and returned the party safely home at about eight o'clock in the evening. Three cheers for the conductor followed the debarkation, and the passangers dispersed."

The *Mansfield News* for 1874 reported that there was soon to be a railroad from Mansfield to North Bridgewater (Brockton). That is yet to come.

The first rails used in this country were shipped from England. For some time the early rails were half-inch strips of scrap iron, fastened to four-by-eight inch wooden "stringers." These quickly flattened and frayed out. The repair of such rails became a business for some blacksmith. Sim Clark, that genial soul who engineered the Horrible Parades at Fourth of July celebrations, was the rail mender for this section. Rails from a distance were brought to his shop on flat cars attached to the engine, but the rails nearby were carted on a small car drawn by a horse. The way that Martin Shea drove the old white horse down the track was almost equal to the speed of the train. When the car was empty he often gave school boys a ride. Jim Bellow drove over the rails with a black horse named Doctor. It was not until 1879 that steel rails were used throughout the line between Boston and Providence, though some steel rails were used as early as 1873.

Just as the first rails were imported from England, so too, were the first engines, crude little affairs of scarcely ten tons weight and developing but fifteen horse power. Under ordinary conditions they made ten miles an hour. A slight grade, or a short curve, frequently proved too much for these engines. Passengers were sometimes called upon to help push the train.

Directly behind the engine was a box car, or tender, to hold the fuel, which was pitch pine from the south. It was years before it occurred to anyone that the wood growing so abundantly beside the track could be utilized to fire the engine. To overcome the expense and uncertainty involved by depending on the the native southerner, the railroad companies bought large tracts of land in Virginia. As late at 1853, the Boston and Providence railroad company paid $13,500 for 1753½ acres of woodland in that state. There they built a railroad into the woods, built a sawmill, bought scows or lighters, opened a company store, and employed a good many men.

When the war between the north and the south came on in 1861, it became an exigency to find fuel in the north and the railroads turned to their local woods. Here was a chance for the farmers of Our Town to add to their incomes by hauling their wood, cut in four-foot lengths to the depot woodpile. A supply of about two hundred cords was kept on the west side of our railroad station. As Our Town was the fueling point, the woodpile here was larger than that of other towns through which the railroad passed. Day after day, three men sawed at the pile, one cut a stick, at sixty cents a cord.

As far back as anyone knows there was a wood-pile at the depot, at first, merely for use at the station. In 1841, Fred Paine, a twelve-year-old lad, sawed wood for Jim Green, the station agent. By the time Mr. Paine was thirty, Jim Green had to retire because of a fatal illness. At his request Fred Paine was appointed to his place. Perhaps that was the time Mr. Paine began wearing his tall silk hat, which he wore as habitually as he did his coat, at any rate it was the time when local wood was being introduced to fire the engines. Paine then conducted the wood business, buying the wood, hiring the sawyers, and selling to the railroad. Not until years afterwards did the railroad manage its own wood transactions, thereby saving the profit which the middleman had pocketed.

In time, there developed another wood yard and shed in Our Town. This one furnished wood for the Boston, Clinton, and Fitchburg Railroad. Here the wood was sawed by horse power and later, by steam.

It was around Civil War times that some coal burning engines were introduced. Experiments with coal as fuel had proved it practical in 1857. When coal was first used on this line a new fire was started with wood each morning. One night Herbert Brown, a fireman of West Mansfield, tried keeping the fire over night. It worked. Thereafter the wood-pile which had been diminishing, vanished.

Besides being a fueling station, Our Town became a watering place for engines. An engine today can carry from twelve thousand to fifteen thousand gallons of water, but when an engine had a capacity for not more than fifteen hundred gallons, the stops for water had to be frequent and Our Town was one of the chief stopping places. Practically every train going through here on the Boston and Providence road had to stop to fill the boiler. There was a time when a hundred trains halted daily for that purpose. So great was the amount of water taken from the Rumford River that the factory and mill owners noticed that their water power was diminished, especially the Fisher brothers at the last of the mills on the Rumford River. The matter was taken up and the corporation was obliged to give the Fishers compensation. In time, the corporation sank a well, but as it was within six feet of the river, doubtless some of the water was still drawn from the river bed.

Up to 1860, first- and second-class tickets were issued for passengers. The holders of the first-class tickets, of course, expected more luxuries, though in the present days we should hardly recognize their comforts. Since more people chose the cheaper mode of travel it often happened that the second-class car would be full, and in order to give the second-class ticket holders seats they would be allowed to go in the first-class car, provided there were vacant seats there.

There was laxity in the matter of passes. Not only could an employee take whom he pleased, but his wife was allowed to take her friends as well. A conductor had a chance to show favoritism. One conductor used to look into the baggage car, packed to the limit with men. "All trainmen?" he would call out. "Yes," somebody would answer. "All right," and he would go back to his passenger cars. Somehow the same bunch of "trainmen" managed to come back with the same conductor on his return trip. The rules of the modern engineer are hard, fast, and numerous. He may take no liberties with his engine, or railroad property. We are told that seventy years ago, when the "scoot" came down from Walpole in the morning, and the passengers had left the train at the station, the engineer, and as many of his trainmen as wished to, made a run down to Fruit Street, where they left the engine on the single track and strolled over to Holme's Trotting Park. After getting what beer or other drink they wanted, they returned to the engine and backed up to the Mansfield depot to be ready to take the "scoot" on a return trip to Walpole. They were not stingy, those men, they often stopped on the way to pick up any friend who wanted to ride down to the Trotting Park.

There was at least one convenience of travel in the old days that is absent today. Now, if a restless child wants a drink of water, the tired mother has to reel her way through the aisle to the tank at the end of the car; then, she simply waited in her seat until the water-boy came through. As sure as germs he came, bearing a tray with six glasses and a tea-kettle of water. Each passenger in turn had a drink, or as many drinks as he liked, during the trip. Many a trainman, who has attained fifty years of honorable service began his railroad career at ten years of age, as a water-boy.

It was a proud day when a water-boy rose to the place of engineer. A present day locomotive is a beautiful piece of mechanism, nothing more. It is known by its number, and is run by one engineer and then another. After a few years it will be junked for something more up-to-date. In years gone by, especially in the eighteen-seventies and eighties, every engine had a name and was run exclusively by one engineer, who cared for it as solicitously as any horse lover grooms his horse. Engines going through Our Town bore such names as *Providence, Boston, Sharon, Attleboro, A. A. Folsom, J. I. Ives, Iron Horse, G. S. Griggs, Thomas E. Wales, Henry A. Whitney, Washington, Gen. Grant* and *W. H. Harrison.* The engine that drew the "Tin Kettle" train to Providence (bearing men with their dinner pails for a day's work) was called the *Mansfield.* The scoot to Foxboro was the *Foxboro.* Several on the Taunton Branch were named for the planets, while on the Providence road there were Dickens characters, such as *Pickwick, Macawber,* and *Mark Tapley.*

Even the barren railroad station assumed a personality and had a life history. Take for example the original station that was built at East Foxboro, when the road was put through in 1835. For thirty-five years it served very well, then around 1870, when the corporation had so much money it didn't know what to do and put the surplus over and above the ten per cent dividend allowed by law, into buildings, it was East Foxboro's turn to have a new station. Our Town already had one. Old buildings were not demolished in those days, but moved to other sites. The discarded East Foxboro station was loaded on two flatcars and run down the track to Mansfield, where it was put on a foundation and served as a dwelling house for railroad employees, first on one spot, and then moved to another. Before a satisfactory site was found in Our

Town it rested in three locations. After being a home many years, it became a railroad paint shop. In 1931, the building once more got uneasy and went for an automobile ride over more than a mile of a crowded street, detouring traffic as it went. Once more it settled down to be somebody's home.

The railroad station in the west part of the town put West Mansfield on the map. The stop between Mansfield and Attleboro was originally called "Tobit's Corner," because John Tobit lived near, and was so designated on the railroad tickets. About 1860, the station agent had two young ladies visiting in his home. The guests were interested in the depot and village, and asked,

"What part of Mansfield is this?"

They were told that it was the west part. Thereupon they went to work. In the course of time they produced a large cardboard sign, which bore two words in large printed letters, "West Mansfield." This they nailed to the station building, where it remained until it was replaced by a more permanent sign. Not long after that the name, "West Mansfield," supplanted "Tobit's Corner" on the railroad tickets.

It was John Bayley, the second station agent, whom the girls were visiting. Mr. Bayley was agent from 1855 to 1885, and began on a salary of twenty-five dollars a month. Many today would feel that that would hardly support a family. So thought Mr. Bayley, and in 1858 persuaded the corporation to move the depot to its present site by the railroad crossing and thus enable him to earn an additional twenty-five dollars as crossing tender. A little more money came in from the express business. Later his salary as agent was raised to thirty-five dollars a month. When he retired he was succeeded by his son, J. Frank Bayley.

It was during J. Frank Bayley's agency that an experimental telephone cable was laid in West Mansfield, in the latter part of 1882. The telephone company wished to prove that it was possible to telephone by means of an underground cable and made arrangements with the railroad company to use the ground between the tracks from West Mansfield to Attleboro for the trial. A locomotive was used to plow the furrow for the wires. One receiving station was at West Mansfield, the other was in a little shanty built for the purpose just above West Mansfield. After the feasibility was proved, the line was discontinued.

Railroading, like the ministry, seemed to run in families. Besides the Bayley family, there was the Paine family, which was a particularly good example.

The first generation of Paines to have connection with the road was Nelson, the cobbler, who became baggage master, and held the position until he dropped dead at his post.

Nelson's son, Fred, worked for the road long before his father became baggage master. He it was who sawed wood at the railroad station, when he was twelve years old, in 1841. When he was married, about 1856, he went to housekeeping over the station and soon was given charge of the station and allowed to run a restaurant there. While Mr. Paine had charge of the restaurant much of the cooking was done in his own kitchen. Meats and delicious squash pies were cooked by his wife and Mrs. Baggs, the Irish servant, who cooked the beans. Luscious great doughnuts were made by Mrs. Paine's sister and sold for five cents apiece. In the last years of Mr. Paine's life he was caretaker in the Old Park Square Station in Boston, after it was supplanted as a depot by the new South Station, in 1899, but still used for other purposes. There the somewhat short, rather thickset man, always wearing a tall silk hat, was noticeable among other men.

Nelson Paine's second son, Henry, made his first contact with the railroad in the character of expressman, bringing from Foxboro straw shops cases of hats to be sent on the Boat Train to Providence for New York. When eighteen or nineteen years old he came into the employ of the railroad as fire-man. After eighteen months as fireman he was given an engine to run. For thirty-seven years he was on the road. When the Old Colony Railroad bought out the Boston and Providence, in 1889, he voluntarily retired.

Most of Hen Paine's driving was on the famous old *Boston*, which was built in Roxbury. The engine, designed to run from Boston on the New York express, was given to Hen Paine to "shake down," or in other words to try out to see if it was all right. On the second day the railroad president rode in the cab with Paine. At the end of the trip the president asked the engineer how he liked it. A surprise came to Mr. Paine a few days later when he got his orders to run the *Boston* as his engine, between Mansfield and Boston. The train that the *Boston* hauled was the New Bedford express, going out of Our Town at 8:41 A.M., and returning at 5:10 at night. Some other engine pulled the train up from New Bedford. On arriving in Our Town, the passengers and train-men stayed on the train, but the engine was changed. This was where Henry Paine and the *Boston* came on the scene. The usual day's work was the run into Boston in the morning and the return at night. Between trains Mr. Paine had the time for loafing in Boston. For about two years, in the summer he ran a train out in the middle of the day, and for a time he ran a "scoot" to Foxboro, early in the morning. Mr. Paine was worked no harder, and no less, than other engineers of his time. When the old *Boston* had served its time, eighteen years, it was junked. For years Henry Paine had the cab in his yard, and it was a favorite place for him to go and sit.

Nelson Paine's third son was Edward. His first contact with the railroad was more painful than his brothers'. When he was thirteen years old he sold papers at the station. In some way he made a misstep when getting on or off the train and he lost a foot. At eighteen he began work in the telegraph office.

When Fort Sumpter was fired upon in 1861, it was Ed Paine who took the message as it came through, the first to get the news in Our Town. Sometime, around 1870, he became ticket agent, which position he held until the time of his death, in 1894. Mr. Paine also succeeded his brother, Fred, in the restaurant business at the station.

In the third generation, one of the family, first as fireman and then as engineer, worked for the road for forty-four years; a third spent his entire working life as a railroad man, in one capacity or another; and two others have held responsible positions over a considerable period of years.

We might fill several pages with family histories, for in the eighteen-nineties about every third man in Our Town was connected in some capacity with the railroad. Many worked about the freight house. Favored by position at the junction of two, or it might be said three, roads, Our Town was an important transfer point for southeastern Massachusetts. Within the yard were fourteen miles of rails,—fourteen tracks of one mile each. Under ordinary conditions scores of men were employed there. During the war days of 1917-19, about seventy-five men were at work on the platform, some forty-five at the switches, besides a dozen more in the offices. When, a few years after the war, the freight was handled largely at another junction, a hundred permanent men were thrown out of work.

Near the freight house was the stone round house, built in 1872, and enlarged in 1893. In our busiest times four men were employed there at night, wiping engines, at a dollar and seventy-five cents an engine.

Work on, and for the railroad, was the men's job, yet the women at home carried a constant anxiety much like that of the wives of seafaring men. The railroad took its toll of life and limb.

The casualty list began in 1835. One opponent of the new

road in Our Town was so wrought up over the matter that he wrote a poem of one hundred and eighty-eight stanzas. Here follow a few:

> A cow here got upon the road,
> The pasture she deserted
> And there remained until
> Her life and body parted.
>
> Now Jacob Bailey's case comes on,
> He's had his share of losses,
> When the steam-cars against him run
> And tore his cart to pieces.
>
> In Roxbury, a fatal stroke
> Which seemed beyond expression
> Some joints put out and bones were broke
> By means of this concussion.
>
> The Providence and Dedham cars
> With ram's play interlocked;
> The battle came at unawares,
> Because the road was crooked.
>
> One steam-car was so driven back
> It tore two cars to flitters;
> And every piece they had to take
> To rig out biers and litters.
>
> This fracas did the fire-man kill,
> Of course his wife's a widow;
> I hope the corporation will
> This woman's case consider.
>
> Among the rest one Thomas Brown
> Had his neck so distorted
> That o'er his back his head hung down,
> And was almost inverted.

> But finally his head arose
> > Which placed his neck beneath it;
> And now if he does turn his nose
> > His body must turn with it.

It is a pity that this rhyme maker had not lived to tell of Ham Nason's calamity fifty years later. Ham was a conductor, and as he served in a time when no special uniform was required, his head covering was just like every man's, a tall silk hat. The time of the accident was in the winter during a heavy fall of snow. The train was trying to plow its way through the drifts and the conductor was standing on the platform to watch the progress. A sudden jolt. Conductor Nason was bounced from the train, head first into a snow bank. The plug hat did not save him from ridicule, but it protected him from head injury.

Elwood Grover's stylish working clothes got him into trouble. The indispensible garment of the seventies and eighties was a linen duster. Grover wore his when he was working the crank on the hand-driven service car of the section men. The wind blew the billowing robe into the simple mechanism. There was no lasting damage to anything but the duster. It was not, however, a pleasant experience for Grover.

Let us hope that the present uniformed employees of the streamlined trains lighten their responsibilities with laughter.

CHAPTER SIX

Coal Mines

THE YEAR 1835 was an era of great expectations in Our Town; in June, the first train from Boston to Providence passed through here; in October, coal was discovered.

The uncovering of a vein of coal was quite unexpected, though State records say that coal was found in Mansfield, in 1810. The 1835 discovery was in the west part of the town, not very far from the then newly built railroad.

On that October day Alfred Harden was digging a well and came upon a black substance that caused him to pause in his work. Without doubt his practical New England temperament led him to finish his well. He did, however, tell what he had found, and before long, scientists and engineers were on the spot and pronounced the black mineral coal. Soon everybody was digging. More coal was found on a farm not far away. Farmers at the south end of the town unearthed coal on their property. Men in the east part found some. Taunton, Boston, even New York newspapers carried items about the Mansfield coal mines.

Anthracite coal had been in use in the United States less than twenty-five years. In 1803, a load of "stone coal" was brought into Philadelphia and was rejected for everything except to be broken up to make sidewalks. In 1812, seven wagon loads of coal were taken to the same city, and failing to find a market, the traders who brought it gave it away. As soon as people learned how to use it as fuel, it became valuable.

The coal discovered in Our Town was pronounced by Dr. C. F. Jackson, the Geological Surveyor of Massachusetts and Rhode Island, nearly equal to that of the purest Lehigh beds in Pennsylvania. He called attention to the fact that the quality of the Pennsylvania coal had improved since the beds were opened and predicted that the Mansfield coal would do the same. He made it plain that coal taken from a new region might be expected to require a little different mode of management to make it burn. Dr. Jackson continued his interest and gave valuable advice and suggestions to the operators of the mines as soon as companies were organized and the mining begun.

Before the end of the month in which coal was discovered, a mining company was formed and was buying or leasing land under the name of the Massachusetts Mining Company. Alfred Harden was the first landowner to sign. He was paid $1800 outright and was to receive six per cent of the actual value of the mine and of the coal at the time it was thrown out of the pit. Two shafts were dug in West Mansfield, one on the Harden farm, and the other on what is now known as Tremont Street, three quarters of a mile away.

At the Tremont Mine a shaft, sixty to seventy-five feet was sunk, but presumably no drifts were made. After a short time work suddenly stopped, either from lack of funds, or because the work at the Harden Mine seemed more worth while. The miners who were thrown out of work were thoroughly disgruntled. Tools were left in the mine and many were wilfully damaged. Some years later farmers in the vicinity used their oxen and filled the hole with gravel. Around 1920, when there was an attempt to open the mine, the tools were found. One man took out and used a wheelbarrow that had been in the mine more than eighty years. Another found a heavy four-foot rod that angry workmen had bent into a triangle.

The thing about that early mine that seemed to make the greatest impression was the death of an Irish miner who met his fate in the shaft. The coal and debris were primitively brought to the surface in buckets controlled by a rope. Men, too, rode up and down in the same conveyance. One day the rope that held the bucket carrying a single occupant, broke. The wake that followed was a fireside tale for generations. It was an innovation in West Mansfield, for by 1836 there had been few Irish deaths in town. The wake was an elaborate and hilarious affair, just the kind that the men, recently come from the Emerald Isle, were accustomed to at home.

About the same time that the work was going on in West Mansfield another organization, called the Mansfield Coal Company, was at work on land at the south end of the town. Several shafts were sunk, one of them sixty-four feet deep. Drifts may have been made at this mine. The attempt was no more successful than the Tremont Mine and the holes were soon filled in, or at least boarded over. In the early nineteen hundreds, rotted timbers in the main shaft most unexpectedly gave way and there was a cave-in during the night, leaving an ugly and dangerous hole, which, until it was filled, was fenced in and looked upon with awe.

The Massachusetts Mining Company, working on the Harden farm, was more persevering and more successful. Having gone twenty-five feet, they struck a bed of coal five feet wide, and another seam a foot thick, separated from the first by only ten inches of rock. Later the shaft was carried down sixty-four feet. From the bottom of this shaft drifts following beds of coal were dug one hundred and fifty feet in opposite directions. A railway for bringing the coal to the foot of the shaft was laid. For the first few years the coal was brought to the surface by a windlass and hand power, but before 1841 steam power was used. In less than three years from the time the work was commenced, they had already raised fifteen hundred tons of coal, a small amount judged by modern machinery and equipment, but not so bad for a hand windlass. In addition to the tunnels already mentioned, another drift had been started in a southeasterly direction from the bottom of the shaft in search of a new bed.

The work of exploration was carried on by General Samuel Chandler of Lexington, Massachusetts. General Chandler was very optimstic. In his report to the State, he said, "The quality of this coal has given good satisfaction generally to the purchaser, notwithstanding it was taken out under unfavorable circumstances. Many competent judges who have had the opportunity for testing its qualities thoroughly, say that it is equal to Pennsylvania anthracite in its essential properties."

Edward Hitchcock, State Geologist and Professor of Geology at Amherst College, visited the mine in 1838, and also later. In 1841, he turned in a somewhat lengthy report on coal deposits in Massachusetts. The report stated that coal was found in various parts of Plymouth, Bristol, and Norfolk counties. That found in Plymouth County was not in sufficient quantities to be worth mentioning. The same condition existed in Raynham. In Norfolk County the principal deposit was in Wrentham. There, too, according to the report, the deposit was not worth exploring. Along the borders of Mansfield and Foxboro, where Bristol and Norfolk Counties come together some coal was found, but with so much waste and earthy matter that mining was out of the question. The results of investigation in Rhode Island were better, but that is far removed from this story.

Of the mine in West Mansfield Professor Hitchcock said, "The bed has been considerably explored and with others in that place has proved more important than any other, and excites sanguine expectations that the region may prove an extensive and valuable field." Further along in his reports he adds, "In spite of stagnation in business and general incredulity in respect to the existence of valuable coal, they have been so successful as to satisfy any reasonable men acquainted with coal formation that a great deal of that mineral may

exist beneath the deep alluvial coat of that region." Professor
Hitchcock considered that General Chandler had managed
the whole concern with remarkably good judgment.

Few, if any native born Mansfield men, had any part in the
mines. The superintendents and engineers came from outside.
The miners were practically all of them Irish, some of whom
came especially to work in the mines, and some had come to
build the railroad and had remained. There was quite an Irish
settlement around the mines, and in its most active years the
little No. 6 schoolhouse, built for twenty-five or thirty children,
had to accommodate sixty or seventy.

In general, the people of Our Town were inclined to be
skeptical, even in the face of proof that the coal would burn.
Robert Davis, a blacksmith, used it in his shop and said it was
as good as any Pennsylvania coal. The directors of the mine
used the coal in their open grates, cylinder stoves and cooking
ranges.

More interesting than the fire in the blacksmith shop, or in
directors' homes, was the coal fire used to heat the *S. S. President*,
which plied between Providence and New York.

It was on Christmas Eve, 1836. The steamer, under the
command of Elisha Barker, started out from Providence with
thirty-five passengers aboard, people from Maine, New Hampshire, Massachusetts and Rhode Island. On board were three
barrels of coal dug at the Harden Mine by the Massachusetts
Mining Company. The fires on the boat were started with coal
from Pennsylvania, but after they got burning they were kept
going with Mansfield coal. Because of the extreme coldness
of the weather it was to be a good test. Captain Barker was
interested in the Mansfield coal, but more than that he was
anxious to have his passengers comfortable. After supper he
gave his time to watching the fires and observing the action
of the fuel. Everything was entirely satisfactory. At nine o'clock
he called to the attention of his New England passengers that

they were being kept warm with Massachusetts coal. Captain Barker afterwards made a written statement that on this trip from Providence to New York the Mansfield coal had been used in the various stoves on board the Steamer *President*, and that the result was as hot a fire as from any anthracite coal as he had ever used, and fully equal to Pennsylvania coal in all its properties. His testimony is recorded in the State House in Boston. This was a little over a year after the mine was opened.

Another enthusiastic booster of the Massachusetts Mining Company was the clerk of the corporation, William B. Dorr, Esq. In his report to the State, he said:

"The Massachusetts Mining Company, at an expense of less than $15,000, with all the discouragements of a novel undertaking, with almost an entire lack of knowledge on the subject, and the cost of experiment, which experience would have rendered unnecessary, have been able to raise 1200 to 1500 tons of coal, worth from $5000 to $6000 at lowest estimates, both of quantity mined and of its true value . . . . The directors have unhesitating confidence in the eventual success of mining operation on a scale commensurate with their confidence and importance of the subject."

It was unfortunate that the opening of the mines came at the beginning of the seven-year business depression which affected the United States, England, France, and Belgium. The depression was brought on, in part, by railroad speculation and resulted in bank failures, unemployment and hard times. After struggling for three years with lack of funds, the mines were closed, in 1838.

The outlook for Mansfield coal was now rather disheartening; three mines opened, and work on all suspended. There was, however, one man at least who was not discouraged. That man was Foster Bryant. Mr. Bryant had discovered Our Town when Our Town discovered coal. He came here in the employ of the Massachusetts Mining Company, either as superintendent, engineer, or perhaps promoter, and remained until his death, some forty-five years later. During those forty-five years he was usually hotly championing some cause, coal mines, the institution of slavery, or the system of education. He was over forty years old when he came here and had already been a building contractor and had built part of Girard College in Philadelphia; he had been a newspaper man and had edited a newspaper; he had been an educator and had prepared an arithmetic, which was said to have considerable merit.

Mr. Bryant was not very well liked in Our Town. He was too outspoken for popularity. His friends and his foes, nevertheless, gave him the credit of being sincere and steadfast in his convictions, and courageous in upholding them. Some people go as far as to say that he was too brilliant for his contemporaries here. In the light of the present day he appears narrow and bigoted, especially in his attitude in regard to slavery.

For more than forty years his voice was heard in town meetings and more than once he represented the town at hearings before the Legislature. His first appearance before the Legislature in Boston was in 1839, when he went in behalf of the town to ask state aid in working the Mansfield mines.

Mr. Bryant's argument covered twenty-three finely printed pages. He appeared familiar with Pennsylvania mines and stated that the Mansfield coal was better than the coal from the Little Schuykill in 1831, and altogether better than that taken during the first years from the Lackawanna mines. The coal taken from the Mansfield mines in the first twenty-five to fifty feet was scarcely capable of combustion, but that taken from a depth of sixty feet, or more, was equal to Pennsylvania coal in all respects, except a larger portion of waste.

With the Bryant statement went the certificate of sixteen citizens of Our Town, who had used the coal in their stores and homes, and also a petition to have the State explore to a depth of four hundred to five hundred feet.

Mr. Bryant called attention to the nearness of the Taunton River, thus connecting with the seaboard from Bangor, Maine, to New York. Professor Hitchcock's statement that "A more favorable spot could hardly have been chosen on account of the close proximity of the new Boston and Providence Railroad," was added.

At that time a geological map was prepared showing that coal deposits were found over an area of four hundred square miles in this section of Massachusetts and Rhode Island.

The State Committee, in reporting before the House, said that the gentlemen who acted as agents for the petitioners exhibited with commendable industry a great variety of argument and evidence to show the importance and propriety of granting public aid in developing coal mines in Massachusetts.

Under the date of February 25, 1838, the bill, recommended by the State Committee, was signed by J. Daggett, who, if we are not mistaken, was the representative from Attleboro and years before had taught school in the very district in Our Town where coal was discovered.

One advantage that our committee brought out was "that it would give work to our own men, work which would be congenial to the citizens. No field of enterprise could be better adapted to the present worth and capacity of the State."

Herewith are given extracts from the bill.

Section 1 recommended that a commission of three, entitled the "Commission of Mines in Massachusetts" shall be elected by joint ballot of both branches of the legislature.

Then followed four sections dealing with the duties of the commission.

Section 6 recommended that a loan, not exceeding $150,000, be floated. To raise this the State Treasury would issue certificates on "A loan for developing the coal mines of Massachusetts." The certificates were to be issued "In sums which may be divided without a remainder, by $500. The next four sections were in regard to this loan. Section 11 arranged for the salary of the commission.

Just what happened to this House Bill, No. 33, does not appear, but on March 2, 1841, two years later, House Document, No. 66 was presented before the Senate. The report was given before a special joint committee, to which had been referred the argument of Foster Bryant, concerning coal mines of Massachusetts, and the petition of the inhabitants of Bristol County. The Committee was unanimously of the opinion that the subject matter was highly important to the whole people of Massachusetts. They said that no little commendation should be given Mr. Bryant for his research. They called attention to the heavy outlay of $5000 every day for coal brought into the State, with the money paid to strangers, when it might be paid within the State.

All arguments appear to have been fruitless. The coal mines of Our Town got no help from the Commonwealth.

Foster Bryant, finding the Massachusetts legislators so shortsighted and niggardly, apparently lost his enthusiasm for mining, and retired to devote himself to town affairs. He held few public offices, but his voice was heard at every town meeting. He bought a small farm where he did farming after his own way, raising among other things a small quantity of tobacco, which he offered for sale. In the days long before sundials were used here to decorate the flower gardens of Our Town, Foster Bryant's sundial in his front yard attracted a great deal of attention.

On Dec. 3, 1884, in his eighty-seventh year, Mr. Bryant died in Our Town, of old age.

The withdrawal of Mr. Bryant from the active promotion of the coal industry did not decrease the interest of geologists or mining men. Professor Hitchcock persisted that there were four beds of coal in Mansfield of sufficient thickness to be worked. The fossils of fruit and ferns found at the beds were similar to those of Pottsville, Pennsylvania, and to him indicated a similar quality of coal.

In the meantime mine operators in Rhode Island were faring better than those in Massachusetts. The General Assembly of the former state granted a lottery to raise $10,000 to search for coal.

About 1842, without state aid, or lottery, a new corporation, the Mansfield Mining Company, came into being. William Coolidge and Nathaniel Dorr, each connected with the previous mines, headed the new venture. It was backed by merchants and speculators in Boston. William D. Clapp was engaged as agent and work began in earnest.

The new field of operation was half a mile west of the Harden farm and was called the Wading Mine. A shaft was sunk and a drift dug horizontally to the southeast. This had not been pushed far when a bed of coal ten feet thick was struck. Twenty-five tons of coal, some of it of superior quality, was thrown out. Aaron White, whose father, years before, when the lad was but ten years old, had come from Easton to that district to set up machinery for the Williams cotton factory, was the engineer.

He ran a six horse power engine, operated by steam made by a combination of Mansfield coal and wood, a layer of one and a layer of the other.

In a few years the Mansfield Mining Company went the way of our previous mining organizations.

Even then the matter was not a dead issue. The people at the south end of the town, as well as West Mansfield, did not forget that there was probably coal under the farm land. Or was it that the mining promoters prodded them on? At any rate, in 1848-9, new mining companies were formed to work in each section of the town.

At the south end, six farmers owning a block of some 867 acres on both sides of South Main Street and on both sides of Rumford River, held meetings at the District No. 3 school-house to draw up articles of agreement with the company. The company is not named, but Thomas S. Ridgeway, a mining engineer of Philadelphia, and Stephen M. Allen of Roxbury, the agent for the company, and six land owners signed the agreement.

These six Yankee farmers were a canny lot. They left no undetermined questions.

The lease, giving right to bore and examine for coal and iron ore, was to run for fifty years, but the excavations were not to come within four hundred feet of the dwelling of any one of the lessees. Realizing that the company needed some time to prepare, they were allowed nine months. If at any time the working of the mine was suspended for a year at a time, after coal was found, the lease was to be terminated. In case of failure the owners reserved the right of buying back their property. The coal company was instructed that it should not sell its rights to the Massachusetts and Mansfield Coal Company operating in West Mansfield. A dividend of six per cent of the value of the mine, minerals, and ore, was to be paid semiannually to the owners, according to the number of acres that each held. In addition to that, the farmer, on whose land the excavation was made, was to be paid outright for the damage to his property, and also for a right-of-way out to the road or to the river.

It was estimated that the company would get annually fifty thousand tons of coal, which would sell for four thousand dollars.

If air castles were built with the income, they fell to earth, for the undertaking never materialized beyond three or four large holes.

The above agreement was signed on March 9, 1849. At the same time, or a little before, the Mansfield Coal and Mining Company was formed to work in West Mansfield, at the already excavated Wading Mine. Benjamin F. Sawyer, a lawyer from New York, came to manage the operation. The mine soon took his name and was called the Sawyer Mine.

Mr. Sawyer, like Foster Bryant, was a man of importance before he came to Our Town. He was a lawyer of some distinction, and held offices in Brooklyn, New York. In appearance, a more imposing man to look upon than was Mr. Bryant. Mr. Sawyer was a big man and walked with an air of authority. This stately man with black whiskers that never turned gray to the end of his days, and always wearing a tall silk hat, hardly fitted into the picture of the coal mine neighborhood. No more did he fit into the social life, but he did, however, make a good manager of the mine.

Besides managing the mine, Mr. Sawyer, with the aid of his boys, ran the company store, the store that had once been the store for the Williams Cotton Factory people.

The mine, under the control of Mr. Sawyer, seemed to prosper. The Massachusetts' State Report for March, 1853, says that in 1848, "The Mansfield Coal and Mining Company, through the enterprise and perseverance of Benjamin F. Sawyer, Esq., sank a shaft of one hundred and seventy feet, ten feet in diameter." Thomas Ridgeway, Esq., the mining engineer, it says, carried the tunnel, six feet high and five feet wide, six hundred and sixty feet. There were other tunnels that amounted to seven hundred feet more. Thirteen beds of coal were found. These, however, were irregular, being in some places six to eight feet thick and pinched to a few inches.

A strange thing about this mine was that thought it was only a short distance from the Harden Mine there was little similarity between the two; the Harden Mine was tunneled through solid rock which served to hold up over head, while the Sawyer Mine had to be bricked up in places. The Tremont Mine received still different treatment. That was shored up with wooden supports. Much more slate was mixed with the coal in the Sawyer Mine than in the Harden Mine.

Referring again to the State Report: A letter from Mr. Sawyer is quoted, in which he said, "In 1848 my attention was called to the subject. I examined the field and procured 'mining leases' for about 1600 acres, which were conveyed to myself. Since then the Mansfield Coal and Mining Company purchased some portion, so that they hold it in fee simple." He went on to say that with the help of friends he had done all he could. Though he had exhausted his resources he was still trying. "I have expended nearly $98,000 to $100,000." (The earlier company had spent $20,000 to $25,000.) "The general embarrassment of the period which shook to the very center the whole commercial and mercantile world," was the cause of the failure, he said. "The company under my immediate charge," continued Mr. Sawyer, "has accomplished a large amount of work, set up an engine of fifty horse power and sunk a shaft." He went on to give the figures, which we have already given. In the north tunnel, he reported, they had mined twenty-five hundred tons of coal of fair quality. Most of that was used in their own boiler.

Under date of September, 1853, Thomas S. Ridgeway, the mining engineer, recommended that the government of Massachusetts drill holes at the Harden Mine, and also trench across the ridge on the highway from Mansfield to Foxboro, and at another point.

In all, perhaps five thousand tons of coal was taken from the Sawyer Mine. This was used for smelting bog iron ore, for power, and for heating, both in Our Town and in Foxboro.

Again money was lacking and operations stopped about 1854-5. Never again was that mine worked. In all these years the shaft has remained open, a dump hole and a seeming danger spot, though nothing has happened there. Close by, the old boiler is rusting.

From 1854 until 1883 coal mining in Our Town was at a standstill. Some didn't care; others nursed disappointed hopes; scientists never lost sight of it. Professor Louis Aggasiz of Harvard expressed an interest. Likewise, Professor Shaler of the same institution examined specimens and asked for fern fossils to add to the Harvard collection.

In the spring of 1883 a new company was formed and the following item in the *Boston Globe* in March of that year, said:

"A party of scientists arrived in Mansfield last Friday from Boston and vicinity on a prospecting expedition to consult upon the probable success of the expenditure of $100,000 in developing coal mines in that town. A company, of which Professor Shaler of Harvard is the leading scientist, has been formed."

Great interest was once more aroused. In March, an engine, boiler, and other pieces of machinery arrived. Twenty-five owners of land, consisting of over one thousand acres in West Mansfield, signed leases of the underground portions of their premises, on the condition that the work be commenced within one year.

The owners stipulated that no underground passage should be nearer than twenty rods of any homestead building. The leasees were to receive twenty-five per cent for three years. If at the end of that time the coal were found in sufficient quantities to be mined, the company was to pay the leasees fifty cents per acre, and ten cents a ton on coal mined, and in event of success, the lease was to run for ninety-nine years.

By the last of May, 1883, the engineers had diamond drills working on the field. The first week in June saw more people at work. There was a rumor that soon the mine would be operating day and night, that, however, proved to be nothing but rumor. In fact, all effort ceased after a few weeks. In the winter it was again resumed and more machinery arrived. Though the shafts and drifts of the Sawyer Mine were cleared out, it was found that vein had been very nearly worked to its limit. Drilling continued wherever there were suspected coal beds. The greater part of the work was done around the Harden Mine. Pipes were sunk there in one place to a depth of eleven hundred feet and in another eight hundred.

For about eight years the engineers remained in Our Town, drilling more or less of the time. While that sort of work was going on night and day, it became a form of amusement for the young people from the Center to go down to watch the drilling during the evening. There were really no actual mining activities during that period.

After the efforts of 1883, there was a lapse of twenty years or more, then came the Massachusetts Coal and Power Company. One had to but listen to the agents of the company to realize the great things they intended to accomplish. It seemed as if all New England was to be heated by burning coal from Our Town. The Company set about buying West Mansfield property in the coal mine region. Altogether, they bought fully twelve hundred acres, including in the purchase whatever buildings were on the land. That meant sixteen or seventeen houses, as well as barns, shops, poultry houses, and other small buildings. Many thousands of dollars were involved in these transactions, and to that amount enriched the people who owned land in that region. Stock was offered far and wide, but in most cases the people who invested never had any returns.

At about the same time the Cumberland-Mansfield Coal and Power Company bought two hundred acres not far away, in the hope that coal was to be found there. Apparently they never found anything.

It is a question how much coal the Massachusetts Coal and Power Company mined. They got enough to send five or six tons to the Food Fair in Boston. The lumps were just as they came from the mine, some as big as a bushel basket. Though the new mining engineer did not dig deep enough, or stay long enough to find much coal, he did find a wife here.

After the company retired from the field there was a foreclosure auction sale at which some of the original owners bought back their farms at half the price that had been paid to them by the coal company.

The next move was in 1917, or 1918. This time, Walter Packard of Avon leased the old Harden Mine. Probably under the right conditions Mr. Packard would have been successful. He was young, energetic, and an upright business man. But he chose a bad time to begin.

One coincidence noticeable in the history of mining in Our Town is that practically every attempt was made when the country was going through some unusual condition. The first attempt, in 1835, was at the beginning of a seven year financial crisis. So again, in 1848, there were numerous business failures, followed by the panic of Wall Street, in 1854, which was the time when Mr. Sawyer was obliged to suspend operations at his mine. The next attempt, in 1883-84, was also a period of financial depression, due to railroad speculation, and low prices for American grain.

Mr. Packard's attempt was at the closing days of the World War. He found it impossible to get the machinery he needed. For instance, he needed a grader for sorting the coal. Nobody would take an order with a promise of delivery. He sought a secondhand one in Pennsylvania, but it was not to be had. In spite of handicaps, such as shortage of equipment, and the mine flooded with water running in at the rate of a foot an hour, he kept at work for many months. He employed some twelve or fifteen men, among them Lewis Harrington, who with his father had done so much drilling around 1883, and who had also worked for the Massachusetts Coal and Power

Company in 1910, or thereabout. Eight experienced miners were on the pay roll, which amounted to a thousand dollars a week. The trucking was done by Henry Hallett.

It is a wonder that Mr. Hallett is alive to tell of working there. One day his work was to take several loads of something from the West Mansfield depot to the mine. There were six tons in the lot. He made three trips, taking two tons each time. When he had dumped the last load he discovered that he had been carting dynamite, which according to law should not be carried in more than five hundred pound lots. The secret of his safety in this particular case was that the dynamite was frozen.

It seems to have been a custom to keep the driver ignorant of the nature of his load. Back in 1850 William Brown carted for the mine. The day that he had a large load of boxes to carry, Mr. Sawyer cautioned him to handle them carefully. He later found that he had carted dynamite.

Dynamite certainly was used at the mine in Mr. Packard's time, for in all he took out some hundred thousand tons of coal. Some of this was used at the mine, some was taken to Brockton and Avon, and some was used here in Our Town. Mr. Hallet, the man who was not killed by the dynamite, heated his house one winter with the coal from the mine.

As long as the mine was worked during this 1917 spasmodic attempt, Mr. Packard financed the project himself. More money was needed and he hoped to interest his friends. About that time the Regal Shoe Company, in which corporation Mr. Packard was financially interested, got into difficulties, and Mr. Packard could not afford to spend any more money in Our Town.

The man to whom Mr. Packard sold was a typical promoter. ready to spend other people's money, but none of his own. He did little mining. The next owner was a crook and finally landed in jail.

People from the Mount Hope Finishing Company in Dighton were the next on the field. It was their intention to get coal for their plant. They wanted the Harden Mine, but for some reason could not get it. The Sawyer Mine had too much slate to be practical, and also was pretty well worked out. They took the Tremont Mine and set up an electrical equipment. When they got to work they found the mining conditions there were bad, the shaft was too far away from the vein and other things were inconvenient. They abandoned the project.

The people of Our Town are no richer for having coal under their farm land and probably never will be.

CHAPTER SEVEN

Basketmakers

It is strange, the way the town divided itself. East Mansfield and West Mansfield were as distinct as though they were many miles apart. They had their separate military companies and tax collectors; there was little courting and marrying back and forth; many of their industries were different. In the east part, a hundred years ago, there were any number of shoemakers who made, or at least soled, shoes in their own homes, or in little shops set apart for the purpose. There was hardly a man who made shoes in the west part, but any number of them made baskets, a commodity practically untouched in the east part. The center of the town had some of each.

In 1837 four thousand dollars worth of baskets were produced here. If any town anywhere made as many we have yet to hear of it.

When, where, and by whom the first baskets were made in Our Town by white men no one can tell. The first basket-maker recorded is Abner Bailey, a grandfather of George E. Bailey, the bakeshop and oven man, of whom we shall write in another chapter. In 1795-7, when Abner Bailey was buying the land that years later became the site of the bakeshop, was building himself a house, and getting married, he was listed as farmer and basketmaker. When the inventory of his property was made at the time of his death, in 1837, the year that the basket business in Our Town was valued at four thousand dollars, Mr. Bailey had a saw and basket machine and fifty-eight unfinished baskets among his effects. He is also said to have invented some sort of basket machine.

The industrial survey for 1845 gives the number of baskets made here as 35,200, valued at $5,228. Ten years later it was

56,000 baskets, valued at $13,560. Naturally in 1865, just as the Civil War was coming to a close and when so many of our men were in the army, the basket business decreased. Baskets, however, could be and were made by old and less active men. Women, it has been said, then and at other times did some of the light weaving in their kitchens. We find there were forty-two men at work in 1865 and 3,040 baskets were sold, valued at $18,385. The price shows the post war inflation of currency.

All sorts of baskets were made here. Bushel, half-bushel, peck baskets for farmers and cranberry growers, bobbin baskets for cotton factories, charcoal baskets, market baskets, signal baskets, eel pots, fish baskets, clothes baskets, and wood baskets were made in quantities. Special orders took care of other varieties. We read that in the summer of 1883 J. D. Draper and Velorous Hodges started a new venture of making basket canoes. These were ten feet long and had a three foot beam, were thirteen inches deep and weighed forty pounds. They were designed to carry two people and cost a third of the price of an ordinary canoe. How they were made water tight does not appear. Probably they were canvas covered. Since we have never heard that the men became famous by making basket canoes we conclude that their attempt was not successful, or popular.

Most of the baskets were made of oak, white or black; some were made of red oak. A few lighter baskets were made of ash. Of the oaks, the white was the tougher but the black was the more durable. When ash was used the black was preferable, because the layers separated easier. The handles of the baskets were sometimes made of ash or walnut, but usually of oak.

Although there seems to be plenty of woods in Our Town today, in the height of the basket business the demand for oak was greater than the supply. The heaviest of the timber was sent to New Bedford for the building of whaling vessels; the of wood annually were being bought for firing the locomotive engines; and until 1857 charcoal was used exclusively for producing intense heat in the jewelry shops and forges. Trees did not grow fast enough. Basketmakers, producing on the average fifty thousand baskets a year, were, therefore, forced to go to Rehoboth, Middleboro, Easton, Medfield, and other places that were not railroad centers and where there were no basketmakers. It was even contemplated at one time to go to Virginia, where good oak was plentiful and cheap.

Logs three feet to twelve feet long and of any manageable size were brought to the basket shop. Usually the basketmaker had a brook or small pond handy and the logs were placed there until they could be used. Under water the logs kept much better than on the ground. They could be left in water as long as twenty years without serious deterioration.

When ready to be used, the logs were hauled out of the water. If they were very large they had to be sawed in two. They were then split by means of iron wedges into halves and quarters, and finally made still smaller with a frow and wooden maul. The resulting sections were called bolts. Through a machine that had a sort of knife, like that of a carpenter's plane, the bolts were run to be split into strips. In the earliest days these strips had to be pulled through by man power; later, waterpower or horsepower, and finally electricity was used. The strips were required to be of various sizes for standards, bottom fillers, setting-ups, and fillers. Basketmakers also had to make hoops, handles, and yokes; the last were used principally in coal baskets.

The ash logs responded to a much simpler treatment. These were simply beaten with a wooden mallet until the layers formed in growth separated and could be pulled apart to work up into strips.

After the strips, ash or oak, of the desired width were made, the next step was the steaming to make them pliable. Steam in the olden days was produced in a farmer's boiler, such as was used for scalding hogs at butchering time, a boiler holding twenty to fifty gallons of water. Over the boiler was placed a long wooden trough or box, six or eight feet long and fifteen inches square, with an opening to admit the steam. The strips of basket stuff were placed in the box and left until they were thoroughly heated. This took from twenty minutes to half an hour.

The forms on which the baskets were built were called drums and were made of white pine by the basketmakers themselves, or by neighboring carpenters.

Basketmaking seemed to go in families. There were Hodgeses, Grovers, Whites, Skinners, Coreys, Shepards, Fishers, and Treens, to mention a few that stand out in our history of basketmaking.

Of the Hodges family there was Milton of West Mansfield, and James, Isaac, Edward, William and Velorous at the Center. The first four of the group at the Center were brothers and Velorous a distant relative. William Hodges, the youngest, though he drove a baker's wagon for the Baileys a number of years, spent thirty-five years of his life making baskets. In the 1860's and 1870's James L. Hodges and Isaac Hodges worked in a long basket shop that stood near Murphy's cutlery shop and used the power from there. That was a three room building. Velorous Hodges and Jacob A. Blake occupied the other two rooms. It is said that Blake's shop was a popular gathering place for local politicians and that more political questions were settled there than in any other place during the decade that followed the Civil War.

In 1880 the long three-room shop was destroyed by fire and the basketmakers were scattered. James L. Hodges built a new shop, twenty by thirty feet, a story-and-a-half high, just below the dam at the foot of Kingman's Pond. In it he installed a three horsepower engine in order to be independent of freshet or drought conditions that sometimes existed in the Rumford River. Mr. Hodges employed several men and in the 1890's had the reputation of doing the largest basket business of anyone in Our Town. He made bushel and two bushel baskets and sold them in Providence.

Then there was the Corey family. Leonard, the cabinet-maker, also made baskets and taught his sons the art. Charles B. made that his life business, and in 1871 built himself a new shop. John Corey, the other son, became a minister and paid part of his way through school by making baskets. At his new shop, Charles B. Corey took his son, Charles L., into the business. Their card shows that they made round and square baskets. The square ones were large and shallow, perhaps four by three feet across the bottom and three or four inches deep. Their market was Boston and in the earliest days the Corey baskets had to be carried over the road with a horse and wagon, or Corey may even have tied them together and thrown them over the back of the horse he rode.

The horse deserves credit for the promotion of the basket business. Not only did he travel miles delivering baskets, wholesale and retail, but he walked miles in circles at the horsepower windlass used by many basketmakers to draw the strips of basket stuff through the knives. In Charles B. Corey's new two-story shop he had the windlass in the well-lighted basement. Mr. Corey's horse walked alone in the basement while Mr. Corey worked in the room above. As the horse grew older he sometimes lagged on the job. A sharp rap on the floor above set him going again at his regular pace.

Charles L. Corey, of the third generation of basketmakers, worked in the straw shop in the straw season and at basket-making in the off season. In the middle 1880's he built himself a shop and hired men to work for him. After he gave up basket-making the shop was moved and converted into a dwelling;

so also was his father's. It is surprising the number of one-time basket shops that are now homes.

On Main Street three Grovers, Alfred, Lewis, and Arnold, made baskets. Arnold made fish baskets which were used not alone in the fish trade but in department stores, where they were put on runners and used to move the goods through the aisles. Mr. Grover's children found them nice hiding places in their play.

Not far from Main Street, at the south end of the town were the Fisher brothers, David, George, and Jasper, who had a mill. There were two other Fisher brothers; one had taken up a claim in Kansas in 1873; and when he died a few years later, from the poison of a rattlesnake bite, the other went out to hold the claim and remained there. Of the three who stayed at home, David and George were the basketmakers. Jasper was more occupied with the various activities of the farm, but during the off seasons of the farm work he worked in the basket-shop. The shop had been started years before by their father, Daniel Fisher, as a gristmill for grinding meal, first for neighbors and later for the storemen, S. C. Lovell and Rogerson Brothers, both of whom bought their meal from out of town. The Fisher boys, with their ox team, used to haul the grain from the freight house to the mill and, after it was ground, to the stores. With the same waterpower that ground the meal they sawed lumber for themselves and for the community. After a time they enlarged the mill and used one end for making baskets of all kinds, though chiefly the baskets were the various kinds of farm baskets and the large two bushel crockery baskets of red oak.

The Fisher brothers found that their basket stuff could be used for another product, namely wooden shanks for men's shoes. These wooden shanks were sold in Brockton to shoe manufacturers, who used them to give spring and elasticity to men's shoes.

The Fisher's mill was more than a workship; it furnished sleeping quarters for some of the Fisher boys. Three of them swung hammocks in the upper part of the mill. Perhaps they had acquired a liking for that sort of berth when they were at sea,—two of them were in the navy for a time. That upper floor, sixty and more years ago, was sometimes used for dances.

Just as the mill was used for more than one purpose, so the land was used for more than ordinary farming. On the side they started the cranberry business. As the cranberry business increased in importance the Fishers devoted more attention to that. At length, they greatly enlarged their cranberry bog and gave up the mill entirely.

Less than a mile beyond the Fishers' were two more basket shops; one used by the Farrington brothers; the other by the Skinners. Both Skinners and Farringtons made the usual kinds. Charles Farrington, however, used a different method to dispose of his product.

Spring and fall, Mr. Farrington went off, usually to Cape Cod, on a selling tour. He had a large wagon planned for the purpose. On a platform body, hung on heavy express wagon axles, were arranged stakes spreading outward. Six inches from the top was a light frame of three inch furring, having holes for the stake ends. This was hung over the stakes to hold them firm. In this rack were packed the bail-less baskets of all kinds, fitted together by size, and tied with tarred rope. The baskets with bails were hung on the stakes. As many as two hundred baskets could be carried on a single trip. The driver's seat, built like a box with a back, was useful to Mr. Farrington to carry anything he might need during his seven-day absence. By the time he got back his box was always full, and more besides, for he had bartered many of his baskets along the way for farm produce. In the same way he had paid for food and lodging for himself and stabling for his horse. On such a trip he got a pretty good idea of the kind of baskets he could sell next time, and in the long intervals between trips he worked on those.

Continuing on about a mile beyond Farrington's, toward West Mansfield, was Adoniram Skinner's basket shop. Here were some rather unusual types. For example, Mr. Skinner made signal baskets for the railroad. This was before the days of the interlocking system and the signal towers; yet some manner of signaling was necessary. Someone devised a basket signal. Who that was we do not know, but we do know it was Adoniram Skinner who made them, hundreds of them, for the railroad. In the *Mansfield News* for 1874, we read that "A. J. Skinner has just finished an order for one hundred signal baskets for different railroads." Most of his orders were for Fred Paine, the station master at our own station. If Mr. Paine wanted some of these baskets, he put on his tall silk hat, mounted an engine, and ran down the track to Skinner's crossing. When he was a few rods from the crossing he began to blow the whistle and kept it up until he arrived. No one could help hearing his call and Adoniram Skinner knew what it meant. It meant that Fred Paine wanted signal baskets and wanted them right away! These baskets were shaped like an egg, two and a half by three feet and covered with canvas. Before they were used they were painted black. They were hung from the arm of a pole thirty or forty feet above the ground. Hanging from the bottom of the basket was a lantern for night use. The signal baskets were operated by a double chain system at the nearest station. So far as is known no other basketmaker made signal baskets. Some railroads used tin signals of the same shape painted red.

Besides having a corner on signal baskets, Mr. Skinner was alone in making eel pots out of basket stuff. These were four feet long and at the largest end almost as big around as a water pail. The small end tapered to four inches and was covered with canvas. Just inside the large open end was a funnel

of loose basket strips that gave as the eels swam in, but closed
so that the fish could not make their way out. Mr. Skinner sold
a great many of these in Boston, from which point they went
to the Cape and other fishing grounds.

No other basketmaker made the quohog-shaped baskets
such as Mr. Skinner made for the Ames' shovel factory in
Easton. These baskets, used to hold waste, brought Mr. Skinner fifty dollars a dozen, an unusually good price for baskets.
Adoniram Skinner's fan-shaped charcoal baskets and coal
baskets did not differ materially from those made by his
neighbors.

It will never do to take the space to list every basketmaker
and his products. Those mentioned above are typical.

The Shepard firm is the only one doing business today.
Their business was started years ago by Henry Shepard. He
may not have made baskets himself, but he was an agent who
went around collecting baskets from small producers and then
shipped them to market in Boston and Providence. Some of
the baskets were sent by freight and some were carried over the
road in wagons.

Henry Shepard's sons, Elmer and Everett, became actively
engaged in the manufacture of baskets about 1885. In their
most flourishing days they employed about sixteen men. In
all the years that they were in business no employee was ever
discharged from the pay roll. Thirty-four have died while in
their service. Others have left only because they were moving
from town or going into some other line of work. Elmer
Shepard died nearly twenty years ago and Everett Shepard in
1930. Since the death of Everett Shepard, Mrs. Elmer Shepard
has carried on the business, the only basket shop in Our Town
and doubtless one of the few in the country. Cranberry growers and truck gardeners now use wooden boxes; coal men use
canvas bags; and store men use pasteboard cartons to a great
extent.

Though basketmaking in the nineteenth century never brought large pay, it required comparatively little overhead expense and meant a good livelihood to many a family. Some men worked at it during off seasons in other lines of work. One old basketmaker put it, "Not much money in basket making, but if you want a few extra dollars there ain't no easier way to get 'em than to make a few extra dozen baskets." The really energetic basketmaker made more than a comfortable living. Basketmakers in the olden days, making nine or ten dollars a week, did not worry about feeding and clothing their children. Taxes were low and there was time to produce their own food stuffs. Many a man, untroubled by Wall Street fluctuations, contentedly grew old in the basket business. Horace Shaw, at the age of eighty-six, had a record of having made baskets for sixty-seven years and was still actively engaged at his trade.

Not all of the basketmakers of Our Town were content to remain at home. In the late 1850's, or early 1860's, five basketmakers from here went to Oak Creek, ten miles from Milwaukee, Wisconsin, to engage in the business. They found plenty of wood near at hand and a market in Milwaukee. Three of the men spent the rest of their lives there. After the Civil War two of the group went to Maryland, there to be joined by other basketmakers from Our Town. Baltimore was their market. Still another party of our men went to Lumberville, Pennsylvania, to engage in the trade.

In basketmaking days trade-marks were little known for such products. Wholesale dealers knew the reliability of the men with whom they were dealing, but the basket user gave no thought to its origin, hence basketmaking had no chance to spread the reputation of Our Town.

CHAPTER EIGHT

Cutlery Shops

OUR TOWN grew slowly but steadily. The railroad and coal
mines had brought English-speaking foreigners to work and
make their homes here. Not until the gold rush of 1849 did
many of our men leave to seek their fortunes elsewhere.

In 1844, for the first time since the days of the French
foundrymen (1779-1783), men of foreign birth came here to
establish an industry. The new arrivals were Robert Fulton
and his father-in-law, Robert McMoran.

Though presumably unknown to each other in the old
country, they were both born in the north of Ireland. From
across the water they both came to Boston, McMoran, a married man with a family, and Fulton, a child with his parents.
In 1838 Mr. McMoran, who had been a forgeman in his home-
land, moved his family to Easton where he became a hammerer
in the Ames' shovel factory. About the same time seventeen-
year old Robert Fulton went to work at the same shovel factory as a trimmer.

The lonely youth found friendliness and companionship in
the McMoran family where there were two daughters. This
friendliness and companionship soon evolved into marriage
with Mary McMoran, and a business partnership with the
father.

The two men left the employ of the Ameses, and, in 1844,
undertook the making of knives in a little shop on the Canoe
River in Our Town. There they remained ten years.

There were not a dozen neighbors within a radius of a mile,
and those were genuine country people, born and brought up
on the land. Young Robert Fulton, lately from Boston, made
quite a sensation whenever he appeared with his pretty bride.

Picture him on a Sunday morning going with his wife to the country church: his fine figure topped with a tall silk hat, his coat with brass buttons, his waistcoat of buff, lavender pants encasing his shapely legs, and shoes of patent leather. Mrs. Fulton looked equally fine in a large beribboned bonnet, full silk dress distended with a hoop skirt.

Their Canoe River factory was small. The number of employees was listed as six; their invested capital was one thousand dollars; and their yearly output was valued at four thousand dollars.

By 1851 they needed a larger factory and found the site of the burned Pratt and Bates cotton factory on the Rumford River just what they wanted. This, with the buildings, surrounding land, and water privilege, they bought for $3500 from Samuel B. Schenk, the owner of the machine shop further up the stream. At once they built a three-story factory. On the same land Mr. McMoran built himself a good-looking house; and from the heirs of Solomon Pratt's son, Harrison, Mr. Fulton acquired the finest home in town.

Within the next twelve years many changes took place. Mr. McMoran's daughter, Letitia, married George A. Robinson. In 1863, Robert McMoran sold out his share in the Moran and Fulton business to Robert Fulton for $3500 and went into business with his son-in-law, Robinson, in West Mansfield.

Notice that the *Mc* has been dropped from the firm name. It is no mistake. In stamping the knives with the company name of McMoran and Fulton, the *Mc* kept dropping off. In a new die each letter cost fifteen cents. It was cheaper and easier to drop the *Mc* altogether.

Before the father-in-law had left for West Mansfield, Mrs. Fulton had died. Mr. Fulton did not remain a widower long. His second wife was a stunning young relative from New York state. Though less than twenty years old this capable girl proved a fitting mate for the young business man. She equalled

him in his ability to wear stylish clothes. Her black silk gowns
and her appearance on horseback called forth much admiration, and none wore hoop skirts with more grace.

The beguiling clothes of the Fultons make it hard to stick
to business. We must; Robert Fulton did. He is said by more
than one who knew him to have been the most remarkable
business man that Our Town ever had.

One incident that illustrates his business acumen is shown
in the way he managed during the serious financial panic of
1857. There was practically no money in circulation at that
time and many families throughout the country actually suffered for want of food and clothing. Not so the thirty or forty
men in Moran and Fulton's knife shop; they had enough of
both. Mr. Fulton took his shoe knives to Brockton and traded
them for shoes; another load of shoe knives he traded in Lynn
for groceries; after the same manner he got clothing from some
other place. The attic of his factory he turned into a sort of
store, from which he allowed his men to draw all they needed.
In addition he promised to pay his men when money should
once more be in circulation, which promise he kept.

Besides shoe knives the firm made oyster, cigar, bread, fish,
and other knives. They also turned out large quantities of peg
awls.

Just before Mr. Fulton's sickness and death, in 1865, he was
sending twenty thousand dollars worth of goods yearly to New
York and Philadelphia markets, from which places the goods
were shipped south and west. His reputation was so well established that his regular customers took all that he could produce.

Let us turn back time and visit the factory. As we arrive,
Charles Williams' team is backed up at the door. So many men
are handling the load that we have difficulty in discerning
what it is. A bystander tells us that it is a huge grinding wheel
that weighs tons. It had been shipped from Windsor, Nova

Scotia, where the firm always buy its wheels. When in place it will stand six feet high.

"Better be careful when it is set up," we are told. "The last one burst and went through the side of the building."

"No, no one was hurt, because they knew that just such a thing had happened years before, and they were on their guard."

Lynch and Waters are the grinders for the large wheels. At the smaller wheels, which are the big ones cut down, less expert men are grinding.

The steel comes to the factory in long narrow sheets and the first process is to cut it with machine shears to suit the different length of blades. Next, it is cut into strips, two thirds the width of the future blades. It is now ready to be passed through the die press and then forged to as near the proper shape as possible, with a trip hammer. By hand the shank is drawn into the proper shape and the edge and back trimmed with heavy shears. Up to this point the steel has been kept soft to make it easy to handle. The blades are now ready to harden. A half-dozen blades at a time are immersed in moulten lead until they reach the desired heat, then they are thrust into cold oil and lastly cold water. These operations leave the blade of different degrees of hardness. Now all must be tempered. Good judgment and practice are required to bring the blades to just the right color by heating in a sand bath over a hot fire.

We now go back to the grinding room where we saw the huge grinding wheels being set up. Here the dull black steel blades are straightened and each blade "cross" ground and "draw" ground. On the different grades of emery wheels they receive the final silvery polish. The blades are now ready for the handles, which have been shipped, rough-turned, from New York. The handles receive a polish, and the ferrules, cut from brass tubing, are added.

The peg awls are cut from square wire, called "peg awl plate steel," the required length, each piece forged separately by hand, hardened, tempered, ground, polished, and finally packed in gross boxes for the market.

Mr. Fulton, as already stated, died in 1865. For the next three years the business was carried on by his executor, Judge E. M. Reed. In the meantime the widow had found another husband and the business passed into his hands. For the next thirty-five years he ran the factory successfully, then retired and the shop was closed.

Do not forget that before Mr. Fulton died his father-in-law had gone into the knife business in West Mansfield with George Robinson, another son-in-law. They were on the site of the old Williams Cotton Factory. For a second time in a dozen years Robert McMoran built a knife factory on the site of a burned cotton mill.

Soon they were making butcher knives, oyster knives, bread knives, shoe knives, and cigar knives. Mr. McMoran had retained the *Mc* and the knives made at West Mansfield factory were stamped "McMoran and Sons." "Sons" meant his son-in-law and grandson. After Robert McMoran retired, the firm name became "George A. Robinson and Company."

The cutlery from this factory was shipped to New York, and was sold to all parts of the United States, to Nova Scotia, and other parts of Canada. At the Centennial Exhibition in Philadelphia, in 1876, Mr. Robinson sent a large case of knives made by the firm. There were nearly two hundred and fifty knives in the case.

Mr. Robinson died near the beginning of the new century. After his time knives were no longer made at that factory, though other lines of goods were produced there.

Our Town had still another knife shop. In 1863 John and Robert Murphy of Boston bought, at mortgage sale, a good two-story building which less than twenty years before had been built for a machine shop. They bought it for $6300. Besides the main shop there was the long narrow three-room building, one hundred by twenty feet, already described in the last chapter as a basket shop; a little shop across the river; a two family house; and all the water privilege at that point on the Rumford River. It was a bargain; only three years before the property had carried an eleven thousand dollar mortgage. The small shops all had tenants. As the first floor of the larger building was all the room the Murphys needed, they were able to let the second floor and basement. The Murphys furnished power from their plant for all the small concerns. With the income from their business and the rents, they were able to pay off all the mortgages within five years.

Before the Murphys came to Our Town they had been making dental and surgical instruments in Boston since 1848. Here they continued along the same line for a time. Soon they added a great variety of fine cutlery, oyster knives, shoe knives, paperhanger's knives, cigarmaker's knives, pruning shears, buttonhole cutters, tobacco shears, pinking irons, butter tryers, cheese tryers, can openers, cork screws, cigar box openers, and skates. Perhaps it was by their skates that they were best known. They made plain and fancy skates, some of them inlaid for the fancier skaters. The steel they used was imported from England. They employed twenty or more men, the most skillful being Germans and Englishmen who came to Our Town to work in that shop. Murphy goods were sold to New York and Chicago and many oyster knives went to Norfolk, Virginia.

John Murphy liked Our Town and settled here to stay the rest of his life. He improved his side of the house and kept his yard tidy. But Robert pined for Boston. He took little interest in his environment and didn't care if his goat did eat up the small trees that were trying to grow by the roadside. After twenty years he moved his family back to Boston.

It was probably the disastrous fire of 1880 that hastened

Robert Murphy's going. After the fire the firm used a vacant foundry until the shop could be rebuilt. Robert Murphy never went back with his brother to the old site. Alone, John Murphy did not try to manufacture as much as when his brother had been with him. After a time he sold his shop to Simon W. Card, who was making taps and dies in the building. Mr. Murphy then did his work in a smaller shop in another part of the town.

In 1906 John Murphy retired, after having been in business fifty-eight years.

CHAPTER NINE

Machine Shops

By 1845 the railroad passing through the town did not seem so doubtful a blessing as when first proposed. Owners of the cotton mills, the nail factories, the bonnet shop, the knife shop, and the basketmakers, found it useful for transporting their products. Furthermore, the railroad attracted new business.

Samuel B. Schenck, who was making carpenters' planes in a small shop in South Foxboro, wished to have larger quarters and to be nearer the railroad. In Our Town, a few rods from the railroad station and on the Rumford River, he found exactly the site and small shop he wanted. He didn't care about the small shop. It was there. He at once built a two-story shop. For ten years Loren Willis and his brother, Ichabod, had been making axles in the shop, but Schenck offered them a price that induced them to sell. For $4500, Mr. Schenck was able to buy the little shop, five and three quarters acres of land, the privilege of the run-way, the privilege of flowage from October eleventh to April eleventh annually, and also an old sawmill.

Immediately, Mr. Schenck began buying more real estate, and commenced building; first, he bought a house for himself and half an acre of land with a string attached (former owners reserved the right to dig for coal, or other minerals, but promised to make restitution, if they damaged any crops); next, he bought land all around him, put up buildings, constructed a mill dam and mill pond; soon, he had a two-story shop that was then considered large, several tenements for his help, and a store where his employees were expected to trade. Later, after the death of Solomon Pratt and the burning of the Pratt and Bates Cotton Factory in 1850, Mr. Schenck bought that property and thus controlled that water privilege beyond his own plant. This, however, he disposed of in four years to McMoran and Fulton for their knife works.

It was, therefore, not long after his arrival in town that the new shop was built and in full operation, doing a twenty thousand-dollar business and by far the largest concern here. He employed from thirty to fifty men. The company was called the Mansfield Machine Company. Samuel B. Schenck was the president and principal owner. The directors were listed as T. J. B. Schenck and John B. Schenck, one and the same person, we suspect, and, in fact, a brother of Samuel, the president.

Samuel Schenck took an interest in the town. At his own expense he built a road three quarters of a mile long, from the railroad station past his factory to the knife shop of Moran and Fulton. He gave thirteen lamps, including a chandelier, the whole costing one hundred dollars, to the Congregational Church, when the building was completely renovated in 1852. He gave his support to the Mansfield Academy, by sending his three children there.

There is a story that Samuel Schenck had political aspirations. He wanted to represent Our Town in the legislature in 1854, so the tale runs, and John Rogers, the straw shop owner, also wanted to go. Mr. Rogers usually had things just about as he wanted them politically and he did this time. Schenck took his defeat so bitterly, so they say, that he moved his family and part of his business out of town.

Whether or not the story is true nobody knows. Certain it is that at that time, less than ten years after coming here, he took up his residence at Fishkill, New York.

The Mansfield Machine Company continued in business after Mr. Samuel Schenck's removal from town, but in a few years it fell on evil days. It had a hard time weathering the business crisis of 1854-7. Samuel Schenck took a personal mortgage of nine thousand dollars and there was already a small mortgage to Loren Willis that had never been paid. Six months after Mr. Schenck took the nine thousand-dollar mortgage, he gave an eleven thousand-dollar mortgage to an Attleboro man. Eventually, the mortgage was in the hands of the Wrentham bank. In 1864 the bank had to foreclose and at once disposed of the factory to the Murphy brothers, whose story was told in the last chapter.

The fiasco of the Mansfield Machine Company was not the end of machine shops in Our Town, nor, as we shall see later, of machine shops on that site.

Before machinery was again made at the Schenck location, cutlery and jewelry were made there and another group of men established a machine shop a quarter of a mile farther north.

This second machine shop was run by men who had come from Providence, in 1868, and organized as the Fletcher Manufacturing Company, incorporated in Rhode Island. As the land they bought was known as the "Machine Shop Lot," perhaps there had been some sort of a machine shop there before they came, possibly it was used for machinery by the Chilson Foundry close by. Anyhow, the building the Fletcher Company found had been used by Mr. Chilson for making stoves and furnaces. It is all rather vague as to what kind of machinery the Fletcher Company manufactured. It is known that, besides the shop, they owned and ran the store that in the early eighteen fifties Schenck had built and operated in connection with his machine shop.

After four years, the property that had cost the Fletcher Company seven thousand dollars was sold for fifty-two hundred to John Birkenhead of Providence. Mr. Birkenhead was not a Providence man. He had lately gone to Providence from Canton, Massachusetts, and before that he had come from Manchester, England, where he was well versed in the spinning business.

In Our Town, Mr. Birkenhead made spindles and lathes.

Some forty or fifty men were employed at the shop. Many of the operations were so simple that boys could be trained to undertake the work. These youngsters, some so small that they had to stand on boxes, were paid from two to two dollars and a quarter a week. One man who learned his trade there said that he began at twelve years of age by taking care of Mr. Birkenhead's three horses, at thirty cents a day. Soon he had a hundred per cent raise and in time was paid a dollar a day for work in the factory. The best paid men received twelve dollars a week.

Mr. Birkenhead was a very ingenious man and saw many improvements that could be made in cotton machinery. These ideas he put into form and had them patented, one such was a patent granted in 1880 for a mechanism to support the spindles of a ring spinning frame. There were other patents equally important. He made several trips to Europe to sell his patents there. In whatever countries he visited he was well received and his ideas found sale.

The Birkenhead inventions were not confined to machinery. There were improvements in office work and card filing that Mr. Birkenhead foresaw and patented.

Mr. Birkenhead ran his machine shop here successfully for nearly twenty years and then sold the factory to a young man who used it for some process in making plush.

While Mr. Birkenhead was in business he was his own salesman and he needed a reliable, capable man to run his machine shop while he was away. For this purpose Simon W. Card came, either with Mr. Birkenhead or soon after. Like Mr. Birkenhead, Mr. Card was full of ideas about machinery and its improvement. While at work making spindles he was thinking of taps and dies.

Up to 1871, according to a brochure on the history of the Greenfield Tap and Die Corporation, there existed no machine either for cutting the external thread on the surface of a

bolt, or for making the internal thread on the walls of the hole
to receive the bolt. The thread had to be produced by "worry-
ing" the thread into the rod with the old style "jamb plate."
It was a tiresome process of rotating back and forth, of "squeez-
ing and jambing the metal out of the grooves until a very in-
different sort of thread was produced." The thread of the
tapped bore was made in a similarly crude manner, being
made by the old form of blacksmith's tape tap. Says the author
of the Greenfield pamphlet, "To fit a nut to a bolt was a very
laborious process." On October 24, 1871, John J. Grant of
Northampton was allowed a patent on a new device of his
own invention that would make the desired threads. He then
went to Greenfield and started the business.

Simon Card in Our Town doubtless had heard of that.
Whenever Mr. Birkenhead was away Mr. Card surreptitiously
made taps and dies and as the opportunity presented itself he
filled his pockets with his products and started for Boston to
sell his wares.

At length Mr. Card decided that he wanted to give his entire attention to the manufacture of taps and dies. The story
is told that when Mr. Birkenhead heard of the decision of his
superintendent he gave him freely what he considered good
common sense advice. He pointed out how foolish it was to
give up a good job of foreman to manufacture such trifles.

"Why," he is reported to have said, "one man and a couple
of boys can make all the taps and dies that will ever be used in
the world."

Whether or not Mr. Birkenhead ever said it, it was not an
unreasonable warning. The taps and dies at first were too expensive to have ready sale. Relying on the Greenfield story we
learn that the new bolt cutter cost eighty dollars compared to
five or six dollars for the jamb plate of the blacksmith. Moreover, Mr. Card had no money to set himself up in business.

Undaunted, Simon Card launched out in the basement of

Murphy's cutlery shop. He had neither milling machine nor lathe, but John Murphy let him use the machines in his shop. In fact, Mr. Murphy, who among other things was getting out cork-screws, gave Mr. Card some points on getting the spiral. There were times when John's brother, Robert, considered Card a nuisance, as he got in the way using their machines.

At the very first Mr. Card worked alone, then he took on a few men and some boys. One of the boys was Tom Hibbert, who ran the errands. Daily, Tom was handed a peck basket of unfinished taps and dies to carry over to Mr. Card's house, where Mrs. Card was expecting them. Tom sat down in the kitchen to wait while Mrs. Card tempered the steel on her kitchen stove. Though she watched her work carefully, occasionally a piece got too hot; then she plunged it into a bowl of water that she kept on the back of the stove for just such an emergency. When the tempering was done the boy took the basket of tools back to the shop.

Another daily trip for the youth was with material to be forged at Chapman's blacksmith shop, and a third daily jaunt was to the express office.

For his labors young Hibbert was paid at the rate of forty cents a day. Pay day for all the employees came once a month, unless funds were low, in which case they had to wait until a check came in to Mr. Card. The men were sure to get the money sometime.

Two men, years afterwards, recalled the time that they did *not* earn a quarter in their boyhood days in the shop. It happened on a Saturday afternoon: Mr. Card was working in a flurry of haste to finish a die that was important to get off at once. The work had reached the stage where it was ready for the final polish on the emery wheel. One of the workmen happened to be perched on the box that served as a stool, in front of the crude polisher. With little ceremony, and with strong language, Mr. Card ordered him down, and in a trice was on the box himself, holding the die over the revolving wheel. Zipp!! Pish!' Consternation. Vehement words. In his nervous hurry Mr. Card had let the tool get caught in the leather covering of the wheel and away it had gone, through the window. Mr. Card looked about at the wide-eyed, gaping boys.

"I know one of you would like to earn some money. I'll gin any one of you a quarter if you will find that thing."

Diligently they searched around Murphy's cow sheds and in the field beyond, but all in vain. The result was that Mr. Card had to pay one of his men a dollar to file another die on Sunday.

The loss of the necessary die was annoying. There was, however, a really serious loss awaiting Mr. Card. On a night in March, 1880, the shop where Mr. Card was doing his work was burned to the ground. Telling of it afterwards, Mrs. Card used to say, "We lost everything but the door key."

It was little enough that Mr. Card had to lose. Though working hard for six years his profits had been slight and he had been able to acquire very little machinery of his own.

As Mrs. Card watched the fire, she began to cry.

"This is the only dress I've got," she wailed. "And when shall I have another?"

Perhaps that night the Cards wished they had followed Mr. Birkenhead's advice. But with the dawn came fresh courage. He decided to go on. Mr. Card was not without friends. John W. Rogers, one of the partners of the Straw Shop, went to him.

"Did you lose everything, Mr. Card?"

"Yes, everything."

"Will fifty dollars help you?"

It was the confidence more than the monetary value that helped.

Mr. Card set up his business in the unused attic of Matthew George's knife shop (formerly Moran and Fulton's). Mrs.

Card then lost her job of tempering. That was done by the temperer of the knife shop.

John Murphy immediately rebuilt the shop and it was not long before he and Mr. Card were back there, not, however, in exactly the same relation as formerly. Before the fire, the Murphy brothers had occupied the most space and Mr. Card had small quarters in the basement, or wherever John Murphy would let him use machinery. Now it was arranged that Mr. Card should have the most room, for Card had expanded his business and Murphy had reduced his, after his brother Robert retired from the firm.

Mr. Card was ambitious and optimistic. He needed more machinery and as his purse was still flat he sought financial assistance. First, he approached his friend, Charles Williams, silent partner of Doliver Spaulding in the jewelry business. Mr. Williams failed to have faith enough in the taps and dies to invest any of his money in their manufacture. Next, Mr. Card sought out David Harding, who as a partner in the Rogers' straw shop had made a little money. He agreed to let Mr. Card have five thousand dollars. Though five thousand dollars looked bigger, and was bigger, in the eighteen eighties, than it is now, it did not go far. Mr. Card asked for more. Mr. Harding let him have another five thousand, which was probably a loan, as the records show only the first five thousand as actual investment. Even then Mr. Card was not satisfied; he asked for five thousand dollars more. This almost staggered Mr. Harding. Before he could make up his mind he talked it over with friends on Main Street, as was his way. They advised him that since he had already let Mr. Card have so much he had better let him have this, with the hope that in so doing he would get returns on his original investment. Harding took the advice. He was never asked to put in any more. Within a few years, money was coming back to him, and in time, as treasurer, he was drawing five thousand dollars a month from the company.

Much happened before Mr. Harding began to receive so large a return. There was another fire. The second fire came just ten years after the first one, and was disastrous.

The night of March 3, 1890, was chilly and there was snow on the ground. By eleven-thirty the good people of Our Town were sleeping soundly in their beds, as the good people of those days were wont to do. Suddenly the neighbor nearest to Card's shop was awakened by a snapping noise and found her room flooded with light. In no time her husband was out of the house, spreading the alarm. Town water had recently been installed in Our Town and following that, a fire company had been organized, but it was all so new that no fire alarm had been arranged. Cries of "Fire" echoed up and down the street. The firemen arrived promptly, but immediately had trouble with ice, and then a hose burst. On through the night they fought the fire. By three o'clock in the morning it was pronounced out. Though the building was not entirely burned, there was a damage of $8,750. The firemen had worked well and had saved a large consignment of valuable stock that was all packed, ready to be shipped. In appreciation, Mr. Card gave the firemen one hundred dollars.

Fortunately, seven new machines that had come to town the day before were still at the freight house.

Next day, Mr. Card put a force of thirty-five men to work cleaning the fine steel that would otherwise have been ruined by the water. Mr. Card was very choice of that fine English steel and had constantly warned the men about wasting it. It cost a dollar a pound.

On the fourth day after the fire the men were at work in the basement, manufacturing stock and filling orders.

In the years that elapsed between the first and second fire, a partnership known as the Card Company was formed, with

Simon W. Card the head of it and David E. Harding the silent partner. The company had bought the building from Mr. Murphy.

In 1894 another business adjustment was made; the firm became a corporation, issuing stock under the name of the S. W. Card Manufacturing Company. Mr. Card was the president, Mr. Harding, the treasurer, and Mr. Card's daughter, Miss Lulu Card, the secretary.

Miss Card died, in 1896, at thirty-one years of age. Her death was a great blow to her father and mother. They not alone lost their only child, but Mr. Card felt that he had lost a business companion and associate. In memory of the young woman, the sorrowing parents built a beautiful Card Memorial Chapel at the entrance of the cemetery in Our Town. Three years later Mr. Card died.

Mr. Card was genuinely mourned by his employees. All bore testimony that he was an honest, upright man. If he thought that a man deserved more money than he was receiving he raised his pay without being asked.

"Tom," he would say, "I'm going to gin you twenty-five cents more a day. Try and earn it, won't you?"

As president of the company Mr. Card was succeeded by Frederick J. Smith, the very first man that Mr. Card had hired to help him, in 1874. Mr. Harding remained as treasurer until his death, in 1909. Then Mr. Smith became treasurer, as well as president. After Miss Card's death, John W. Rathbun, who had worked up from the position of book-keeper, became secretary and held the office until 1913, when he became sales manager.

In 1913 there came a distinct change. The plant, though retaining its name and the good will of its customers, became a division of the Union Twist Drill, the other divisions being located at Athol, Massachusetts, Derby Line, Vermont, and Rock Island, Canada. Mr. Smith was general manager of the local plant for one year, then retired and was succeeded by Mr. Rathbun.

During all the years of the firm, whichever name it bore, the same class of goods have been going out from there. Up to the present depression many of the same men continued to work in the factory, some for a generation, some longer; even for fifty-two, or fifty-three years, some men had worked on dies that were stamped with the name of Card. Hence, the general public took little cognizance of the administrative changes taking place.

What the public did notice was the external growth. For some years, even after the second fire, the small one-story and semibasement frame building was sufficient. About 1896-7 the company built a narrow, wooden addition, some seventy feet long. This was also one-story and semibasement. At the time of the merger with the Union Twist Drill, in 1913, a two-story brick building was erected in front of the previous buildings. Then came the great war with the increased demand for the products of the factory, and, in 1917, two stories were added to the brick structure and a four-story addition built up against it.

Many of the men working in the factory at that time had seen its growth from the days when Mr. Card was able to carry his output of dies in his pocket to its position of shipping goods to every part of the world, to every spot where there is a manufacturing concern that fastens two metals together. To-day, England alone has more than half a dozen wholesale houses where Card's taps and dies are sold.

The Union Twist Drill has a capitalization that runs into millions and the division in Our Town is no insignificant part of it.

Up to the time of the war the work in the factory was considered solely a man's job. Then, as the men enlisted, about forty girls went in to supply the shortage of man labor. Once admitted the girls have continued to work there. The greatest number of employees, both men and women, was during the war-time rush, when three hundred and fifty were at work. At all times during the present century it has been the busiest factory in town.

The Card Company has served as a school for die makers. John and Murray Winter, owners and operators of the Winter Brothers' tap and die works in Wrentham, received their training here. The men at the head of the Bay State Tap and Die Company of Our Town are also graduates of the Card shop.

The Bay State Tap and Die Company, organized by local men in 1903, has a brick factory and is a firm of which Our Town is proud, but since it is a twentieth century plant it does not come into this story.

CHAPTER TEN

The Bailey Bakeshop and Ovens

FROM 1840 to 1850 Our Town had made a gain of over four hundred in population, an advance not to be equaled by any other decade before 1890. Many small industries had come into existence. One of these was a bakery.

The making of bread commercially in Massachusetts towns was an innovation in the eighteen forties, though in Boston there were forty-six bakers in 1841. Not many housewives were then ready to relinquish the homemade product, the real pride of not a few; and, furthermore, these thrifty New England women felt that the buying of bread was an extravagance. Yet there were enough purchasers to warrant the starting of bakeries throughout the state. Before 1820 the Boston bakers employed boys to carry the bread about in covered wheelbarrows. The first carts distributing rolls and brick loaves on the streets of Boston were introduced in 1840, and were two-wheeled vehicles which opened near the top on each side. The number of bakeries in the state were few at first and the first Baker's Exhibition, held in 1843, attracted little attention, but the fifth one, with prizes, in 1847, aroused an interest that called out numerous bakers and flour merchants. Two years later, the California Gold Rush gave a boost to the cracker trade. Sailing vessels filled with expectant gold diggers needed a bread that would not mould during the many weeks that would be spent on the way around Cape Horn to the west coast. With this impetus, little bakeries began springing up in small towns all over Massachusetts; one in Our Town. A large number of these attempts failed after a year or two; ours survived.

The bakery here was established a year before the Forty-niners started on their long voyage. It was begun in a small way by Jacob Bailey, a farmer and basketmaker, son of Abner Bailey, the farmer-basketmaker, whose story was told in a previous chapter. Jacob Bailey was at that time forty-seven years old, too old by the age standard then to be entering upon a new enterprise. According to the family tradition, he did not actively engage in the baking of bread but started the business to keep his children from wandering too far from the parental roof. His ambitious son, George, then nineteen years old, had already gone to New Bedford to buy and sell ship timber for New Bedford whaling vessels. Jacob, a staunch deacon of the Orthodox Congregational Church, would have preferred to have his only son become a minister. Jacob's only daughter had a beau who came selling bread from a bakery in Medfield. The deacon feared that she might marry the itinerant bread man and leave home, and he tried to solve the problem by settling Charles Turner, the prospective son-in-law, in a bakeshop in Our Town. Deacon Bailey furnished the land for the building and the money.

Son George married and settled in the west part of Our Town, still buying and selling ship timber. Daughter Deborah married her baker and all went well for a time. Charles Turner, however, after being tied to one spot for four years by a bakeshop had a return of the wanderlust. Then it was that Deacon Bailey made so strong an appeal to his own son that the young man came home, built himself a house near his father and sister, and went in business with his brother-in-law, Bailey doing the baking and Turner going out on the road with the bread and crackers. In a little while Bailey was in sole control, building up a good business and absorbing the trade of the surrounding towns. Turner kept up his line of work, buying at the bakeshop and selling from house to house, both here and nearby.

Charles Turner established a reputation all his own.

Through a long period of years he made himself an institutional part of town meeting, during the days when the spring voting was an all day affair. In the back of Central Hall, where town meetings were held, Mr. Turner set up his tables and the aroma of his coffee stimulated the voters. At the noon adjournment the men hurried to his stand and each one bought a big mug of coffee and a great town meeting bun, made at Bailey's bakeshop. In later years old folks seldom spoke of town meetings without mentioning those buns, each a meal in itself. Many remember Charles Turner because he was the first man in Our Town to make and sell ice cream.

About the time that George Bailey dissolved partnership with his brother-in-law, Turner, and went on alone, his capital investment was five hundred dollars, and he was consuming four hundred barrels of flour a year to put out seven thousand dollars worth of bread and crackers. In his employ were four men. Ten years later, 1865, his capital was three thousand dollars, the value of his stock twelve thousand, and though he was employing but five men he was putting out twenty thousand dollars worth of bread in a year. In time he was one of the largest wholesale bakers in this part of Massachusetts.

When the bakeshop was started in Our Town very few bakers anywhere were using machinery. The bread was mixed by hand and anything that required a batter was hand-stirred with a wooden paddle. The ovens were after the style of the old brick ovens seen today in ancient houses, only of course, the bakeshop ovens were larger. The fagot fire was built in one side and kept going until the bricks were thoroughly heated. Two doors to the oven allowed the baker to put the bread in one and clean out the ashes through the other. The baking section was built two-story and the brown bread and beans were put in the upper section to be left all night.

After the Civil War there was a distinct change in ovens. George C. Jennison of Walpole, New Hampshire, invented a mechanical reel oven, which consisted of a series of large iron pans revolving in a framework, similar to the later Ferris Wheel. The mechanism was placed in a great brick oven, so arranged that as the reel came in front of the door, the pan could be emptied and refilled. A complete circuit was sufficient for the baking process. This invention revolutionized the cracker business. According to Arthur Brayley in a book on "Bakers and Bakery in Massachusetts," an oven using a reel could consume forty to fifty barrels of flour, an advantage compared with a half-dozen to twenty-five or thirty barrels used for baking on the flat tiles.

Mr. Bailey never used a reel oven, because he was contriving an invention of his own. Having an inventive and mechanical mind, he was constantly endeavoring to improve the methods of baking. At length, a few years after the reel oven was put on the market, he had an invention that has been of lasting advantage to bakers. The first Bailey bread oven came out in 1871 and was patented in 1872. Within four years the Massachusetts Prison Commission placed three of the Bailey ovens in the State Prison at Concord, and one at the Reformatory at Sherburn. Other Bailey inventions and patents followed.

One of his inventions that was a great aid to him in baking crackers was an endless pan. This steel pan was eight feet wide and seventy-five feet long and was arranged to pass over the large drums of three fires, at graduated speeds. Thin, quick-baking wafers could go through in two minutes; thicker crackers could have twenty-eight minutes, if need be. All were sure of an even bake, top and bottom. Before this time, the baking was laborious and slow, and the results often unsatisfactory.

The little original bakeshop would hardly hold the new lengthy oven that had to be forty feet long to carry the traveling crackers, consequently Mr. Bailey built a fifty-foot addition. That was in 1879. The next year he added another room for more of his patent bread-baking ovens. The original old brick oven was still retained for brown bread and beans. These additions were necessary to fill his orders. He was having to run the shop night and day, and even then, at some seasons, was a week behind. Thirty barrels a day of some single articles failed to fill the demands.

By 1880 all the first-class grocery stores of New England were selling crackers, fancy biscuits, and cakes, made in Our Town. Bailey cakes had been on the market only a year at that time. To introduce his cake, Mr. Bailey had put out neat sample packages, with a printed price list. The boxes contained a slice of each variety made in the bakery.

A little before this time, George E. Bailey had taken his sons, George P. and Frank H., into the business with him, and the firm name had become George E. Bailey and Sons. With the support of his sons, he was able to carry on the growing oven business and the ever-increasing baking trade.

Some of the Bailey baked products were shipped by train to New York and parts of New England, though most of the goods were carried out on bread wagons. At one time there were perhaps twelve or fifteen bread carts going out from the factory, some on short trips through here and neighboring towns, others went as far as Boston, Providence, Taunton, Fall River, New Bedford, and even to Lowell. Part of this trade was wholesale and part was retail. For the most part the drivers of these bread carts, bought of Bailey and made what profit they could. Be assured it was no small profit. Some men did this for a few years, others made it a life long work. Charles Turner, except for the few years that he ran the bakery, never did anything else. William Hodges drove for eighteen years and then gave it up to settle down at home and make baskets.

When Mr. Hodges was peddling bread he made two trips a week, through Foxboro, Walpole, Wrentham, Plainville, North Attleboro and Easton. He drove two horses and carried about a hundred loaves on a trip. Each loaf weighed a pound and sold for ten cents, or three loaves for a quarter. Besides the bread, he had cakes, cookies, pies and crackers. He had his regular house-to-house customers, and also a wholesale route to Walpole and North Attleboro.

It was Lysander White who had the longest route and the largest bread cart. His loads were so heavy that four horses were required to draw the bread wagon. Now it can be told about his Canton trip, and how he got his money for the crackers. The goods taken there, like the rest of his deliveries, were for wholesale trade, and were carried from the Bailey bakeshop in forty-barrel lots, each barrel weighing more than one man could lift. At Canton White drove into a certain field and in an old barn, out of sight of the road, he deposited the forty barrels, then went in search of his pay. And this is the secret: He lifted a particular stone and there was the money. White made big money. It was not unusual for him to take in thirty-five dollars a day.

Bread carts going hither and yon every day; orders coming in by mail; four and one half tons shipped by freight in one day! The little shop with its additions was hard put to keep up the supply. Two shifts were at work there; two shifts, also, were occupying each bed in the little boardinghouse that had been Abner Bailey's home. Big wholesale bakers today would sneer should they read that Bailey was employing thirty, or more, at the shop. This, however, was fifty years ago in a small town. We were proud of the Bailey business and happy to see it expand and require a new factory.

The new building went up in 1883. Near it they built a new office, and used the old office for storing spices and sundries connected with baking. A brick and stone engine- and boiler-house was put up, with two tanks just outside to hold three thousand gallons of water for the boiler and for other purposes. What changes! In the beginning, a boy on the end of the crank was the motor power, then, a horse attached to a revolving windlass, and in 1883, a thirty or forty horse power steam engine. In 1848 there had been not more than a man or two at work, while in 1883 seventy or seventy-five were needed.

Under the improved conditions, two traveling ovens put out 320,000 ordinary crackers daily. If it happened to be oyster crackers that were going through, they came out at the rate of 3500 a minute. It took about thirty barrels of flour a day to make these crackers, and such crackers! The best that could be bought anywhere. Nor is this mere hearsay and local pride. There was every kind of cracker: common crackers, extra common crackers, soda crackers, graham crackers, zephers, wine crackers, amber biscuits, three kinds of oyster crackers, and others, to say nothing of the specials that came out now and then, such as "The House That Jack Built," "The Maiden All Forlorn," and "The Rat That Ate the Malt." About six barrels of flour a day went into cookies.

The bread making was a department by itself, and the work done at night, when none of the other workers were around. Bill Gaffney and his helpers came in early in the evening and started the bread, which came out of the ovens before the day workers came on. At four o'clock in the morning Gil Leavitt, and a helper, appeared at the shop to start the crackers. Thirty barrels of flour went into the batch, and the two men mixed it by hand, dipping into it up to their elbows. By early breakfast time that part of the work was done. At seven-o'clock the cracker crew were back again to attend to the baking.

The doughnut making was even more apart. That had been ostracized to a different building, separated from the main factory by the track of the Boston and Providence railroad, which ran through the Bailey land. Too many times, before it was moved, had the doughnut fat boiled over and endangered the whole factory. The Bailey men had such a fear of frying doughnuts that they never allowed any doughnuts to be made in their own kitchens. There was a fear of fire inbred in the Bailey family, and with reason.

Early one Monday morning, November, 1888, the Bailey bakeshop, through no fault of the arson-committing doughnut kettle, got on fire and was burned to the ground. Sparks from a passing steam-engine probably perpetrated the deed. It had done so before, but never with such disastrous results. The fire worked quickly. A young man passing along the road saw the building as usual; fifteen minutes later it was a mass of flames. Shrieks from a locomotive gave the general alarm. It was a spectacular fire, seen for many miles around. In two hours the main building, where the large cracker and cookie ovens were located, was in ashes. All of the valuable machinery, bought not long before by Mr. Bailey on a special trip to England, was destroyed. Large quantities of flour and other material stored in the basement were burned. One heavy team, loaded with the usual amount and variety of food, ready for an early start on Monday, was turned to cinders. Bert Rand, the man of all work, asleep in the factory, was rescued in a nearly unconscious condition.

The bread, pie and cake rooms were saved, and the big ovens, though crushed, were still usable. The offending doughnut kettle was left with its building across the railroad track, untouched by flames.

The big bakery was never rebuilt. The Baileys used to capacity what was left, until that was burned in 1890, and turned their greatest attention to the oven business which had been growing apace all those years, under the firm name, The Bailey Oven Company, with the father, George E. Bailey, president, and George P. Bailey, treasurer. Their oven, the "Continuous Baking Oven," was the one that George E. Bailey had developed in the original little bakeshop in 1871 and had

had patented in 1872. Charles Goodrich of Charlestown had the agency for Maine, New Hampshire, Vermont, and Massachusetts, and Jesse A. Lock, for New York and the rest of the United States.

In 1886, two years before the fire, the elder Bailey took his oven to England for display at the Healtheries' Exhibition in London. The oven was well received, but George Bailey himself nearly fell into disgrace. He had arrived before the exposition grounds were entirely ready and one day stood watching some English workmen awkwardly trying to fell a tree. It was more than the New England Yankee, once a trader in ship timber, could endure. Off came Mr. Bailey's coat and he seized an ax from a laborer. The superintendent of the grounds, chancing by, was consternated to see the foreigner at work. The tree was down before Mr. Bailey resumed his coat and pacified the Englishman.

In England, Mr. Bailey made contact with Joseph Baker & Sons, extensive manufacturers of bakers' machinery. The Baker firm took over the British agency of Mr. Bailey's oven, putting it out as the "Bailey-Baker Oven." In 1889 the oven was exhibited at the Paris Exposition. Joseph Baker and Sons even sent it to the World's Fair in Chicago in 1893 as part of their exhibit. With branches in all parts of the world, the London company sent the Bailey-Baker oven to distant countries, to India, to Russia, even to old Jerusalem.

On this side of the water, by 1890, the Bailey oven was installed in many public institutions and bakeries in the United States and Canada. For this trade the oven was beautifully advertised (we use the word advisedly). In the center of the advertising circular were three pictures, the faces of George P. Bailey's baby daughters. The annotation stated: "These children were brought up on bread made of Duluth Imperial Flour and Baked in a BAILEY PATENT OVEN." The proud

grandfather always said that he was the first man to use children's pictures in advertising.

Although the Bailey family are not actively engaged in oven
business, the Bailey ovens are still in use and were on exhibition at the Century of Progress Exposition at Chicago.

CHAPTER ELEVEN

Yankee Peddlers and Soap Makers

PEDDLING WAS the means of livelihood of many a New England man fifty and seventy-five years ago. We might make the range of years greater, for there were peddlers a hundred and twenty-five years ago; and at the beginning of the present century, peddler's carts drew up at our door, not to mention the fishman and vegetableman today.

The original Yankee Peddler was a man of a different order. He was not a man with a license for selling, a man starting out in the morning and returning to his home at night; nor was he down and out, traveling aimlessly; nor yet an elderly individual driving leisurely about the country. He was young, and up and coming. Richard Wright in his *Hawkers and Walkers of Early America*, says that the first peddlers had to be reckless, bright young men, with abundant grit and virility, capable of taking care of themselves.

Although such peddlers were found in all the thinly settled parts of the United States, practically all of them were natives of New England, and for that reason Yankee Peddler was the name applied to all.

A certain technique of salesmanship was required of those first peddlers. Wright says that their most effective sales talk was the "soft sawder of flattery," and that they had the genial habit of giving their customers the feeling of being "accommodated."

In the *Penny Magazine* for 1837 an Englishman gave his impression of the Yankee peddler of that time. He said they were mostly "active, handsome young men, shrewd, witty, intelligent, insinuating, wheedling, not always altogether down right particular honest."

Wright in his book points out that the Yankee peddler was not really considered dishonest, but was simply acting according to the standards of his time. It was a part of salesmanship to outwit the customer. When the buyer realized that he had not been as keen as the trader there was nothing he could do but laugh, and try to be more wary next time. The peddler joked about it when he got home. We have previously told how Sam Tolman boasted that he had sold to the women on Martha's Vineyard Island two small bonnets apiece, by explaining to them that the style that year was to wear two of the saucer-like affairs at a time, one on front, and one on back, over the bun.

One reason for the adaptability of the young New Englander to this kind of trading as suggested by Wright was the climate; the New England climate makes for a keener and quicker pace. Another reason was the soil; the native of this section of the country in the early days had to fight for every necessity of life.

The Yankee peddler was really a boon to the country people. How else would the women have obtained their new straw bonnets had not the peddlers from Rogers' bonnet shop in Our Town, or from some other straw shop, brought the bonnets to their doors? Rogers' men, even John Rogers himself, used to go to Maine and Cape Cod, and perhaps other places, selling bonnets, some of them, alas, slightly out of style, or seconds.

Didn't our mothers and grandmothers depend on the tin peddler coming around once in so often to take the old iron and rags (white and mixed colors carefully separated), in payment for brooms, milk pans, bread tins, pails and every kind of tin utensil?

As far back as 1845, according to a State record, Our Town had a little tin shop where two men were working. That is too long ago to locate, or even tell who the men were. Perhaps

Joseph W. Foster of Attleboro may have been an apprentice at the shop. At any rate, in 1852, when Joseph was twenty-three and marrying a widow four years his senior, he was the owner of the tin shop, and in 1855 was doing a business of one thousand dollars a year. Of course somebody, perhaps he himself at some seasons, was going about the country selling his wares.

In 1865 George L. Wheeler, who had previously run a tavern and livery stable here, was doing the work of a tin-smith and selling his goods to tin peddlers. One of these, a man named Baker, used to buy in large quantities and store his supply in the east end of the old Mulberry Tavern.

The peddler certainly was a benefactor to the farmer's wife. From him she bought not only tinware and straw bonnets, but yard goods, thread, needles and pins, elastic and laces, buttons and beeswax.

The first dry-goods peddler known to us by name was John Middleton from the west part of Our Town. He dates at least to 1848 and probably earlier, and for years traveled about with a wagon fitted up with shelves and drawers to hold his merchandise.

Oliver P. Cook, the shoeman, beginning in 1886, drove through West Mansfield, Norton, Easton, East Foxboro, Foxboro, and all over Our Town, for twenty-three years, then settled down, for fifteen years, with a shoe store of his own on Main Street.

Our Town had women peddlers, as well as men. One of these was "Old Lady White."

Old Lady White was, according to tradition, born in England of "high-toned" parentage. She suffered disinheritance because she ran away to Canada with the man of her own choice, the man of whom her parents disapproved. In Canada six children were born to the pair and they were destined to live happy ever after, when suddenly the cholera or some such scourge took husband and children all at once. Then Mrs. White came to the States.

Why she came to this section, or how she got here, no one knows. Judging from her later pedestrian feats, some say she walked. It was her common custom to walk to Taunton, twelve miles, to buy her supplies; and she not infrequently walked as far as Canton, fifteen miles, and even beyond, selling her goods.

She first went to Norton where she was cook at Wheaton Seminary. After that she went to keep house for Parker Makepeace, whose wife had just died.

Something led her to Our Town, probably around 1850. Here she settled herself in a little one-room house in Sodom. Her abode was so tiny that when J. Arthur Wheeler went to paint her house he first set the furniture out-doors and then went to work. When the day was over his job was completed, inside and out.

Mrs. White was an asset to the neighborhood. When needed, she went out nursing. The neighbors found her little store (part of her one room) convenient. She sold Arnold's Balsam, a popular home remedy of the day, tobacco, candy, pins, needles, pencils, skein thread, shoe strings and such small wares, the same sort of things she took peddling.

Little children, for some reason, were afraid of her, but young people as well as their elders liked to drop in of an evening to see her. She was a hospitable soul; if she happened to have gone to bed when there came a tap at her portal, she graciously arose and opened the door, and if she found neighbors or acquaintances she invited them in and entertained them with her nightcap on, and in her nightie. As they sat by the fire and chatted, she smoked her clay pipe.

On the street one noted her as tall, straight and slim, and in a certain way, graceful. She is said to have been a good dancer.

The story is told that when Woodward, the dancing master, saw her coming up the street with her basket of wares he would begin to dance and then she would put down her basket and dance too.

To all appearances she was very poor. People pitied her and gave her food. Besides going out nursing, and selling Yankee notions, she picked berries to sell and she also dried apples for sale. Because he was so sorry for her, Crocker Lovell, the storekeeper, paid for her dried apples two cents a pound more than the retail price.

In her eighty-fifth year, Old Lady White fell sick and died. Just before her death she confided that there was money under a barrel in the tiny cellar. Moreover, those who took care of her found bills pinned all over her underclothes, and after her death several hundred dollars were found pinned in an old dress. In all, there was from a thousand to two thousand dollars; some say more. The hope of finding further hidden treasure led to ripping up the boards in the floor, pulling out chimney bricks, and otherwise mutilating the house; the entire cellar was dug over; the ground outside was pretty well spaded up; yet nothing additional was found, not even with the help of Mrs. Briggs, the clairvoyant.

Mrs. White had expressed a desire to have a good funeral with singing. Her wishes were carried out.

Another woman peddler was Mrs. Georgiana Foster of Norton. She drove about in a buggy, the seat and floor of which were packed high with all the notions a housewife could possibly need for her sewing. She came regularly to her customers in Our Town.

Besides the peddlers who came periodically and were looked for to supply household wants, there were unexpected and often unwanted packpeddlers. Earliest of these was the "Image" man, who, instead of pack on his back, wore on his shoulders a sort of framed board with a hole through which his head protruded; surrounding the peddler's head were the small statuettes that he had for sale. Men of his trade were of Italian birth and shouted "Imagig, imigig," as they approached the door, seventy, even eighty years ago.

A quieter peddler was the man with the pack containing writing paper, pencils, and handkerchiefs. He, nevertheless, was just as insistent as the image seller.

Of greater importance to Our Town was the manufacturer and peddler of soap.

The making of soap and candles was for many years a home industry, as much a part of the seasonal routine of the Housewife as the weekly baking of bread and pies. Then some enterprising Yankee began making soap to sell, and peddled it around the countryside. Many women thereafter traded the grease that they had been saving, for the peddler's soft soap, and the soap man also bartered his goods for wood ashes. Soap making became a business in many a Massachusetts town. Foxboro had a soap factory, and Theodore Carver, just over the line in Norton, made soap.

In Our Town, eighty-two years ago, Jason Belcher was a soap maker. How long he had been at that work nobody knows. The Belchers, Jason and Robert, lived on what we now know as Ware Street. Robert, too, made soap, perhaps in the beginning with Jason; at any rate, he later made it by himself.

At the other side of town, Captain Schuyler Shepard made both hard and soft soap and employed Daniel Martin as soap peddler. Martin drove a little old brown horse that moved at about three miles an hour. In the back of his wagon he had two good-sized barrels, or tanks, filled with soft soap to be dipped out for the buckets or pitchers of his customers. On the wagon seat he had just room to sit, for on each side of him was a box of hard soap. By the time he had sold all his soap, his wagon was full of ashes and grease, taken in exchange.

The lye for soap was made by pouring water over the

ashes and leaving them to leach. Nothing was wasted. After the alkali had been extracted the ashes were still good as a fertilizer, and Captain Shepard once traded his ashes for a piece of land. His old soap house still stands back of the New Mansfield Hatchery off School Street.

Albert S. Shepard, the son of the Captain, took up his father's business, though in another building with somewhat improved methods of manufacture. In company with Shepard was Frank Drake. Drake attended to the making, and Shepard did the selling on the road. In later years, after the soap business was given up, the soap factory was converted into a house and is now a comfortable and attractive home.

Looking backward once more, we find according to the State records, that in 1855 there were two soap makers in Our Town who made both soap and tallow candles. The two men, with a capital investment of $1,200, in a year produced a thousand tons of soap valued at four thousand dollars. It is our guess that the two soap makers of that time were Captain Schuyler Shepard and Jason Belcher.

Ten years later, 1865, there were still two soap factories here, though presumably Captain Shepard had been succeeded by his son and Frank Drake; and perhaps it was Robert and not Jason Belcher, who was making soap in the east of the town. The value of the stock used by these later men is listed at $600; their yearly output of soft soap, three hundred barrels valued at $1,200; one thousand pounds of hard soap valued at $120; and other kinds of soap to the value of $500. Their working capital was only $500.

Just about sixty years ago James W. Cobb began his career as soap maker and soap peddler. He was not a young man then, indeed, he was fifty, an age when many men were content to plod along in the business of their earlier years. He was a frail-looking man, the sort of man one would expect to be seeking the comforts of the fireside, rather than the adventure of the highroad. Mr. Cobb, a trader, buying pigs by the hundreds at the Brighton Stockyards and selling from his own yard had, however, been on the road and had enjoyed it. He had been at one time a peddler of dry-goods and on his trips had been a keen observer of human nature and alert for opportunities. He saw the soap that was being sold and decided that he could make soap as good or better. His two sons, James R. and Dallas W., were then getting big enough to help, but until they were old enough he hired Jasper Fisher and Gillis Parker, neighbor's boys, to work with him.

The process of manufacture employed by Mr. Cobb varied somewhat from the methods of earlier soap makers in Mansfield. For example, the days of collecting ashes and grease from house-to-house had gone by and Mr. Cobb bought the best beef tallow from the slaughter houses, and the alkali he used was imported from England.

Soft soap was Mr. Cobb's specialty. James Cobb's "Wonderful Soap" was widely known and came boxed in twelve, twenty-five, fifty and hundred-pound lots. The hard soap, similar to the soft in content, with the addition of resin for hardening and palm oil for coloring, was put up in one-pound bars and sold as "Cobb's No. 1 Laundry Soap." A soap trade name was then new in Our Town.

The winter months was the off-season for making and selling soap. Mr. Cobb took that time to study railroad maps and lay out his route for the opening of spring. At the same time Bill Ingraham, the carriage painter, was dressing up Mr. Cobb's wagons. Cobb had two or three; one for his own long route, and the others to be used on short routes by his agents. Those soap wagons were wonderful creations. It was Mr. Cobb's intention that they should equal in splendor a caravan in Barnum's circus parade. From all accounts we think they did. The wheels were red and there was plenty of color about the body. All over the sides one could read from a distance, the inscription, "Washing Made Easy by Using James W. Cobb's Wonderful Soap." This was in gold leaf stripe, real gold leaf that Mr. Cobb bought in book form.

The gay wagon with the bright letters was not Cobb's only way of advertising. He got out show cards and handbills. On these were three views of his factory, taken in such a way that it looked like an immense plant. Mr. Cobb was not the last advertiser to exaggerate.

The factory was large enough to do a pretty good business. Ten to twenty tons of soap a week was the average output during the selling season.

The selling season began in April and lasted until nearly Thanksgiving time, depending on the weather. Daniel Leonard was one of Cobb's earliest salesmen and one of his best. R. J. Paine came a little later and took to the business so readily that he eventually went into the soap business for himself.

The longest journey and the largest and gaudiest wagon, James Cobb, generally known as Jim, took for himself. With his two boys, who stayed at home to make the soap, he left the outline of his route and the list of shipping places, the result of his winter's study and planning. Though Mr. Cobb occasionally came home for a day or two, his two-horse soap wagon did not return from April until late November. One year it was even after Thanksgiving before he returned. That was the time he got caught in a snowstorm. It was a real one and as the roads became blocked beyond the use of wheels, he drove home on runners, with the red wheels fastened to the sides of his wagon.

James Cobb became inured to the unexpected and to emergencies. One time as he was passing over a toll bridge the bridge collapsed, and man, beasts, and wagon went through. We suspect that the water was a bit soapy for a time and we understand that Cobb did not get his toll back.

The route laid out by Mr. Cobb took him through Massachusetts and Connecticut, and one year into Pennsylvania. His procedure was to start from home with his wagon, which was fitted up with doors at the back and sliding doors in front, loaded with soap, both hard and soft. He managed so well that he usually sold out his stock by the time he reached the first shipping point agreed upon with his sons. There he refilled his wagon and moved on until his supply was again exhausted and he had reached the next loading station. Accompanying him were some young men who ran on ahead to distribute the handbills apprising the people of the approach of James W. Cobb, the soapman, with his "Wonderful Soap." On the circulars was a lot of reading matter that told the qualifications of the soap. Mr. Cobb usually put up at the traveling men's hotels and paid for his food and lodging with soap. Never was any cash paid to the hotelkeeper. If any money changed hands, it was the landlord who paid Cobb, for Cobb often sold him enough soap to last a year.

According to his own admission, Jim Jr. was never as good a salesman as his father and could seldom barter enough soap to pay hotel bills. Consequently, the younger man lodged at some unpretentious farmhouse. Somehow, Jim Jr. did not take to the salesman end of the business. His trips were few, but on one, at least, he had high adventure. He and Walter Foster of Norton started for New Jersey, with all the courage and assurance of youth, but when they reached the Housatonic River they arrived at a point where the river was wide and shallow, but bridgeless. Inquiry revealed that the nearest bridge was eight miles distant. Did the boys intend to go that much farther out of their way? They did not. A native told them that they could ford the river, provided they followed the ripples and avoided the smooth places, which indicated holes. The two spirited horses plunged in, and Cobb drove, oh, so carefully, until, sure enough, they were in a hole, with water up to the horses' bellies and to the bottom of the high-hung wagon body. After a long moment of suspense they got out of the hole and across the river. On their return trip they kept nearer to the shore line of Long Island Sound. Once more they came to a river, minus a bridge. In substitution for a bridge was a raft, not much larger than a good-sized room. This was propelled by two men, father and son, with poles. Cobb and Foster drove aboard and they started across the river. Perhaps all would have gone well had not the polemen got into a disagreement and begun fighting. The tide then took charge of the raft and the soap wagon landed two miles farther up the river than was expected.

Not all Cobb adventures took place in Connecticut. One happened right in the soap house at home. The soft soap was made in two great kettles that were set level with the first floor and were heated by fires in the cellar below. Each kettle held three hundred and fifty gallons of water and was capable of producing a ton and a half of soap. One morning, when by good luck the kettles were empty, Dallas Cobb found his handsome colt in the kettle. Here certainly was a pretty kettle of horse. And how to get the colt out! It took all the neighbors and plenty of homemade tackle to lift the animal out bodily. When the act was accomplished the colt stood on his own feet, unhurt.

The time finally came when James Cobb, the father, had to admit he was getting too old for travel; his bones creaked as he climbed on and off the showy wagon; and after twenty-five years in the business of making and selling soap, he gave it up. Neither of his boys had any desire to continue making soap. Dallas Cobb went in business with some other men, manufacturing electric switchboards, and later worked in Cobb's jewelry shop. James R. Cobb devoted himself to the teaming and wood business.

Not a mile from Cobb's soap factory was the soap plant of

R. J. Paine.   Two men more unlike in appearance would be hard to find.   Cobb was tallish, lanky, and almost cadaverously wan; Paine stood six feet, but his three hundred and ten pounds, protuberant in spots, made him look shorter, his color gave the semblance of health.   As often happens, the thin, sick-looking man had a longer span of life than the fat one. Both men made good soap salesmen.

Paine, in his young manhood, came from Rhode Island to work with Lysander White, selling crackers.   His good salesmanship in that line led James W. Cobb to engage him in his employ to take "Cobb's Wonderful Soap" on the road.   Paine enjoyed traveling through the country in Cobb's two-horse wagon of color and when Mr. Cobb decided to get along without him, Paine undertook the selling of sewing machines. Sewing machines, however, did not appeal to him as soap had done and he decided to make soap of his own to sell.   By no means was he a rival of his former employer.   He left the field of soft soap manufacture to Cobb and made a soap powder called "Puritene."

Rufus J. Paine said his middle name was Jinks and termed his company The Jinks Soap Manufacturing Company.   His trade-mark was his own portrait, which faced the reader on circulars, in the newspapers, and on the Puritene boxes.   "Don't be a Dunderfunk," he advised and added, "We live in an age of progress."   Of course being progressive meant to use Puritene, which had every attribute possible in a soap powder; in fact, he advertised that Puritene was the greatest invention of the nineteenth century, imitated by many, equalled by none. The pasteboard soap packages were covered with reading matter that was intended to leave no doubt in the mind of the reader.   Mr. Paine had a convincing way with him, and sometimes on the road he made use of the sharp Yankee peddler methods that had not entirely gone out of use.   More than one country storekeeper could tell of the purchase he made of Paine.

According to the story of one proprietor of a Connecticut crossroad's store, Paine, in a nice wagon (body painted olive brown, gears red, wheels red, striped with black, and letters in gold leaf), drew up at his store and inquired if he used Puritene. On learning that the storeman not only did not use Puritene but had never heard of it, Paine proceeded to enlighten him by giving a demonstration of how Puritene would take out gudgeon grease stains, the most difficult smudges to dissolve. Paine went over to his cart, removed one wheel, wiped the axle end with a spotless handkerchief. After ostentatiously greasing the wheel, and replacing it, he picked up the handkerchief. "Now," said Mr. Paine, "I'll show you what Puritene will do." The storeman offered to bring out hot water, but Paine assured him that Puritene was effectual in any kind of water. It was just as had been said; Puritene made the handkerchief perfectly clean. In the face of such proof a good sale was accomplished. A few days later, with plenty of cracker barrel loafers for witnesses, the storekeeper thought that he would advertise his newly bought soap powder by showing what it would do. He brought out a fine linen handkerchief, recently given him by his wife, and smeared it with grease from a wheel. He washed, he rubbed, he scrubbed; he tried cold water, he tried hot water, and warm water; the spot remained. The Connecticut merchant was clever enough to realize then what had happened. Are you? To his friends Mr. Paine readily acknowledged his system. He bought Packer's Tar Soap by the box and always carried with him a can of it to grease the wheel, always the same wheel. In his coat, and in the coats of his helpers, he had rubber-lined pockets inserted to hold wet handkerchiefs. On one journey he had a green hand, a man who had worked for the Babbitt soap people. The new man took off the wrong wheel!

Like Mr. Cobb, Mr. Paine took the best and longest route himself, though one of his men, a man named Cook from West

Mansfield, was once away from home four years. By going south, Mr. Paine was able to travel through the winter and early spring months. He started these trips by driving to Providence and there taking his horse and wagon by boat on the Baltimore and Ohio line to Norfolk, Virginia. From Norfolk he took the road, receiving consignments of Puritene from time to time.

At the home plant, while Mr. Paine was on a southern trip, Enoch Thayer, an acquaintance from his home town in Rhode Island, attended to the manufacture of Puritene. The grease was gathered here and there; kitchen grease, butcher's waste, and condemned animals (cows preferably, for there is little grease in horse flesh). Mr. Paine was particular about his home and neighborhood, consequently he set his rendering tank in a field, away from any house, and as it chanced, the very field that Captain Schuyler Shepard, years before, had bought with the leached ashes of his soap business. Even then the odor was obnoxious in summer and Mr. Paine finally invented a chemical that made the tallow and bone keep indefinitely, without causing too great annoyance. As a by-product, Mr. Paine made glue and considered using the bones for fertilizer, but died without accomplishing the last project.

In Paine's factory the soap was made in a great kettle, ten feet across and deep enough to hold fifty gallons. The caustic was bought in solid form and melted. The ingredients were stirred together by hand in a special tank, but the cooking and mixing of the emulsion was done by machinery. (Mr. Paine was the only soap maker in Our Town to do his work by steam-power.) A little of the soap was run into frames to be sold in bar form, but most of it, as soon as it hardened, was ground up for powder. It was also rolled and sifted, before it was boxed. The sealing of the boxes, or packages, was done by four or five neighborhood girls, who did it by piece work. Sixty of these one-pound packages went into a wooden box. The plant put up fifteen to twenty boxes a day, amounting to over a thousand pounds a week. Three or four men were employed.

To stimulate his trade, Mr. Paine offered premiums. By mailing to him a certain number of trade-marks and return postage, the purchaser was sent a large chromo picture, suitable for framing. Some of his packages contained as hidden treasure, a nickel, which was the actual purchase price of the package.

Every correspondent of Mr. Paine's, and every caller at his factory, received a little card that carried the advertisement of Puritene on one side and the following legend on the other:

DON'T SWEAR
Give this card to all you hear using profanity, and
You will never swear. Four weeks will effect a cure.
Card free, except postage.

Besides making and selling Puritene, Mr. Paine sold machine, sewing machine, bicycle, harness, and axle oil. He bought the oil by the barrel and bottled it at the factory. It was sold as "Paine's Sewing Machine Oil. This Excels Every Oil in the Market."

Paine was also a famous auctioneer and advertised, "Sales attended to in all parts of the State."

By his various lines of work, Mr. Paine made a pretty good living. In the early eighteen-eighties, to benefit the town he gave a fine granite drinking trough for horses, to be placed in a prominent location on Main Street, believing that it would be a lasting memorial. On the base was cut in large letters, *PAINE*. A similar trough was set in front of his own residence.

His neatly kept lawn was decorated with a cast iron fountain, silver-painted, and with a terra cotta figure of a woman, nicknamed by someone, Aunt Hannah. As Aunt Hannah was more than life size, and had to be taken into the factory every winter and have a new white dress of paint every spring, she was something of a nuisance to those who had to care for her. After Mr. Paine's death she disappeared. The Paine drinking troughs are still in existence, though not in their original positions, and are perhaps destined to follow the route of Aunt Hannah.

Even more remunerative than the making of soap was the making of a patent medicine. No widely known quack remedy was made in Our Town, but two of our musical youths, Alson and Elbridge Cobb (not closely related to the Cobb soapmen), went out on the road selling Dr. Tucker's "59." Dr. Tucker, a Norton man, began as a "sleepy doctor": that is, by hitches and twitches, he went to sleep, or into a trance, and while in that state could diagnose a patient's disease and what to prescribe for him. Dr. Tucker made his own medicine and soon found that keeping wide-awake to sell his medicine left little time for the sleeping process. He reasoned that since a man could always tell for himself when he was sick, and as he (Dr. Tucker) could make a medicine that would cure everything, why bother with the sleeping diagnoses? After that, New England could not hold him. He established himself with a home and factory in New York. Besides his widely known "No. 59 Compound," he manufactured a less known concoction, "No. 64," a fever medicine.

He opened an office in Providence. There the people flocked, and one often found fifty waiting in line. His next move was to put agents out on the road, and he found in the Cobb brothers the men he wanted.

The Cobbs had a special wagon, made with side seats, and in this they traveled all over New England, and even beyond. Both men sang, and Elbridge played the fiddle. To see and hear them was enough to release one from the blues and make him want to be well. The Cobbs knew all the popular songs of the day, and if those gave out, they improvised as they went along. They sometimes took a banjo player with them, and sometimes, Pliny, another brother, joined them with a portable organ.

When they made a stopping place, they gave a concert to attract a crowd and with a sufficient number gathered, Alson began his sales talk and the other men were kept busy handing out the small bottles of medicine at one dollar a bottle.

Taunton Cattle Show was one of their most favorable selling points. Everybody looked forward to seeing the Cobb brothers with Dr. Tucker's medicine and were never disappointed. Dr. Tucker, himself, was sometimes present and helped with the sales. He brought with him a cure for deafness. It was his custom to call for volunteers from the crowd, the assurance being that by having some of the Tucker ointment rubbed on the head, the deafness would disappear. Now it happened that there was a young man in Our Town, named Nathan Wood, who was very deaf. It was arranged that Nathan should be on hand to come forward for treatment. With remarkable rapidity young Wood's hearing was restored, but by the next Cattle Show, he was deaf again, and was ready once more for the experiment.

With such a thriving business Dr. Tucker became a rich man.

CHAPTER TWELVE

Foundries

THE SECOND half of the nineteenth century saw a new industry coming to Our Town; the making of stoves and furnaces. Not for seventy years had there been iron work in the town worth mentioning, other than nails, blacksmithing and rail repairs.

The incentive of the eighteenth century had been the easily mined bog iron, and in the last quarter of the period, the demand for cannon and cannon balls. Before 1800 bog iron began to be replaced by the stronger and better pig iron. After the French foundrymen left, no one here seemed interested in casting hollow ware. Between 1800 and 1846, General Leach in Easton was the only one hereabouts who ran a blast furnace for casting.

It was a stranger who introduced the making of stoves and furnaces in Our Town.

The people of Our Town were beginning to get used to strangers coming here to engage in business. They looked upon them with tolerance, slightly tinged with suspicion. The cottonmen coming from outside had not been any too successful; the coalmen surely not. McMoran and Fulton were doing well, but they, especially Mr. Fulton, were exceptional business men. Schenck's machine shop seemed to be on the verge of tottering. The town waited to see what Gardner Chilson would do.

Mr. Chilson was born in Thompson, Connecticut, on December 21, 1805. Like many poor boys of his time, he served an apprenticeship away from home. His line of work was pattern and cabinet making. When he became of age he went to Providence and let himself as a carver to Asa Eames, a stove dealer. It was not long before young Chilson developed an aptitude for the construction of improved stoves, which were by no means common at that early date. In the country, at least, most people were still using fireplaces for heating and cooking.

By 1837 city people were beginning to use coal. That necessitated the use of stoves, for gas fumes from a fireplace were intolerable. Mr. Chilson saw an opening and moved to Boston to set up a stove business for himself. He had no money, but he did have indomitable energy, courage and inventive genius. In a modest way he opened a tin and stove store on Blackstone Street and began selling stoves. His sales that year did not exceed one thousand stoves. That, however, was as well as he expected, and as good as other dealers. Stoves were a luxury. Year by year he enlarged his business until at the time of his death, forty years later, his was reputed to be the oldest firm for the manufacture of stoves with a salesroom in Boston, and one of the largest in New England.

Following closely after the introduction of stoves was the introduction of furnaces for heating houses. In 1838 Mr. Chilson included these in his wareroom. These furnaces were even more of a luxury, and, as a matter of fact, were still in the experimental stage. Mr. Chilson sold about thirty that year.

No one more than Mr. Chilson realized the uncertain advantages of these new furnaces. He began to experiment. In 1844 he invented and patented an air-warming and ventilating furnace that was better than anything thus far produced. A Massachusetts State report for 1852, commenting on the subject, said: "Mr. Chilson undoubtedly has given more attention to the subject of warming and ventilating than any man in this country. His inventions are based on strictly scientific principles which govern the elements of air and heat in harmony with the laws of nature . . . . A new era came with the Chilson Furnace." This commendation was probably brought about by the fact that the year before (1851) he had exhibited his furnace at the World's Fair in London, where he received the Prize Medal. The furnace had previously been exhibited at all the principal fairs in America and had received one gold medal, three silver medals, and numerous diplomas.

In the illustrated program of the London Fair, plans of the construction of the Chilson Furnace were pictured. The Secretary of the Fair testified over his own signature that "This compliment was paid to no other article in the American exhibition *unsolicited*." The Earl of Carnovan was the first in Great Britain to use one of the furnaces.

Mr. Chilson was still unsatisfied. He continued his experimental work until he perfected a cone furnace, operating on the radiation principle. This was in 1854, and the year he came to Our Town.

Whether the town appreciated it or not, it was a wonderful thing to have a man of such ability and prominence start a business and make his home here. Even in Boston he was an outstanding man. In 1853 he represented the city in the Legislature. He had large investments in real estate and was much interested in the construction of model dwellings in the city. In Ward 7 he had the honor of having a short street named Chilson Place.

No one now knows what brought him to Our Town. He bought a large tract of land on both sides of the railroad near the station. On the west side of the tracks he built a large stone factory. Somewhat back from the station on the east side was his residence, formerly the home of Samuel B. Schenck. The house, of course, was not new, and in a little while Mr. Chilson moved it away and built himself a much more elaborate home. Nothing in town, before or since, ever compared with the new Chilson home and grounds when completed. Workmen came from out of town to do the work. They liked the town and stayed for years to work on other buildings. The granite foundation of the house cost fully $6,000 and the whole house has been estimated from $30,000 up. For years it was the only house in town with a bathroom. It made the people look and talk. There was a stable, too. Such carriages! In 1872 the assessors valued two of them at $600. The carriage of John Rogers of the straw shop (the next richest man in town) was valued at only $150. The Chilson's winter carriage was in the style of a coach or landau, with the coachman's seat high up in front. The summer carriage was open. It was either a victoria or a landaulette, with the top folded back. The carriage was drawn by a large, valuable sorrel horse. The harnesses, one with silver trimmings, and the other with brass decorations, were kept highly polished.

It was Gardner Chilson's son, George, and his wife, who furnished the most style. When they went out to ride people liked to look, for Mrs. Chilson brought her clothes straight from Paris. Children on their way home from school hoped to catch a glimpse of the splendor. If the carriage was standing at the door, the children usually waited until they were rewarded by seeing the young couple sweep down the front walk. The coachman stood by to wait on them and place a stool for Mrs. Chilson.

Behind the house was the garden, laid out by John McGrath, a young Irishman, in conformity with the manner of Lord Ormond's estate, where he had work on the Emerald Isle; walks, flower beds and greenhouses. In the greenhouses were Hamburg grapevines and peach trees, as well as plants. In time the Chilson greenhouses contained 12,000 feet of glass. For several years the beautification of the grounds continued according to the Irishman's ideas. Then one day his views and Mr. Chilson's clashed and the hot-headed son of

Erin flared up.   Before either of them hardly realized what it was all about, McGrath was out of a job.

However, he was not out of a job long.   John Rogers, the bonnet shop man, had looked with envy on the Chilson gardens.   Now was his chance.   Soon John McGrath was laying out walks and starting Hamburg grapes south of John Rogers' house and now there were two lovely gardens for our people to look at, instead of one.

Once again the British Isles furnished Mr. Chilson with a gardener.   The Scotch burr instead of the Irish brogue was now heard.   The new man, trained at Fyvie Castle under an expert gardener named Farquhar, knew his business thoroughly when he came to Our Town.

The arrival of the Scotchman, William Winter, was the beginning of a small Scotch colony.   Some came to work in the garden; among them Robert Farquhar, son of the gardener of Fyvie Castle, and himself later to be a prominent American seedsman; others came to work in the foundry.

That brings us back to the foundry, which is really the subject of this chapter.   The house, the carriage, the garden, the clothes of Mrs. Chilson, offered so much romance to Our Town that we have been constrained to linger around the premises.

As soon as Mr. Chilson bought land in Our Town he began the erection of his large stone foundry.   Up to that time there had been no stone factory in town.   Nobody had had the money to build more than a wooden building.

It would take months to complete his foundry and he was eager to get to work.   Close by the new plant was a small factory recently started by Terry, Shurtliff and Company.   Mr. Terry and Mr. Chilson got together and it was readily agreed that Mr. Chilson should hire the company's building and that Mr. Terry should do Mr. Chilson's work until the new building was completed.   The plan worked to perfection and when the Chilson Foundry was done, in 1853, Mr. Chilson bought out Terry, Shursliff and Company, and hired Terry as his superintendent. After a time, Mr. Terry left Our Town and Mr. Chilson engaged one of the Whites, who had been left stranded when the White brothers had dissolved their tack business in the Whiteville section of the town. It was said that Mr. Chilson did not hire James White so much for his knowledge of iron work and his business ability, as for the purposes of keeping him in town and in the Baptist choir, in which Mr. Chilson was much interested. Mr. Chilson's selection of a superintendent was justified. As long as Mr. Chilson lived, Mr. White was his right hand man, and was remembered at his employer's death with a small legacy.

Mr. Chilson always kept his store and warehouse on Blackstone Street, in Boston, and was there every day, leaving the foundry in the hands of Mr. White. Before starting for Boston, he went to the foundry at 7:30. There he gave close attention to his work until the arrival of the 8 o'clock train for Boston. He was at his store on Blackstone Street, Boston, until five-o'clock.

He was a good man to work for. He demanded capable workmen, but when he got the service he wanted he paid well and promptly. He was much more reasonable as to factory hours than most employers of his time. Nine hours a day he considered sufficient, though most foundrymen were working ten and even twelve.

Mr. Chilson during his years in business had to meet the financial crises of his time. In one of them he failed and many of his workmen became frightened and left him. One man, besides his superintendent, stuck by, and in gratitude for his loyalty and faithfulness, Mr. Chilson left him $500.

The failure was only temporary. The Chilson stoves and furnaces were built upon honor and had a good reputation wherever they were sold. This fact, coupled with Mr. Chilson's business integrity, carried him through and he was soon on his feet again.

Mr. Chilson practiced in his business the religion that he professed. He had joined a Baptist church in Boston in 1842, but as the years progressed he had not been especially active until, by the great religious revival that swept the country in 1865, he became spiritually quickened and transferred his membership from the Boston church. From that time until his death he was most devoted. Always, when his health permitted, he was at church on Sunday and at the midweek prayer meeting. Never did he allow his horse to be taken out on Sunday. Both he and his wife always walked to church. He frequently affirmed in public that his wealth was consecrated to God, and he lived as he spoke. When the Baptist Church was remodeled, in 1869, Mr. Chilson gave generously to the fund. He also gave a new pipe organ and the cushions for the pews, as well as other things. At his death he gave $5,000 to the local church, $2,000 to Welcome Lewis, his former pastor, and the bulk of his large fortune to Baptist Missionary Societies.

It is interesting to note that at about the same time that Mr. Chilson was giving so generously for the remodeling and renovation of the Baptist Church, John Rogers, the bonnet shop man, was being equally generous in the remodeling of the Congregational Church. John Rogers also gave a fine church organ.

Mr. Chilson had but one child, George (already mentioned), who was twenty-one about the time that the family moved to Our Town. It was the father's hope and ambition that his son should enter the business and carry it on after him, but his desire never came to pass.

Young Chilson did not have the advantages that his father had had, or to put it in other words, he had the disadvantages of being a rich man's son with plenty of money to spend. Without doubt he had much ability and had he been obliged to

take the responsibility and initiative that his father had to
take in his youth, he might have shown as much steadiness.
But for him money and the things he wanted came without
much effort on his part, and when he showed a tendency to
kick over the traces his father began to pull the reins a little
too tightly. The youth had too much spirit and energy to submit willingly.

For a time the young man was put to work in the office at
the foundry as assistant to the bookkeeper. He was very quick
at figures, being able to add two, three, even four columns at
once, and in other ways to expedite bookkeeping. The work
was not nearly exacting enough to fill all his time. His being
in the office was not as strenuous for him as it was for Superintendent James W. White, who was supposed to keep an
eye on him. Mr. White could watch him about train time to
see that he did not start for Boston, but he could not do his
work in the foundry and be on the lookout to see that the
young man did not skip out and hasten to East Foxboro to
take the train. They say young Chilson was "smart as lightning, but a devil on wheels."

Young Chilson tried to please his father in some things.
He confided to someone that it was to please his father that he
joined the Baptist Church and was immersed in Fulton's
Pond.

After a time, the elder Chilson decided that it would be
better to take George to the Boston office and make him a
salesman. He should have made good at that, for he was the
kind of young man who could make friends wherever he went.
Presently George Chilson found for himself a wife in Brook-
line and made his home at the Parker House, Boston, coming
to Our Town only occasionally. Next, his father transferred
him to England to look after business there. The young people, however, preferred travel and spent most of their time
in France or Italy. It was then said that they were there on ac-

count of George Chilson's health. Now and then they arrived in this country for a visit. Always a sheaf of bills arrived before them.

In November, 1877, just as George Chilson arrived in Liverpool, for one of his European stays, Gardner Chilson, then a widower, died suddenly. (Just one hundred years before, another Mansfield capitalist, Ephraim Leonard, had died with his only son in England.) Gardner Chilson was genuinely mourned in Our Town. His funeral was conducted by a large number of ministers. The pastor of the Congregational Church, as well as the Baptist minister, had a part in the service. Twenty-five carriages of church members and citizens followed the body to the grave. Very touching was his own horse drawing the empty Chilson carriage.

It was but natural that at Mr. Chilson's death there was much speculation as to what would become of the foundry and much curiosity about the way his money had been left, until it was learned that the executors of the estate, ex-mayor Eustice C. Fitz, of Chelsea and Judge Edmund Bennet of Taunton, would carry on the foundry until the estate was settled. Much to the annoyance of the townspeople, it was not settled for several years. Mr. White remained as superintendent of the foundry and Mr. Fitz ran the business office. Finally the estate was settled, and the foundry was sold to James E. White, who had succeeded his father as superintendent. Mr. White ran the business under the name of Chilson Furnace Company until about the time of the world War, when, partly because of his health, it was given up.

As for George Chilson, he was not at all pleased with the way things were left. The first item of the will read:

To my son, George M. Chilson, an invalid, the net sum of $100,000 the income to be paid by trustees. (In trust, not for want of affection, but because of his health.) As he has no children, I hold it my duty to direct the bulk of my money to

*religious and charitable uses.   Also, I give my son my Fradsham
watch.   To him and his wife, their heirs and assigns, all furniture and bedding in rooms occupied by them in my house in
Mansfield, my pianoforte, and my French clock, which my son
brought me from Paris, my library, paintings and prints, my
silver and plated ware, and my best horse and buggy.*

Item 2.   To my son's wife, Mary, in her own right, $15,000.

Inasmuch as George Chilson's regular expenses amounted
to about $15,000 yearly, he failed to see how he could live on
the income from $100,000.   He forthwith contested the will.
Ultimately the case was settled by compromise and he relin-
quished all claim to the real estate in Our Town, other than
the right to live in the house when here.   It was in this house
that he died, nine years after his father's death.

After George Chilson's death the house became a hotel.
Years later, Walter M. Lowney bought it, removed it so that
he could build the Mansfield Tavern on the spot, and the
Chilson home was then converted into the present First National Bank Building.   The greenhouses became the property
of the Scotchman, William Brown, who was Mr. Chilson's
last gardener.

One of the Englishmen who came to Our Town to work in
the Chilson Foundry was William Bird.   He came in 1856 and
worked for Mr. Chilson eighteen years.   Bird's skill as a molder
was known everywhere in this vicinity.   He had known foundry work all his life.   He brought with him a cripple foot that
in his childhood had been terribly burned in an English
foundry.   In this country he had worked for a heater company
in Boston and in Nashua, New Hampshire, where it was said
that he was the first one in the United States to sweep a pulley.
In the Chilson Foundry, Mr. Chilson soon recognized Bird's
ability by paying him five dollars a day, which was an extremely
high wage for that time.

In the 1860's Mr. Bird's sister and her husband, Joseph

Rider, came to America and to Our Town. Soon after they arrived, Mr. Rider died, leaving Mrs. Rider with two infant boys. As Mr. Bird had no children of his own and was very fond of his sister and her children, he gave the boys almost a father's care and attention. As soon as the boys were old enough to leave school, Mr. Bird got them jobs in the foundry. William, the younger, was only fifteen when he started work there. As small lads they had become familiar with the place when they brought noon dinner pails to their uncle and other workmen.

In 1874 Mr. Bird decided to build a foundry of his own. It was called the Central Foundry, and was located on Central Street near the railroad track. In May, the building, forty-two by eighty, with a wing twelve by twenty, was under construction. In this he installed a ten-horse power engine for a blower furnace with a capacity of four tons of metal daily. Of course, he took his nephews to the foundry to work with him. By the middle of the summer, they were beginning the work of general jobbing; before fall, Mr. Bird was taken sick, and in December, he died.

Here was the widow left with the new-built foundry on her hands. Luckily, the young Riders, though only twenty-one and nineteen, had already had several years of training in foundry work in Chilson's foundry and six months in Mr. Bird's foundry, working more or less by themselves, because of Mr. Bird's failing health, yet with Mr. Bird's guidance. They had the courage and assurance of youth, and were ready to go on. They justified the wisdom of the venture by sticking to it for thirty-six years. The business had its ups and downs, but never a failure.

The boys got practically all the general jobbing from the factories in town. Their first job was a grate for the boiler in John Rogers' straw shop. Later, when the same firm, then under the name of the Comey Company, decided to put in some sewing machines, the Riders made the running gear for the first fifty machines that were used in the shop.

In 1910 death claimed Joseph E. Rider. William H. Rider no longer had the same interest in the business and soon decided to retire. Joseph Rider's son, William E. Rider, carried on the foundry for eight or ten years, then sold out to the Mansfield Foundry Company.

Two other young men who learned their trade at the Chilson Foundry and then went into business for themselves were Alec and Wallace MacRae. In 1885 they left the Chilson place and as the Mansfield Cooperative Foundry began making gray iron castings for stoves and furnaces, for repairs, and for the Bailey ovens. Though both MacRaes, and their father, Charles, as well, worked in the new foundry, it was Alec who was the principal owner and the treasurer of the new company. In the height of their business they employed a dozen men. In 1902 the firm was incorporated as the Mansfield Furnace and Coal Company, and finally became the Mansfield Coal and Grain Company, doing business here; and the Foxboro Coal and Grain Company, in Foxboro; both parts run by Alec MacRae's son, Frank, after the death of the older man. The casting business was given up a short time ago.

There was still another foundry started in Our Town during the lifetime of Mr. Chilson; this one by Simeon Clark, the blacksmith, as a repair shop for the frayed and broken rails of the railroad. Sometime, probably after Mr. Clark's sudden death, in 1872, it was sold to George E. Wilbur of Foxboro. Mr. Wilbur was not successful, and in 1885 the place was offered for sale at auction. Patrick Shields, working at Belcher's Furnace in Easton, bought it.

In Easton, Mr. Shields had been making malleable iron and it was his intention to follow the same line when he went into business for himself in Our Town, but after he became established, it seemed advisable to go on with the kind of work

that had already been done at the foundry he had bought.
That was gray cast iron. He soon built up for himself a reputation in general castings, making a specialty in stove repair-
ing for jobbers. As furnaces and boilers became more widely
used, he also added that line.

This firm, begun in 1885, is the oldest, doing business under
the same family name and run by members of the same family,
in Our Town today. It is there that the romance of industry
exists, if it is to be found anywhere in the foundries and factories of this twentieth century. A new man has little chance
of getting a job there, even in the best of times, unless he waits
for someone to die, leaving a vacancy. Most of the workmen
have been there at least twenty years. The late foreman had
been there more than forty years, and then retired on account
of failing health. The present foreman has been with the firm
more than thirty years. Two Swedes, one of them a molder,
are in the same class. The shipping clerk has been there forty
years. There is such a story for every man on the pay roll.
Each man is thoroughly interested in the work of the firm and
his faithfulness is not just taken for granted; there are remem-
brances at Christmas.

Though the business is in Our Town, it is probably more
widely known outside than it is here. In its fifty years of existence it has done very little local work. Besides stove repair
work for jobbers, and in the last twenty-five years repair work
on boilers and furnaces, they have also made a line of fireplace goods. They have some fifteen or eighteen styles of and-
irons. The market for these is mostly New York and Philadelphia. Their repair work was originally for large jobbers in
New England; now their work is well known throughout the
iron trade. They have the largest line of patterns in the east.
For the past twenty-five years, George Shields, the president
of the company, has been the secretary of the National Protec-
tive Repair Association.

CHAPTER THIRTEEN

Geese

IT IS not necessary to have a factory to be an industrialist of importance. The Austins of Our Town proved that.

Their story started about 1859, with George M. Austin buying and selling poultry in a small way. The name was not unknown in our small business world. Nearly fifty years before, George Austin's father, Stimson Austin, was one of the owners of the Mansfield Union Cotton and Woolen Company. This earlier Austin was by trade a housewright and cabinet maker. Aside from business, the family had two distinctions. Stimson Austin's father had left his family, in 1799, to go to England to fight in the war with France. Soon after he arrived, he died, when only thirty-four years old. Stimson's mother was the twentieth child of Zebulon Field of Taunton.

George M. Austin had two sons, George F. and Charles M., who joined the father in the poultry business. George F. came into the poultry business early, but Charles M., not until he had done considerable butchering. Although in time the goose business became the main trade at the farm, in the early days the Austins had any number of side lines, among them pigs.

In the spring of each year two men from the Austin farm went to Brighton to buy pigs. After selecting fifty, sixty, at times even seventy porkers, they started for home, driving the creatures over the road. They planned to make Norwood the first night. Here the men put up at a tavern. The pigs, meanwhile, were safe in a large yard built for the purpose. By the next night they reached the Austin farm. Next morning, the pigs were again driven out; this time to the Common in Our Town and there the Austin's set up a market. Hither the farmers from miles around came to buy. In those days, pigs were as essential on a farm as a cow, and many a man in the village owned a hog. One can guess that the noise at the pig market, as the farmers bargained and loaded up their purchases, might have far exceeded the noise of mechanical squawkers and squealers of later day carnivals on the Common. By nightfall the pig sale was about cleaned up. The few that remained were taken back to the farm and sold from there.

But pig selling was not the only side line at the Austin farm. In the dull season of the poultry trade, the Austins dressed beef. For heavy beef, they brought mostly steers from Brighton and from Canada. Charles M. Austin was the butcher after 1872, when he returned from the Gowards, in Easton, where he learned the trade. He joined his father and brother at the farm, where they were already dressing beef. Besides the heavy beef they also did a considerable business with calves, killing as many as twenty or twenty-five in a week.

The beef killing opened up another line of trade, namely hides. Not only were the hides from the animals that they killed, shipped to market in Boston, but they bought a quantity of raw hides in Bristol, Rhode Island, for selling.

Poultry was the line in which the Austins made their reputation. It was in 1861 that George F. Austin, then a lad of thirteen, drove to Boston, thirty miles, by night with his first load of dressed birds. He was then considered a member of the firm, and continued taking dressed poultry to Boston for the market men at Fanueil Hall. His business the second year is said to have netted, on the average, seventy dollars a week. After his brother Charles came into the poultry business in 1872, the brothers leased a basement stall on North Market Street, Boston, and sold poultry under the firm name of G. F. & C. M. Austin. In 1887 the father joined them and as G. M. Austin and Sons, they enlarged their business and leased a stall in the Fanueil Hall Market. Eight years later, they enlarged their space by adding another stall. George F. Austin died in 1897.

The firm then changed the name to G. M. Austin and Son, under which name the firm is still doing business in the same location, though there is no one by the name of Austin now connected with it.

Let us return to the more picturesque and romantic aspects of the business. In 1867 they began collecting geese. They also bought some turkeys, for in those days many local farmers raised turkeys.

Up to, and during the Civil War period, Boston was the only market for geese. New York ordered from there. At the close of the war, George F., who was a keen young business man and progressive, went to New York to tell the dealers there that they could buy directly from the Austin Farm, without the bother and expense of the Boston middleman.

These geese that he offered for sale were collected by his brother Charles, and from men who drove the Austin goose carts, mostly in Bristol, Compton, and Little Compton, Rhode Island and Westport, Massachusetts.

With the advent of motor drawn vehicles, trucks took up the work that horse drawn wagons had done in collecting live poultry for the farm.

The early collectors used to make two trips a week during June, July, and August, and were gone at least three days on a trip. The average load that they brought home was about 225 geese.

The enterprise was built up by the wise business acumen of the men concerned, yet at times an element of chance entered in, or shall we say the door of opportunity opened and the Austins entered in?

One can readily see that it was necessary to have good horses for this business, which in its most active days required about ten horses. At one time they had twenty. The best horse market seems to have been Quebec, and thither George F. went to buy. Not only did he buy his horses, but he unexpectedly discovered a man, named Jones, who had geese to sell. Thereupon, he bought geese. It was long a family joke that he successfully instructed Jones how to pack the live geese for shipping when he had never packed any himself.

For perhaps twenty years, the Austins continued to buy geese in Quebec. They probably secured 3,000 or 4,000 a year that way.

The muscovy ducks came mostly from the southern shore of Long Island, and the turkeys from Bridgehampton, Long Island, and Rhode Island.

Around fifty or sixty years ago, a sailing vessel came into Boston from Prince Edward's Island, bringing on it 400 live geese. By chance, the Austins heard of it and it was "Georgie on the spot" at once. From that time to the present, Prince Edward's Island has been the principal source of supply, though some are still procured from Rhode Island. Geese have been bought from some of the western states, but they had not proved as satisfactory.

The busiest season at the goose farm is from October first to the first of January.

In the days when George M. Austin and his sons were doing the most business, they employed sixty-five men about the place.

In 1876 they made their record. That year they handled 25,000 geese, 12,000 ducks, 14,000 turkeys and 100,000 hens and chickens. In the record week they dressed 2,205. The largest day was credited with 519. Small wonder that this was then called "The Largest Goose Farm in the World." In October the geese begin to arrive at the farm, coming to the freight house in 1,400 and 1,500 lots. They traveled three miles over a comparatively little used road to the farm. Six men were able to handle the emigrating birds, and during the two hour trip, seldom a bird went astray. In the most active days at the farm, car loads of geese came at intervals all through October and November.

Turkeys and chickens were killed as soon as they arrived, for these birds lost weight, if kept. Geese and ducks, on the other hand, were in poor condition and had to be penned and fattened. In the eighties, it required twelve bushels of grain daily for this purpose. The food was prepared in a huge iron vessel that had formerly been the bread mixer at the Bailey bakery. When thoroughly mixed the feed was carted to the pens in great tubs made from discarded whale oil barrels bought in New Bedford and cut in two. These were placed on wheels and drawn by a horse.

Geese are wise birds; they once saved Rome. The geese in Our Town look out for themselves. At night they huddle together and one acts as sentinel and keeps awake. An unusual noise may mean a fox and the watching goose at the farm rouses the rest. Much cackling brings help from the farm house. In recent years the pens have been lighted by electricity and the sentinel can tell whether the noise comes from a falling branch of a tree, blown off by the wind, or from a marauder. Two American eagles have descended upon the geese in the day time.

The fatted geese go from the pen to the picking house to be killed and dressed. Poultry picking is a profession in itself. At one time the Austins employed twenty-three pickers, some of them champions in their line. One man is reputed to have picked sixty-seven geese in nine and one half hours. Ordinarily, a practiced hand can dress for the market, sixty chickens a day, while twenty-five geese, or fifty turkeys, is a good day's work. With some men it is a life work. One man in this vicinity has been at it forty-five or fifty years, part of the time at the Austins.

In the picking house, the pickers sit in rows. Beside each one is a tin can in which he drops a token, given him as he finishes a bird. Feathers are everywhere, though most of them are supposed to go through holes to the basement below, where they can be baled and sold. Next to the picking room is the storage room where great ice chests, which in the Austin's busy years required a hundred tons of ice a season, hold the dressed geese. (The Austins cut and store the ice on the premises.) When the birds are ready to be shipped, they are weighed in a swinging pan that is big enough to hold a person.

The Austins have made a reputation for their geese throughout eastern United States. In 1928 two of their dressed geese started on a mission of good will to England. At that time there was a budding friendship between Mansfield, Massachusetts, and Mansfield, England. In October, the British town, which is located in what was once the heart of Sherwood Forest, holds its Swainmote Feast, a merry festival reviving the memories of the olden days when the "agisters" or forest officials, used to meet to collect the "pannage" due from the yeomandry whose pigs roamed the forest lands and ate the beech and acorn nuts that fell from the trees. Conviviality had a place at the early meetings. The occasion is now one of the social events of the year, and is attended by the Mayor, the Corporation, someone from the Duke of Portland's estate, representing the Lord of the Manor, and citizens of prominence. The menu is made to follow closely those of a century and more ago. A roast of English beef is always an important item. There is always a stuffed boar's head, garnished with rosemary, brought in on a platter, carried by a white garbed chef, who is attended by a bevy of singing girls, dressed in old English costume. Each year there is an effort to have a surprise dish. For the 1928 feast, Our Town sent two of the Austin geese. They were received, first with skepticism, then with acclaim. London papers featured the two Mansfields and the two geese in head-lines. Newspapers on the continent copied the item.

The friendly feeling fostered by the geese has been followed by many more exchange gifts and by exchange visits of citizens of both towns.

CHAPTER FOURTEEN

Jewelry Shops

THE BUSINESS men of Our Town in 1859 were progressive; they wanted their town to grow. The neighboring town of Attleboro was getting rich through the manufacture of jewelry and there was no reason why gold and silver articles of adornment could not be made in Our Town as well. To offer an inducement for jewelry manufacturers to settle here the erection of a jewelry building was proposed. Probably Gardner Chilson, the rich man of the town, the man who was making stoves and furnaces, was the leader in the movement. He gave the land on which to build, with the provision that the stock should be subscribed within sixty days, and specified the size and kind of building. He also became one of the principal stock owners, taking the first ten shares at fifty dollars each. Samuel Chandler Cobb, a carpenter, and Moran and Fulton, the firm that was making knives, took ten shares each. Men taking four to six shares were Charles Ellis, a manufacturer; James Green, station agent; William B. Bates, whose principal business seemed to be settling estates; William Graves and Charles Hallett, both employed at Rogers' bonnet shop; William Robinson and William Bessom, storekeepers; James L. Hodges, basketmaker; and Elijah Copeland, farmer.

The company was formed in the spring, and by fall the building was commenced. It was a good-sized frame building, eighty feet long by thirty-two feet wide, two stories high, with a basement and attic in addition. There was, also, an engine house attached. It was lighted by seventy-five large windows.

Either it took more money than was expected, or else not all the proposed hundred shares were subscribed. At any rate, both in the fall and in the next spring, the directors had to borrow money to complete the building. Moreover, Gardner Chilson, himself, took twenty-six additional shares. Even these helps were not enough. By June the building was mortgaged.

Whether or not they had a prospective tenant when they began building, no record shows, but almost as soon as it was done, two Sturdy brothers, jewelers, of Attleboro, moved in. Their rent was two hundred and fifty dollars a quarter. With a debt and a mortgage, and only the yearly thousand-dollar annual income, it looked bad for the stockholders. Worse than that, the Sturdys did not stay a full year and the building was idle. Three years after its erection, the building was sold at mortgage sale, and the liquidation of the Mansfield Jewelry Building Company soon followed. Shares, once valued at fifty dollars, became worth eight dollars and ninety-six cents.

It was nearly 1870 before another jewelry business was actually located in this building. Meanwhile a new jewelry firm had started a few rods away. In the beginning it could hardly be called a "firm." It was in reality a one man affair.

In June, 1862, Francis G. Hodges of Attleboro, a young man, not yet twenty-six years old, married Harriet, the seventeen-year-old daughter of Henry Kingman of Our Town. Young Hodges came to live with the bride's parents and began making gold- and silver-plated bracelets in one corner of his father-in-law's barn. His machinery was simple, literally one-horse power, and probably his father-in-law's horse, at that, for Mr. Kingman kept horses and entered into the local horse races. Slowly but steadily the business increased.

About two years later Mr. Hodges somewhere saw some imitation jet jewelry, which was really made of horn. He thought that he could do this, also. From cattle horn he succeeded in making enough samples to fill a small case and started with them for New York. He is said to have been the first to show horn jewelry in that city. So successful was he in interesting the retail jewelers that he returned full of enthusiasm, and induced his father-in-law to go in business with him, under the firm name of Kingman and Hodges. For two years they continued to work the horse. By 1866 their business had increased to such an extent that a six-horsepower engine was installed in the barn. For a little while three other men were in company with Kingman and Hodges. Four years more, and they had outgrown the barn. At just that time an old cotton mill of the Mansfield Cotton Manufacturing Company, on the Rumford River, was for sale. In 1870 Kingman and Hodges bought the property for $8,990. At the new location business boomed. They employed fifty men, twelve or fifteen of whom were skilled hornworkers, induced by Mr. Hodges to come here from Leominster, where horn was being successfully used to make combs.

The material for this popular "jet" jewelry was made from the horns of Texas steers shipped here from the slaughter houses of Chicago. The solid end was sawed off and sent to New York to be used for knife handles and cigar holders. After being sorted, according to quality, it was placed in water to prevent its becoming brittle. The horn was then sawed into eight-inch lengths, and again sawed, this time longitudinally. A soaking in hot oil made it soft enough to be pressed by means of hot plates into flat sheets. Shaved and scraped to uniform thickness, it was ready to manufacture. In the machine room was a stamping machine with cutting dies of many different designs. By a secret process it was colored, then ground, drilled, burnished, and made into bracelets, necklaces, "sets," chains, pins, and belt buckles.

Never were the prospects of the firm any better than on the morning of September 15, 1870, when the fall trade was at its height. Before night the factory lay in ashes.

The water power was low just then, consequently the horizontal boiler was in use to supply the power. The fire under the boiler was burning well, sparks were flying up the old stove pipe, and—some fell on the roof. Just at noon the cries of "Fire, fire" echoed up and down the streets. Crowds assembled with fire buckets, but neither the shallow stream in a dry fall, nor the cucumber pump across the road, could yield enough water to quench the flames. Before the fire reached the lower floor many strong men, with the aid of a rope and boys on the end, hauled out the engine to safety.

Lovell's Block was just them in the process of being completed by a Mr. Aldrich, a contractor from Pawtucket. While the fire was still roaring, Mr. Aldrich was in consultation with Kingman and Hodges. Before the fire was out, the order was given for a new building with the understanding that it would be ready in thirty days. In forty-five days after the fire, Kingman and Hodges were in their new building, doing business and delivering their first lot of goods. From then on, their business, equipment, and even their building, grew. In 1874 they added a new thirty-two Angell Turbine wheel, with a thirty-five horsepower engine in reserve to use in the summer drought, or other emergency. At that time they were employing sixty hands, a few of them women. They were turning out annually $50,000 to $75,000 worth of goods, shipped chiefly through their New York office.

An old *Mansfield News* tells us that the mill was "brilliantly lighted when needed," by means of a Drake gas machine. Most of us would not care to exchange our electricity for this "brilliant gas," which was simply air saturated with the vapor of gasoline. There were occasional flare-ups and explosions, but nothing serious.

Kingman and Hodges occupied the first floor of this new building. The rest of it they let to other jewelry firms. In the basement was a firm making jeweler's findings, earrings, Bible and book clasps, and gilt martingale chains. On the second floor was another firm doing a $40,000 a year business in horn jewelry and employing forty-five persons. In the attic, a few men made rings and screws.

About 1876 horn jewelry went out of vogue, but before it was completely passe, an entirely new imitation product was introduced: sour milk turned into "American coral" and "jet"! The milk in the form of curds and looking like popcorn, came to Kingman and Hodges' shop from the butter and cheese factories in New York state. At the factory it went through a secret process that involved great heat and pressure. When finished and colored, it was made up in all kinds and styles of jewelry, and was also sold as culluloid. This use of sour milk was of short duration, possibly because women were no longer buying jet as they had done. Kingman and Hodges then retired from business.

While horn jewelry was popular there were two other firms making that kind of jewelry in other locations of the town. One of these was farther down the same stream, at Cabot's shop. Mr. Cabot, who had come from Attleboro, where he had been making coffin trimmings, continued to make coffin trimmings here, on the first floor of the shop, and on the second floor made horn jewelry. In ordinarily good times, from sixty to seventy-five hands were employed in the two departments, the greater part of the work being on the jewelry. In each department the yearly output had a value of $40,000 to $50,000.

In the coffin trimming business, Mr. Cabot employed both men and girls. The girls received eighty cents a day, and the men a dollar to a dollar and a quarter. Possibly a few were higher paid. Boys were also on the pay roll. For setting up tacks to be soldered, boys received seven cents a gross. One of these boys was elated to be promoted upstairs to the packing room to help the girls. He was now to be paid by the hour, though he was not told how much an hour. Eagerly, he looked forward to pay day at the end of the month. At last, the great day came.

With what pride he bore home his wages to count and figure out what he was getting by the hour. Alas! A month of four weeks, six days a week, ten hours, a day, THREE CENTS AN HOUR! He resigned from Cabot's next day. That was exactly what Kingman and Hodges, also, in their palmiest days, paid boys.

The material from which the coffin trimmings were made was rolled brass, cut and stamped by dies and then silver-plated. The finished product consisted of handles, moldings, and fancy tacks. The tacks, both square and round, were about an inch in diameter and were used as decoration around the edges of the open coffins, which were used at that time. Defective trimmings were thrown out of the window, or in some way got scattered on the ground outside. For twenty-five or thirty years, children delighted to gather these fascinating objects and use them in play.

Mr. Cabot retired between 1885 and 1890.

If the reader has thought that the Mansfield Jewelry Building has been empty and rotting on its sills all these years, while jewelers have been making coffin trimmings and horn jewelry in various other shops, he is mistaken. For, meanwhile, in that building there had developed a jewelry business of greater permanency than any of the others.

It was about 1870, after the building had been idle for a few years, that two men, who had been in the jewelry business in Attleboro since 1855, came to Mansfield and bought the property. With them came several of their workmen and they engaged in a general line of jewelry and book clasps.

At the end of four years, this firm dissolved and each man took in a new partner. One firm worked upstairs and the other stayed on the first floor. That arrangement lasted only a few years and the youngest man in the two firms, Doliver Spaulding, was left in the building alone. He was equal to the situation.

Just previous to his coming to Our Town, Mr. Spaulding had spent some time traveling in Europe, looking over the best jewelry manufacturies of Paris and the other large cities.

The firm he joined in Our Town confined itself almost en-entirely to the manufacture of tortoise shell jewelry, which was very fashionable at that time. The product took the form of bracelets, belt clasps, lockets, ornamental side and back combs, as well as utility combs, napkin rings. umbrella handles, veil ornaments, fans, chatelaines, vinaigrettes, "gent's" chains, and ladies' shell belts. Most of these goods were inlaid with silver or gold. In 1874 thirty men were employed at work on the shell, using machinery of ten-horse power.

The shell that they used was imported from South America, East India, and African waters. The African was the best. A tortoise might weigh from four hundred to seven hundred pounds. Each one has thirteen scales with twenty-six "toe nails" (saw-shaped edge of shell). These shells and "toe-nails" cost jewelers $7 to $11.50 a thousand. The firm used about $15,000 worth a year. The process of preparing the shell for cutting into designs was very similar to that of preparing the horn, such as other firms in town were using for imitation jet jewelry. The scales were soaked in hot oil to make them pliable (how the mess smelled!) and then rolled into flat plates, afterwards shaved and scraped and made ready to cut.

When Mr. Spaulding carried on the work alone, in addition to the shell work, he added the use of gold and silver coin and other forms of fine silver and gold to the amount of about $25,000 in a year. This was made up into chains, rings, sets, studs, and sleeve buttons. He also used some $3,000 worth of precious stones, besides some diamonds. At that time Mr. Spaulding made no plated jewelry, nor did he use paste stones. Everything was genuine. None of his goods were chased, as that process was usually done in filled products. All of his ornamental work was engraved. Mr. Spaulding designed his novelties and forms, but the patterns for the engravings were done by a professional designer.

In those days there was no such thing as white gold. The finish used was known under the terms, gilding, Roman finish, dead luster and satin finish.

The floor of the room where the gold work was done was torn up every few years. Not that the workmen were all heavy footed, nor was it that they tramped about so much as to wear out the floor. "Thar was gold in them thar boards," almost equal to a placer mine. The boards were ripped up and burned and the ashes saved and sent to a refiner. Likewise, the men's overalls and shoes that were used in that room were washed. The water from the washing machine was carried through troughs into a tank, which had a special arrangement for the purpose of saving gold. A surprising amount of gold was rescued, but not all. Gold was found lodging in other places.

One man had a big shaggy dog of which he was especially fond and he did not wish to be parted from him during the day. Every morning he brought the animal with him. The dog slept quietly under the bench and when the day was over, trotted off with his master. Of course a shaggy dog had to have frequent washings, and every washing was profitable.

Another story concerned a man who had bushy hair and a full beard. Greasy hair was common then, and this man kept his especially greasy. What is more, as he worked on the gold, he frequently ran his hands through his hair in a nervous way. You can guess at the rest. There is no data as to whether dog's hair or human hair was more profitable for that particular business.

On the whole, there was less petty thievery in Spaulding's shop than any shop in the east. With so many small articles lying around, and so much gold and silver handy, it might be expected that some would find its way into pockets.

In all shops fifty and more years ago there was very little red tape or discipline. This was especially true of the smaller shops. These had no time clocks. Employees came and went as they pleased. They had their hours, and in general, stuck to them. Shops opened at seven and closed at six, except on Saturday, when the closing hour was five. Fifty-nine hours a week for men and women alike.

There were occasions at Spaulding's shop when men felt at perfect liberty to leave the shop during working hours. The shop was near the railroad station. When some notable person was passing through the town and the train stopped at the station, the men of the brass band, of which there were plenty at this shop, were given full permission to leave their benches, gather up their instruments, which they kept at the shop for noon practice, and go off to serenade Kalakua, King of the Cannibal Island, President Hayes, or some equally notable person scheduled to stop, meant that everybody left his bench, grabbed his coat and hat, and went. Maybe it was somebody getting killed on the railroad that drew a Spaulding crowd. Any real excitement would do it. It was all right with Mr. Spaulding, for he wanted to go, too. Once out, they usually stayed half an hour. On return, each man, and woman (the women were not left behind) checked off half an hour on the big name sheet posted in the hallway. Each was expected to have self-respect enough to be honest and they all were. On the fifteenth of the month, when the pay roll was made out, the bookkeeper deducted the time.

Pay day was the fifteenth. If a man began work in the first of the month, it would be six weeks before he received any money.

Spaulding's shop was a hotbed for politics. It was always said that the way that Spaulding's shop went, was the way that the town would go. Several of the men in the shop ran for state offices and won. First, there was Charles S. Frost, who made chains. He represented Mansfield in the legislature in

1866. Five years later the political lightning struck the gold room of the shop. Up there three Smiths, Abbot and Clifford, of Norton, and Elwin, of Mansfield, sat side by side at the bench, soldering. Along came the fall election of 1891, and then there were two, for Elwin Smith was elected to go to sit in the State House on Beacon Hill. Another five or six years and Spaulding's shop sent another representative. This time it was Frank W. Barnard. Perhaps it was while a boy in the shipping room that James G. Moran, chosen President of the Massachusetts State Senate in 1935, got his political aspirations.

Had the radio existed in his day, Mr. Spaulding doubtless would have installed one for the benefit of his employees. As it was, he did the next best thing; he put up a bulletin board and wrote down the news as fast as he could get it. In the weeks that followed the shooting of President Garfield, Mr. Spaulding kept his help informed of every development in the case as he learned it from the papers or got it from the telegraph office. Items of lesser importance, but of interest to the men, also appeared. It was there that they learned that John L. Sullivan had won the prize fight in Mississippi.

As among most men, a love of sport existed. At the shop they sometimes had fun at each other's expense. Once there was a wager about a walk to Boston, a distance by road of over thirty miles. Two of the men were the victims. The hike was on for April 14, 1883. There was a prize for each one, provided he got there. Somebody furnished cigars for all the men in the shop and it became an occasion. Doubtless all left their benches at 9:30 A.M. to see the start. The men went without retinue. At noon they reached Canton Junction and had dinner. At 6:30 they reached the Boston and Providence Station, at Park Square. Weary and footsore, they took the next train home. Next day they were at the shop to claim their money and tell about it.

Anyone wishing to buy jewelry was welcome at the shop. The way the bookkeeper opened the boxes and undid the carefully folded tissue wrappings made one think that it was a delight for him to show the pretty things. Most of the jewelry was solid gold, or at least heavy plate. Only the dyer knew how the red roses with green leaves were produced in gold.

Expert repair work was done, nothing was too difficult for them to mend, except horn jewelry. Real tortoise shell could be soldered, but not horn. Diamonds were safe in their hands. A man from New York sent on three diamond rings, one valued at five hundred dollars and the others at two hundred and fifty dollars apiece. The diamonds were beautifully set and Spaulding's men did not wish to take them from their setting, nor did they want to submit them to the intense heat necessary for welding, for if there should be the slightest flaw in the stone, the heat would crack it. One of the men devised a way. He took a raw potato and thrust the ring into it, then cut away the part that was around the gold circle, leaving the diamond embedded in the potato. Over the part where the diamond was, he put asbestos to keep out the heat and he put pumice on the sides. Then, without fear of injury to the stone, he turned on the heat and cut away the unnecessary part, bent, and welded the ring. All the men in the shop took pride in the accomplishment.

If the time for visiting the shop should be a dark or stormy day, a stranger might have been puzzled to see men running around with unlighted kerosene lamps in their hands, even going out in the rain with them. They were like the foolish virgins of the Bible, they had neglected until the last moment to get oil for their lamps and have them trimmed. Every man and woman in the shop had a kerosene lamp by his or her side for use when the daylight failed. The overburdened janitor took care of the girls' lamps (filled them with oil and cleaned the globes, and if those globes were not clean he was called down by the girls and had to do it over). The men had to take care of their own. Some were forehanded and took their lamps outdoors to the oil house the first thing in the morning, while others waited until they were needed. Some men could trim their lamp wicks so that they didn't smoke and kept the globes shining by breathing into them and polishing them with soft paper. Others complained because they couldn't see.

Mr. Spaulding had an office in the jewelry mart of New York City, and he also had a store in Mexico City where he did a good business in silver goods, especially chain. Gold was not wanted in Mexico. On the whole, the Mexicans were reliable and good pay. One customer who could not pay presented Mr. Spaulding with two large Aztec gods. These, with some trouble and expense, were shipped to Our Town, where for years they stood on the lawn in front of Mr. Spaulding's house. They are now in the possession of the Public Library. Archaeological specimens of this sort are not allowed to be taken from the country to-day.

Besides selling jewelry in Mexico, Mr. Spaulding accommodated his customers there by sending down plows, or anything they wanted in the way of farming implements. One man wanted horses. Mr. Spaulding bought him three beautiful animals in New Hampshire.

In the 1890's the business was at its zenith. The busiest time was the fall of the year when they were preparing for the Christmas trade and employing one hundred and seventy-five men and women. At other times there were from one hundred to one hundred and fifty at work. While many were old standbys who remained there thirty, forty, yes, even fifty years, the personnel varied considerably, from decade to decade. It sometimes seemed as if everyone who had lived in Our Town during the right years, worked at Spaulding's shop for a longer or shorter time.

With the arrival of the new century the jewelry world

changed. The demand was for less gold and cheaper construction. Bigger firms, with greater outputs, could cut the price below the possibility of his competition. Mr. Spaulding was getting older. He hated to sacrifice his old standard of quality. New methods did not appeal to him. Gradually he was swamped in the maelstrom of the time.

Mr. Spaulding's retirement did not leave Our Town without a jewelry manufacturing plant. Some of the time since then, there have been two; at all times there has been one; good jewelry firms, well run.

Cranberries

ANOTHER NEW industry was started in Our Town in 1862. That year, Elijah and Almond Copeland, two brothers, progressive farmers who had been actively interested in the Mansfield Jewelry Building during the last three years, conceived the idea that cranberries might be cultivated with profit on the large farm that they owned jointly at the south end of the town. Cranberries had been growing wild within the town, but no one in Our Town, or vicinity was cultivating them at that time, though the Fisher brothers started a little while after the Copelands.

The first thing that the Copelands had to do was to decide on a place. The part of the farm that they selected for the purpose was two and three-fourths acres of meadow and swamp land. Right away they began the preparation of the meadow. First, they had to remove the top soil, and then, spread on sand, for weeds and meadow hay would grow quickly in heavy soil and, besides, cranberries like sand. It cost $56 for labor, sanding the meadow, and $10 more, for pulling bushes.

One would hardly expect any returns from that land the first year, but there was. And what? Mud! If you drive through Reservoir Street today you will see a depression, or hole, just after you pass the first house. That hole yielded the most beautiful rich mud, valuable to mix with barnyard dressing and spread on the cultivated land. Not only did the Copelands use a lot of it on their own farm land, but they sold $20 worth that year. The hole left by the mud removal, and ditches leading from the hole, were cleaned out to take care of the water that came from a little brook, which ran under the road, and to drain the swamp, and, also, to supply water for flowage in the meadow in case of drought in summer, frost in spring and fall, and to flood the meadow in winter.

Then in June, when the beds were nicely prepared, at a cost of $38, they set out the vines. That process was back-breaking work. Hour after hour men had to punch holes in the wet sand at fifteen inch intervals and then press into each hole two or three pieces of vine about six inches long.

In 1863, there was more sanding, more bush pulling and more setting out of vines, as well as more mud dug out of the ditches. (For two or three years the beds had to be kept weeded.)

It was not until 1866, that they really began harvesting berries. That year they gathered eighty-eight barrels. The selling price was $13.25 a barrel. To be sure, that did not mean that they cleared $1,166 on their investment and four years labor. There were the pickers and other workers to be paid, barrels to be bought, and always shrinkage, due to certain amount of decay before the berries could be shipped.

Picking in 1866, cost $87.34; in 1867, $148.28; in 1868, $117.68 and in 1871, $118.83. Individual pickers received three cents a quart. An ordinary picker could pick three or four bushels a day.

The next year they had only forty-five barrels and the year after, only forty-one. It wasn't the weather, nor any freak of nature that made that difference. The fruit was set for a bumper crop the first lean year, 1867, then water came over the vines and remained long enough to spoil eighty barrels of berries. It came about by the mind and hand of man.

The facts of the case were that in 1866 there was formed a corporation known as the Wading River Reservoir Company, whose purpose it was to build a dam and thus create a large reservoir, or pond, for storing water, which could be used as power in factories in Norton, Taunton, and perhaps beyond.

The Reservoir Company had been formed with the idea of

turning a part of the Wading River in the west part of the town into a reservoir. When, for some reason, that plan fell through, the company decided to use the Rumford River in the northern part of Norton and in a little of Mansfield. The Mansfield end took in the Copeland cranberry meadow. In 1867, it would seem that the dam was begun and water began to accumulate.

The Copelands had found out, in 1866, what was likely to happen, and at once put in a claim for damage from the Reservoir Corporation. The matter dragged along from December, 1866, until the summer of 1870. Meanwhile, the reservoir dam was completed in August, 1868, and the Copelands had started a new meadow on another part of their property to be ready for use by the time the reservoir should be flooded.

From the cranberry records it looks as if the reservoir was not fully flooded for two or three years after the dam was completed, in 1868, for we notice that in 1868, 1869 and 1870 there was less damage by flowage than there was in 1867. In 1869, there was the biggest crop of all, one hundred and six barrels of cranberries picked, and twenty-five barrels lost by flowage. The berries that year brought $11.65 a barrel.

The Reservoir Company at first refused to come to terms in settling for the damage done to the cranberry property. They even went so far as to say that they had made no agreement about buying up the land used for growing the cranberries, which by that time had increased from the two or three acres originally planted to cranberries, to more than twice that amount. Next, the Company offered $500 for the damage. The case was finally taken to the Supreme Court and the plaintiffs won the case. The award was $4,852.20, but it was considerably less than the Copelands finally received. Of course, the lawyers had a good fat fee. Out of it, also, came $44 for witness fees, and $314.42 for the jury.

By 1870, the Copelands had a new small cranberry bog coming into bearing. They had built a fair sized dam at the north end of the meadow to hold back the water for flowage purposes, and through the meadow had made dikes, ditches, and small dams to control the water. Each meadow, surrounded by dikes of earth, covered about an acre. In time there were nearly ten acres of meadow on this farm in cranberry cultivation. The advantage of having the whole meadow laid out in small plats was that in this way each plat could be flowed separately, and also, it was more convenient in lining off for picking. Then, too, the varieties were kept separate in this way.

A meadow once set out and growing did not last forever, unless cared for. In the beginning, the meadows had to be kept weeded, just like a corn field or a potato patch, except that weeds did not grow quite as rapidly in sand. After the cranberry vines got well grown, common weeds had no chance, but sensitive ferns, (onoclea sensibilis), which are not at all sensitive, and poison ivy, became extremely troublesome pests that had to be rooted out, or killed with salt or acids. After a few years, the vines became too long, and then had to be sanded. The sanding was done in the winter, when the meadows were flooded and under ice, and the ice strong enough to bear oxen and the cart load of sand. Neighboring children dreaded to see this, for the cranberry meadows made smooth and safe skating ponds for them. In the springtime, when the ice melted, the sand settled down in the vines and the new shoots came through. Eventually, there came a time when the vines had to be cut down to the roots and the meadows entirely made over. New vines for planting were obtained in different ways. Probably the first ones were taken from the wild meadows. Later, slips were taken from the most satisfactory vines, either in the Copeland's own meadow or from someone's else, just as in any kind of fruit growing. The Early Blacks, a small deep colored berry that ripened early, were grown in the meadow that could be less easily flowed for protection against frost.

So much for the cultivation. Now for the harvesting, which began around the twentieth of September, and should be through early in October. A stormy fall, or frosty nights, added to the woes of a cranberry grower. A combination of both storm and frost, came in 1900, and the calendar showed November, before the berries were all off the vines and stacked away in crates under cover.

A visit to the cranberry meadow in September, 1883, will show how the picking was then done.

Everything is in readiness for picking on Monday morning, September 17, but much work has already been accomplished. During the summer, the shallow crates, made of laths to let in the air, have been put in repair and new ones made; the meadow has just been lined off with four foot rows; eight quart baskets that cost twenty cents apiece have been procured; and plenty of new tickets have been printed. These tickets are of prime importance, for every picker must be given a red one, marked "Eight Quarts," every time he fills his eight quart basket. Twelve of these red tickets will be exchanged for a blue card, "Ninety-six Quarts." For partially filled baskets at the end of the day, there are white tickets for one quart and yellow ones for three quarts.

The picking date has been advertised in the "Mansfield News" the previous Friday; also, friends have passed along the news by word of mouth. Consequently, by eight o'clock on Monday, the pickers, all native born, begin to arrive, mostly on foot, though a few from a distance come in express wagons. Before nine they are in the meadow at work. J. Henry Clapp, is the boss of the picking. Woe be to the boys who try to scoop the berries from the top of the vines and leave the scattering ones behind. Mr. Clapp's eyes are trained to see berries, even if they are buried deep in the matted vines. Neither Mr. Copeland nor Mr. Clapp will stand for much fooling in the meadow.

The pickers, in 1870, were men and boys. By 1883, women

and girls also pick. There are all ages, the oldest pickers at this time are Dexter Leonard and Charles N. Hall, both of them over sixty. Mr. Hall always comes barefoot. They are from all classes in society; one fairly prominent man from the center picks "because it is such bewitching work." There is a middle-aged woman picker, who loves to talk religion, although she is not a very active church worker. Some of the boys, whenever they can, choose to pick next to her and engage her in conversation. When she waxes most eloquent on her favorite subject, they slip their hands under the line and scoop off the thickest of the berries, leaving her to pick up the leavings, which she does unsuspectingly. She often remarks to Mrs. Copeland that it is surprising that those young boys should think so much of her that they almost fight to pick by her side. They show a remarkable interest in religion, too, she says.

On this particular Monday morning, there is more than the usual amount of excitement for the opening day. Albert Collins, a youth, is pleased to find himself the center of interest, for in a way he had been the hero of an unusual event yesterday. Albert lived beside Cabot's Pond, in Sodom. Further on lived "Lon" Green. Lon Green, a tall, broad shouldered man of fine physique had not turned out to be the kind of man that God had intended him to be. He lived in the time, like the present, when man's independence was unhampered by any 18th amendment. By the time he was thirty-three years old, he had reached a state which was not uncommon in 1883. To raise enough money to buy liquor, which was cheap then, he caught skunks and sold the skins and oil. On Sunday, September 16, as he was passing through Sodom, John Cobb saw that he was on the verge of delirium tremens and told Albert Collins that he had better go home with him. The two proceeded. When they reached the bridge over the stream, Green gave a wild leap and plunged into the river. Alone, Albert was helpless, so he ran for aid, but it was too late. No wonder all the pickers are talking about it and asking Albert for details. Curiosity satisfied, the pickers go to work.

In the meadow, by ten o'clock that first morning, are thirty or more pickers, usually two in a row. On the bank are piles of crates, some of them empty, and some already filled with berries. Beside them sits the bookkeeper, whose business it is to give out the tickets, or send the pickers back, if the baskets are not quite full. Pacing back and forth in the rows is Henry Clapp, watching to see that the workers pick clean. Along the cart road between the meadows, comes a farm wagon with men to load the filled crates. In another meadow, men are lining out rows. By night, tender fingers will begin to be sore, for some of the vines are long and matted. Experienced pickers will soon be covering their nails with shoemaker's wax to prevent hangnails. On Saturday, when children are out of school, there may be sixty to one hundred in all, picking.

Should you happen to visit the cranberry meadow ten years later you would observe some changes. Eight quart baskets have given place to six quart tin pails. (Some boys with an inclination to cheat had discovered that by wetting the baskets the bottoms could be poked up until an eight quart basket would not hold much more than seven quarts.) The men who are lining out are using a reel, which had been invented by David Fisher to use on the Fisher meadow. Heretofore, some man had to tramp back and forth over the cranberries with the line. This new arrangement saves both time and berries. Tickets got lost or stolen, so now the tickets have given way to books where the number of quarts are credited with a rubber stamp by the bookkeeper. The bookkeeper, also, keeps a record in his own book. Throughout the years the price paid for picking ranged from two, two and one half, to three cents a quart, hand work.

If anyone thinks that the daylight hours of the fall was the only time that there was much activity in the meadows, he is mistaken. At midnight, one might frequently see a light moving about. That meant that there was danger of frost and the owner was in the meadow letting on the water. In picking time, neither Mr. Copeland nor the Fishers, liked to flood the meadow, if it was possible to avoid it, for that delayed the picking several hours next day, because pickers did not like to go into a wet meadow and, moreover, wet berries did not keep well. Hence, anxious hours during the evening, watching a falling mercury. Wind, and even clouds, if not too threatening, were welcomed. The same precaution had to be exercised in June, when the vines were in blossom. On the 15th of June, 1884, a frost came unexpectedly and nipped the whole crop, so that there was hardly a barrel to be harvested that fall. Other expedients were used besides water. Both the Fishers and Copeland used kerosene torches. The idea was that the smudge made would keep off the frost, and also that moths would fly into the blaze and be burned. (A certain kind of moth laid eggs that produced fire-worms, an enemy to cranberries.) For some reason the torches did not prove very satisfactory and were given up after a season or two. The same torches were much more serviceable in torch-light parades, though they looked pretty on the cranberry meadows. The Fishers had a still better way of throwing a smoke screen in their meadow. They were also basketmakers, so they took out loads of basket shavings and made piles on the banks of the meadows. Each night, when there was danger of frost, they burned a pile of shavings and incidentally, furnished fun with the bonfire for all the children of Sodom.

After the harvesting season, came the picking over. The berries were first put through a winnowing machine. The earliest machine was a crude affair and was set up where there was a breeze. The berries were turned into the hopper, somebody turned the crank and the berries fell into a box below. As they fell the wind blew the chaff away. The later machine was much more complicated and more useful. From the hopper of this one, the berries fell on moving planes of heavy duck. The sound berries bounded into one drawer and the poorer ones were carried on to another plane and to other drawers. Even then the berries had to be turned into long trays on legs, to be picked over by hand. Lastly, they were barrelled, and shipped, mostly to New York and Providence. The barrels held one hundred quarts. At first, the barrels that the Fishers and Mr. Copeland used, were shipped here by a Mr. Small from Cape Cod, at a cost of forty-five cents apiece. Later, each fall, Small opened a factory here and made barrels to supply Fisher, and Copeland, and also, Turner, of Foxboro. At one time Elijah Copeland, used to hire Leonard Hodges' great lumber reach and drive to Holliston for barrels. In the earliest days, flour barrels obtained at the grocery stores were used.

The Fishers and their cranberry meadow has been mentioned without explaining that they started their cranberry industry on a small scale about the time that the Copelands built their new bog. The Fishers were located on the Rumford River, half a mile above Copelands. Already the story of their mill and basketmaking has been told. The three Fishers and the two Copelands were often in conference over their business and when their meadows grew to considerable size they agreed on picking dates, that they should hire help with no conflict. In the earliest days of the Fisher cranberry meadow, the brothers did all their own work, but when they gave up their mill and enlarged their meadows to five or six acres, they hired pickers, sometimes as many as fifty.

Elijah Copeland died in 1899, and later owners of the farm never did much with cranberry growing. Today, the meadows have reverted to bog and underbrush. The Fisher meadow has now gone to waste. After George and David Fisher died, Jasper carried on alone until 1915, then he too gave it up.

There have been still other cranberry meadows in Our

Town. Near one of the West Mansfield coal mines years ago, the Janes brothers gathered ten or more barrels yearly from wild cranberry bogs, left in their natural state.

At the north end of the town, the King brothers had quite an extensive meadow about the time the Copelands started their earliest one. LeRoy King was wont to say that the first hundred dollar bill he ever saw came from the sale of cranberries. The Kings never did any real cultivation and depended on the Copelands for the use of a winnowing machine. The Kings lost their meadow, in 1869-70, when the Framingham branch of the railroad was built.

Until about 1897, the Copelands and Fishers had their picking done entirely by hand, then, for their remaining years they used cranberry scoops. The Kings, however, even in the early days, used long handled cranberry rakes, which differed from hay rakes only in that the teeth were curved instead of straight.

Today, a few wild cranberries are growing here and there in the outskirts of the town, mostly ungathered.

CHAPTER SIXTEEN

Encouraging New Business

THE TOWN was growing. After the 1880 census was declared people began saying that by the time the State Census was taken in 1885 there would be a population of three thousand. The leading business men were anxious to see new manufacturers come to town. Somebody got in touch with Joseph P. Manton of Providence, founder of the Manton Windlass and Steam Steerer Company, a company with a capital stock of $125,000. Mr. Manton had discovered Our Town, probably from the steam car window, as a desirable place to locate. He seemed to have no desire to remain in Providence where he had been in business with his brother in the American Ship Windlass Company. It was whispered that the two brothers had disagreed to the point of bitterness.

Mr. Manton was a veteran in the manufacture of that type of machinery. He began building iron capstan windlasses in 1857. For fifteen years he spent much time and money trying to persuade owners of sailing vessels to use donkey engines for handling anchors, cargoes, and sails, and for pumping. Strange to say it was on a large Chinese steamer that he installed a steam windlass in 1860. Throughout the Civil War period Mr. Manton labored unsuccessfully to induce the Navy Department to use steam to raise their anchors. It was not until 1872 that Mr. Manton's apparatus became at all popular. That year Charles R. Mallory saw its advantage and installed one on the S. S. *City of Pekin* and one on the S. S. *City of Tokio*. After that the U. S. Navy adopted them on the *Puritan* and the *Meantonomah*.

In 1878 he turned his attention to steering vessels by steam.

The Navy Department then placed his steam steerer on two of the largest vessels of the Navy with complete success.

In Our Town he sought two acres of land near the railroad, a five year tax exemption and $10,000 subscribed by Mansfield people. The local stock was to be put into the main building, two stories high, a blacksmith shop and a machine shop. He said he expected to employ forty or fifty men and to use 4,000 to 5,000 tons of iron a year. A good deal was expected of Our Town, yet with the backing of a man of Mr. Manton's experience and ability it looked good to many people. He was an impressive man when he came to discuss the matter. He carried with dignity the title of Colonel, which he had acquired as a member of the staff of Governor Sprague of Rhode Island. His hair was turning gray, he knew how to wear the tall silk hat that every man of any position whatever wore at that time. He talked well. Although he could not promise the thirty-five per cent dividends that his old company had paid, he did think that he could pay twenty-five per cent.

Public interest was aroused. Howard Perkins, once a cotton manufacturer, now a member of the Board of Selectmen, became the local chairman of the enterprise. On October 14, 1882, a public meeting was called in Central Hall to discuss it. Young men at once circulated a paper with pledges for the first $1,000, one half of which was taken by young men in the Spaulding jewelry shop. The shares were ten dollars each, payable in two equal instalments.

The next week another meeting was held. At this meeting Charles T. Borden, the druggist, was elected president. It was the opinion of that meeting that it would be a good thing to have the windlass company in town, but that it should furnish more security. Mr. Borden was requested to visit Mr. Manton to ask for a first mortgage on the machinery. To this Mr. Manton was not quite ready to agree. Our people had chosen a good man to consult with Mr. Manton, for Mr. Borden, too, had dignity, his hair was snow white and he also knew how to wear a tall hat. And he could talk just as smoothly as Mr. Manton.

Though it was not immediately decided that the Windlass Company would locate here, nevertheless the stockholders decided to build anyway, as there were two or three other companies that had expressed a desire to come to Our Town, if a building were ready. Matters progressed rapidly. The full amount expected of our townspeople was soon subscribed and the building company organized.

Howard Perkins, the selectman who had been so much interested in getting the company here, was elected treasurer. Among the other directors were David Harding of the Card Tap and Die Company, two basketmakers, a storekeeper, a man who kept a stable and sold coal, Francis Spaulding, superintendent at Spaulding's jewelry shop, and the Rider brothers of the Rider Foundry.

The Riders were strong for having the Windlass Company come and they put $500 into the company. That was far more than most people subscribed and a good deal of money for young men who had recently started in business. But they were wide awake and saw in the new enterprise good business for themselves. The plant, if it came, was to be located right at their door and was going to need castings. Their confidence was justified.

By the beginning of 1882 it was certain that the Manton Company would come and building plans were under way. Winter weather and frozen ground hindered the laying of the floor, which was to be directly on the ground. A number of bushels of salt were used to hasten the thawing. At length, the building was done and the windlass company inside it, with forty or fifty men working ten hours a day.

The confidence of the town was such that it was voted in

town meeting to exempt from taxation any building erected for manufacturing purposes at a cost of more than $3,000.

Then came a depression, with business stagnation and ship building especially quiet, but the Windlass company did remarkably well. They were putting machinery on Navy vessels, the coast survey, revenue marines, as well as merchant marines. At the end of the year 1885 the Windlass was said to be the best business in town. Besides that year fitting out three government coast survey steamers, four Pacific Mail boats, four lake steamers, they made a new opening for the Mansfield product by installing the first iron windlass on a fishing schooner. Soon five schooners of the Gloucester fishing fleet were using them. The company also began making dock capstans.

For ten years the company paid steady wages. While they did not pay promptly, they paid fully as high wages as those paid in any other factory in Our Town. Most men received three dollars a day and that was considered good at that time.

About 1892 the Manton Steam Windlass Company went out of existence and Mr. Manton joined Clark Chase in the Chase Elevator Company, of Warren, Rhode Island. Had Our Town been a seaport, the business might have stayed right here, but it was better to have the elevators built in a factory at the dock where they could easily be transferred to the boats.

Mr. Manton became the agent for the Chase company with an office in New York. New York life suited Mr. Manton, for though he must have been nearing sixty years of age, he was quite the gay blade of the nineties. He spent his summers in Barrington, Rhode Island, in a home of considerable style.

Windlasses were still made by this company, which equipped the Nantasket line of steamers out of Boston and the Boston fire boats. The ill fated *Portland* that went down about 1898, and the excursion boat, *General Slocum*, that sank in 1904, were both equipped with windlasses made by Mr. Manton's company, but those were made after the Mansfield days of the Windlass company.

The departure of this company left an empty building, a burden on the hands of the stockholders who had built it. They took the matter philosophically; the town and business men had reaped the advantages of steady wages to the employees through a decade.

Though some use was made of the building for storage purposes, it was not used as a manufacturing plant until the Riverside Japannery came here to japan leather in 1904

After the steam windlass company was well started and was proving successful, it looked as if cooperative building was a good thing. The scheme might with success be extended to houses as well as factory buildings. A group of men associated themselves as the Mansfield Trust Company and began to open up sections of the town hitherto not used for building purposes. They laid out streets and sold house lots.

Next, they felt they must build up after the manner of the House-That-Jack-Built story: that they must attract business, that would employ the men, that would live in the houses, that would be built upon the lots, that had been laid out on the land of the Mansfield Trust Company.

Doliver Spaulding, owner of the Spaulding Jewelry Shop, was one of the principal officers of the land company and he became a leader in the new movement to attract business.

Under Mr. Spaulding's leadership, a number of men agreed to form a building stock company. Before they went ahead with the building, they intended to make sure of a tenant. In July, 1887, Mr. Spaulding received a telegram that set them all agog. "Go ahead with the factory as soon as possible." It was signed by the Rumsey Brothers, shoe manufacturers in Lynn. From then on, Mr. Spaulding and his associates began to hustle. Not wishing to take any chances on a slip, they made an agreement with the shoe firm that the company should come at once, and be housed temporarily in some shop until the new factory should be completed.

Just the building for temporary quarters was waiting for them. The factory that had been the Kingman and Hodges jewelry shop, before horn jewelry went out of style and the men out of business, was partially empty. In the attic a few men were making screws and rings and on the second floor was a man who had come here to make fish lines and had turned to jeweler's findings. That left the entire first floor, the basement and a two story building in the rear for the shoemakers. Moreover, the property was in the hands of Mr. Spaulding and two other men. Mr. Spaulding could, therefore, make an attractive offer to the Rumsey brothers.

At the very end of July, 1887, the Rumsey machinery began to arrive and was set up. By the third week in August, forty hands were at work and more to be taken on right away.

Also during July the Rumsey Building Association was very busy. Money had to be found for the new building and just as important, land on which to build it. Almost immediately $6,000 was subscribed. The Mansfield Trust Company headed the list with the first two hundred dollars.

Mr. Spaulding became president of the directors of the building corporation. The other directors were also all Mansfield men.

The land they wanted belonged to Hamilton J. Green of Oak Bluffs. Mr. Green, a descendant of Rev. Roland Green, the second minister in Our Town, was born here and still interested in the town. He was willing to sell the land at a reasonable price, take the amount in stock, and buy outright one $100 share besides. What could be more generous? On July 29th, the ground was broken. Immediately A. D. King began hauling bricks for the foundation. By September 16th, the chimney, sixty-five feet high, was nearly done. The end of the year saw the new building nearing completion and the Rumsey Brothers' shoe factory one of the established firms in the town. From the temporary quarters on Spring Street, they were shipping thirty cases of shoes a day and employing about fifty hands. That was the dull season of the year, but they had great hopes that with more room in the new building and the spring trade coming on, the industry would greatly increase, and their hopes were justified.

In February, 1888, the shoe firm moved into the new building and on February 22 an auction of the old machinery that they did not want was held in the old building on Spring Street. By the end of the first week in March there were 200 employed in the new factory. Twenty kinds of ladies' and misses' boots, ranging in quality from French kid and fine gondola to American kid, were being turned out.

The concern was owned by the Rumsey Brothers, Bert and Charles, both past middle age at the time they started the business here. For some years before they came to Our Town they had been in business in Lynn. When they came here they still continued the Lynn shops. It was their hope to sometime enlarge the Lynn factory until it should be the largest shop in that city.

The reason for opening a branch in Our Town was a Lynn strike. The Rumsey Brothers took this way to break the strike. When the shop opened they made it plain that no union men should be employed. In fact, when the men and women went to work they signed a paper stating that they did not belong to any union and would not, so long as they worked at the Rumsey shop. The employees stuck to that agreement even when union men came to them and urged them to join.

A few Lynn employees came with the firm from Lynn and boarded at the Mansfield House, the American House, or the Central House, but most of the workers were local people and, of course, green hands at shoe making. These green hands were all paid the same wage, one dollar a day. Soon the firm wanted to put them on a piece work basis. That did not suit, for in their inexperience, many of them could not earn the dollar a day. Finally, an arrangement was made whereby two men working together could finish a given piece of work much quicker than two men working separately. Moreover, they rapidly became so skilled that some men earned from $3.00 to $7.00 a day. A day began at seven in the morning, and with an hour out at noon, closed at six at night, but not infrequently they were asked to come back at seven and work until nine. It required the evening work to make the seven dollars a day. The bookkeeper is said to have made the statement that during the ten years or so that the firm was in business in Our Town, they paid out one million dollars in wages. It is also said that that was the only shop that always paid weekly, regularly, every Saturday.

When it was built the new factory was the highest building in town, four stories with a basement, 40 by 100 feet. One hundred and two windows lighted the building. A small wing on the east side provided a stairway to all floors for the use of the employees. There was also an automatic elevator,—something unheard of in Our Town in 1888. This was before the days of the fire department or the completion of the waterworks, consequently the company installed a fire pump with a capacity of 500 gallons of water a minute, with a reservoir, hose, automatic fire alarm, and sprinkler on each floor.

When the annual town meeting was held in March, there was an article on the warrant to exempt the Rumsey Brothers from taxation for five years. It was so voted. This was nothing new, for two years before, as previously noted, a vote was passed to exempt from taxation any building erected for manufacturing purposes at a cost of more than $3,000.

The Rumseys, though they never moved to Our Town, kept an attentive eye on the business. Mr. Bert Rumsey, the older brother, came here regularly twice a week from Lynn. He was lame. A few minutes after the ten-o'clock train came in from Boston, those working on the east side of the building would see Mr. Rumsey limping along by the aid of his cane. Everyone was on the alert to be up to scratch the days he came, for he had rather a crabbed manner, and was a fault finder, though on the whole a good man for whom to work.

The cutting was all done at the Lynn shop. The cut material, each part packed together, was sent to the third floor when it arrived. Here were some twenty-five to thirty girls at work on the machines. The parts had to be sewed together, turned, and the seams flattened out, the linings sewed in, stitched down the side for the buttonholes, buttonholes made and the buttons sewed on. The shoes made there were all women's buttoned boots, though toward the end of their stay in Our Town, they did put out a few laced boots, for samples.

Eugene H. Walker was the foreman of the sewing room. He was very fair with the girls. Some work was more desirable than others; for instance, for stitching overlap vamps, the girls received thirty-six cents a case, while for a slipper vamp they received just half as much. Mr. Walker saw to it that such work was evenly distributed. The girls, after they reached the shop, were expected to work and not visit or gossip. There was no novel reading, fancy work, nor gala occasions such as often took place at the straw shop. The hours were more strict also. It was easy to get a half-day or even a whole day off at the straw shop, but at the shoe shop there was no such liberty. The girls got out at four o'clock on Saturday afternoon and it was almost impossible to be excused from coming back for the three hours on that afternoon. Most of the girls did not earn over two dollars a day, even by working overtime in the evening, as they often did. Though many of the straw shop girls often earned more money in a day, by the end of the year, the shoe shop girls had earned the most, for their work was more steady throughout the year. In the dull seasons there was usually work, but they made shorter days. Some would go in at seven, do up enough work to last the next contingent for the day and leave two hours early. Another group would not come until nine and would stay the full day or until they had used up the work on hand.

Sometimes the girls made mistakes that turned the shoes into seconds. For such errors they were fined. There was a threat to make the girls buy the shoes that they spoiled, but so far as we know that was never carried out.

A smaller group of girls, perhaps eight or ten, worked on the second floor making pasteboard boxes. Some of these girls had served their apprenticeship at the Sweet box shop in Norton before coming to the Rumsey shop.

After the girls in the sewing room had done all they could to the shoes, the shoes were sent down to the first floor to the lasting room. Here the soles were put on, trimmed off and made ready for the final finishing process. All of the heaviest machinery was on that floor. One of the heaviest machines, called a "beater out," weighed between two and three tons and was run by the smallest man in the shop.

How the girls today would laugh if they could see those shoes after they were assembled. The shoes worn by the women of yesterday bore little resemblance to the foot gear of the present. The shoes made here forty years ago were all boots, practically all of them buttoned. As for heels, well, spike heels were unheard of. Compared with the heels of today, they would be called low. Many of them were concave on the sides, the curve having been made by a special machine.

It was rather interesting to watch a heel being fastened to the shoe. A machine made holes in the heels, which were always of leather, and into these holes, young boys placed the nails and fed them into the nailing machine, which was run by an elderly man. This machine came down on the heel with force and drove all the nails through the heels, thus nailing the heels in place.

Besides setting nails there was another boy's job on the fourth floor. That was blacking the shoes.

After the shoes had gone through all the processes of finishing they were sent from the fourth floor to the packing room, where they were placed, thirty pairs in a case, ready to be shipped. Practically the entire output, thirty or forty cases a day, was sent to Winch Brothers, wholesale shoe dealers in Boston. These shoes sold from the factory at $1.02, $1.20 and $1.40, with a seven per cent discount. Mr. Rumsey is quoted as saying if he had made five cents profit on a shoe he was satisfied. Another shoe was sold to Winch Brothers for about $1.00 and the retailer sold it for $1.25. There was a better shoe sold from the factory for $1.60. That was partly made in Lynn and sent here to be finished.

On the side, they made the "Bijou," a dollar shoe, for the Dexter Shoe Company, which was a mail order house. On these Rumseys made three cents apiece. This business amounted to very little, as the Dexter Company took but small allotments, five or six cases at a time.

Those men who made shoes here forty years ago knew what they were doing. Some of them could make a shoe from start to finish. Once, William Swett made a wager with Horace Tupper that he could make a shoe complete and finish it in the shortest time. Tupper took him up and they went to work. Of course, with their regular work on hand and the machines in use, there was no chance for consecutive work, but at odd moments they worked at their shoes. It was nip and tuck between them until the shoes were almost done when Tupper let his shoe slip and cut the heel. As nearly as can be estimated, if Swett's shoe had been done at one stretch it would have taken one hour and a half to make it.

While there was none of the laxity of Spaulding's jewelry

shop, nor the parties of the straw shop, all of the workers look back to the time they worked there as days of happiness. No one has explained the reason to us, but we can guess. It was understood to be a shoe shop, but from all reports it really seems to have been a "match" factory. It was there that William Fraser met Annie Lowe, whom he married. Annie's sister, Lizzie, met and married Oscar Smith of Norton. Albert Shores met Emma Bonney. Charles Graham met Grace Strople at the Baptist Church, but the courtship went on at the shop. So, too, did the courtship of William Purdy and Lizzie Tremble, Nellie Bragg and Carlton Ring, Frank Middleton and Eva Smith, Charles Chamberlain and Lizzie. Arthur Macleod and Lottie Farrington were neighbors on Willow Street, doubtless the daily trips back and forth to the shop together sealed their fate. Also, Arthur's brother, John, had the help of the shoe shop to aid his courtship with pretty Jessie Fulton, she with the fair complexion and curly hair. William Swett came here from out of town and found Addie Drake in the box room. Martin Shea and Mary Cosgrove trace their romance to shoe shop days. So did Jack Berry and Mary Brady, and Steve Walker and Florence Penfield. Without a doubt there are a dozen more matches of which we have not heard. To help along their social life these young lovers, and the rest of the shoe shop force, had two grand balls in the Town Hall.

Not all of the girls found their husbands at the shop. There were not enough unmarried young men to go around. At one time there were seventy-five girls in the stitching room.

Along in the middle 1890's things looked bright for the Rumsey brothers. The factory here was doing well and so was the one in Lynn, though there were frequent strikes at the Lynn factory. Bert Rumsey built himself a $40,000 house on one of the exclusive streets in Lynn. Soon things did not go so well. Some thought that they were playing the stock market. Along also came one of those depressions which have an ugly way of appearing every once in awhile. The Rumseys didn't have the money to swing the business. Their financial status grew worse and worse. An effort was made to start a local stock company to keep the business in Our Town. Many were ready to subscribe, but not enough to raise the entire $10,000 required, and so the business failed. A local shoe dealer bought out the shoes on hand, the machinery was sold, the doors were closed, and thus ended the Rumsey Brothers' Shoe Factory in Our Town. Bert Rumsey lost his $40,000 house and both men went back to work as shoe factory employees. At one time Bert Rumsey was in the office of the Plant "Queen Quality" shoe firm in Roxbury. At another time they worked in a shoe shop in Newburyport. As both men were about sixty when they came here in 1888, they have long since died.

It was about 1898 that the Rumsey brothers gave up the manufacture of shoes in Our Town and many men and women were consequently thrown out of work. Some went to shoe factories in other towns, while others were absorbed in local industries, like the straw and jewelry shops.

For a little while the building was empty, then came shoe string companies, some of which made corset strings as well as shoe strings.

The first of these new companies was owned by Charles Orr of South Attleboro. He must have come about 1900. Though he did not stay a great while, he put Our Town on the map as a place where shoe strings could be made, for we understand that at times there were two shifts working.

The several shoe string companies that did business in this building, one after another, were succeeded by the C. D. Lyons Company, making jewelry here from 1908 to 1919.

In 1919 the Bay State Tap and Die Company located across the street was in need of room for the expansion of their business and Mr. Lyons readily agreed to sell his factory to them, and move his jewelry business to Attleboro.

The papers were hardly passed when the war ended and the demand for taps and dies immediately fell off. From then on the big building was not much more than a storage plant for the Bay State Tap and Die Company. With the decrease in business, owing to the recent depression, that great amount of storage space was not needed and the building became nothing more than a white elephant. We have read that some circus people have had to shoot their elephants, because since the depression, they have not been able to feed them. The Rumsey Shoe Shop Building, well built and strong like an elephant, and which, less than fifty years ago, had cost Mansfield men considerable money, had to go the way of unwanted elephants, yet not humanely shot, but torn limb from limb by a wrecking company, which, we have been told, paid $500 for the privilege.

CHAPTER SEVENTEEN

Fire and Water

EVERY PIONEER settlement suffers from fire, and not much can be done about it. If discovered soon enough, friendly volunteers can help save lives and movable property, but buildings must go. Mute cellar holes, discoverable all over the New England countryside, tell their tragic story to one who will pause to think.

In Our Town no one has ever tried to list the homes that were destroyed by fire, but many have told of the burning of Sweet's sawmill, of schoolhouses, and of cotton mills. Cotton mills! Of the seven in Our Town, five were burned. How could it be otherwise, with the inevitable lint and cotton waste that was sure to accumulate?

So far as can be learned, Our Town did not have an organized fire brigade. When the railroad depot got on fire, on May 16, 1874, there was an unpremeditated volunteer brigade, without a leader. Citizens came with buckets, pails, axes, picks, and garden force pumps. (Every foresighted man, for his own protection, kept a bucket and garden force pump handy.) Because this fire was discovered promptly, and by hard and intelligent work. the building was saved. The fire was not without its casualties. Fred Paine, so often mentioned in the chapter on the railroads, fell through one of the holes cut in the roof and was so badly cut by the broken glass of the skylight that he had to be taken to the doctor. Jinks Paine, the soap man, ruined his clothes and sent a bill to the town, but never got a cent.

Foxboro, at the time, had a steamer, and proudly and promptly hauled it here by hand. Though they arrived only in time to put a final extinguishing stream on the work of the bucket brigade, they deserve some glory. Fred Paine, who was then station agent, made use of a flat car and sent the Foxboro men and their steamer home by rail.

As early as 1861, someone had the foresight to see the need of a fire engine in town and inserted an article in the town warrant asking for one. The voters at once turned it down. Ten years later, the matter was again before the town and was indefinitely postponed. Time after time the question came up. Those in the outskirts of the town opposed it, because they felt that it would benefit only a few in the very center. Another argument against it was that the introduction of fire apparatus would stimulate incendiaries to set fires in order to create excitement and see the apparatus work.

Somebody came forward with the proposition that to succor property owners, in case of fire, the town vote to insure any building if the owner desired, houses outside the village to be insured at one half to one per cent, and houses in the more thickly settled sections to be insured at nine tenths per cent of the assessors' valuation. No one would overvalue his property, it was thought, because that would increase his taxation. That suggestion was not taken seriously.

The town worried along with garden pumps, water pails, and buckets. Usually after a fire, somebody was sputtering, because he had lost some of his apparatus. After the No. 4 Schoolhouse fire, in 1884, one man who had brought four new pails had to be content with taking away four pails that had seen years of service.

Light began to dawn when the waterworks were installed in 1888. With a force of water available, the citizens of the water district saw the advisability of using it in case of fire. Consequently, the water commissioners bought two hand reels and twelve hundred feet of hose. Immediately, two volunteer fire companies were organized. The first one was formed in a building opposite the Common and that became their meeting place. The next night, another group met in a vacant store at the other end of the village. The latter was called Hose Company No. 1 and they kept their hose in a shed back of King's livery stable. Herbert King was foreman of this company. Hose Company No. 2, at the south end, kept their hose in a shed back of Bessom's store, on Webb Place. Frank Bessom was foreman of that company. Both companies had to drag their hose to fires by hand. There were about twenty-five volunteers in each company. No money was appropriated, and little was needed. If there were small incidental expenses, they were met by the foremen of the companies.

One of the first requests to the companies was to test the pressure of the new water mains and the companies were sent to the hydrant near the new Rumsey shoe factory. They soon found that turning the hose on nothing, or on a building that had no intention of getting on fire, was tame business. Someone in Hose Company No. 1 had a brilliant idea. The nozzle of Hose No. 1 was turned straight at Hose Company No. 2. At once the battle was on and out of control of the foremen of the companies. James G. Moran, later to be president of the Massachusetts State Senate, then but a youth under twenty, held Hose No. 1. George W. Hewitt charged with Hose No. 2.

The streams came fast and furious. The onslaught sounded like artillery, for this was the first time that the mains had been opened and pebbles of varying sizes were hurled through the hose pipes. The pebbles, coming with terrific force, hurt. No one could face the fire. Jim Moran turned, his back to the foe, and fought with the nozzle directed from under his arm. George Hewitt also turned his back, and using his body as a shield, allowed someone else to shoot the stream from between his legs. From the start, Company No. 1 had the advantage, because they had a force of water from a larger main, and moreover, Hose No. 2 was too short to easily reach around

the corner that intervened.   Dutchy Lyons appeared with
fifty feet of additional hose and the company retired to couple
it.   Hose Company No. 1 then concluded that No. 2 had re-
treated in defeat and were about to exult, when a fresh attack,
from around the corner, took them unaware.   Spectators began
to gather.   A horse attached to a butcher cart took fright at the
fusillade and ran away, scattering meat all over the road.   The
butcher did not care; he said the fight was worth the loss of the
meat.

The water fight was the beginning of a feud, or rivalry, that
lasted even after the formation of an officially organized department two years later.   At first, the opposing men would
hardly speak, but as time went on, the feeling showed itself
mostly in the rivalry as to which company could get to a fire
first, and which company could first couple its hose.   Though
the feeling between the men gradually died away, it cropped
out in the bull dogs.   Frank Bessom's Reo and Billing's Tausan
attended all fires and generally got into a dog fight.

The formation and work of the volunteer companies prepared the way for an organized fire department.   The first
move at town meeting was thwarted by George Ware, who was
always moving for indefinite postponement.   At length, a State
law was discovered which permitted the organization of a fire
district and fire department.   Forthwith, a petition went to the
Selectmen and on January 6, 1890, a meeting was held to organize.   William H. Angell, a man older than the rest of the
firemen, was elected Chief Engineer.   He took the bunch of
raw recruits and by his excellent discipline, due perhaps to
his early experience teaching district school in Norton, trained
them into a reputable fire department.   Mr. Angell was not
only a good disciplinarian, but he understood human nature.
He was a Sunday school teacher and for years superintendent
of the Baptist Sunday school.   Some of his colleagues in the
church suggested to him that with the respect given him and

the influence he had over the men, he had a wonderful opportunity to get them into the Sunday school. Mr. Angell sagely replied that a man who made a good fireman would not necessarily become a good Sunday school teacher. One of Mr. Angell's rules was that there should be no throwing of dice in his presence and the rule was observed.

In six months' time a handsome new hook and ladder truck, made to order in Middleboro, at a cost of $427.35, was delivered. Then a fire station had to be built and a Hook and Ladder Company formed.

The new fire company could not reach its full dignity until the men had uniforms for parade purposes. Those were forthcoming and the companies appeared in them on the Fourth of July. Hose Company No. 1 had firemen's red shirts, with blue trimmings, black silk ties, black belts with white letters on red panels, and black trousers. Hook and Ladder No. 1 wore blue shirts with blue trimmings, and the rest of the Uniform the same as the Hose Company. Both companies wore the regulation Boston caps. In those days the firemen were paid twelve dollars a year, the fire police thirty cents an hour, while the chief and his assistants received twenty-five dollars a year. Out of their salary, they bought their uniforms. From some of the money that was left over, they furnished the fire department building.

With all their getting, the fire department had no fire alarm system. At first, the call was by word of mouth and was uncertain. In the volunteer days, two of the men purposely did not call their fellows, in order that they themselves might be first on the spot. Months after the fire department was established, an alarm system, consisting of five miles of wire and nine signal boxes, was set up. A twelve-inch mechanical gong at the fire department building, a ten-inch going at Chilson's Foundry, five six-inch tappers for engineer and foremen, and ten alarm bells at firemen's houses, gave the alarm. A general alarm was sounded by a steam whistle at Chilson's Foundry by Chilson's engineer by day and the watchman at night. A year later, a 1600-pound bell, costing $765.71 was placed in the tower of the fire station. Even that could not be heard in all quarters of the town, so a second clapper was added to the bell of the Congregational Church. For years the town had the duet of bells at every fire, until it was decided that it would be more efficient to have a blast blown from the electric light plant. When the new $50,000 fire station was built, in 1930, the alarm was sounded from there.

In July, 1890, with that new hook and ladder truck and with a fast horse from King's stable, it would not have been prudent to have mentioned to Herb King, foreman of the Hook and Ladder Company No. 1, that the method of getting to the fire was rather slow. No one thought that it was slow. It was such a vast improvement over hauling the hose reels by hand with a rope that before long there was a demand for a horse and shafts for the reels.

Hiring horses was not a great expense. During the first year of the fire department, L. R. King and Son received six dollars for the use of a horse on the hook and ladder truck, and P. A. Drew, three dollars for the use of a horse on the supply wagon. The next year, King's bill was twenty dollars; Drew's four; and Bessom Bros. received fifteen dollars for a horse on Hose Reel No. 2.

A hand reel turned into a horse reel was not very staunch nor very secure for the riders. Once, when going just outside the district, besides the driver there was a man with his arms full of pails. The driver took a plank bridge at a rapid rate. At once, the air was full of arms, legs and pails. On another occasion they crossed the railroad track with considerable momentum.

"Hold on," yelled the rider. "The spokes are flying out."

"Yeh," answered the driver. "If you don't want to ride, get off. Get up, Bill," to the horse.

They arrived on three wheels.

Plenty of stories are told of the cleverness of fire horses, but what about horses that had to play a double role? After a few years, one of King's horses became so alert to the fire alarm that his usefulness in the livery stable service was impaired. The Kings, thinking that by getting him out of town he would settle down, sold him to an Attleboro butcher. All went well until one day the horse was left with the butcher cart on the electric car track. The motorman, when he came along, sounded the gong to summon the driver. The gong awakened old memories and off the horse started, scattering meat as he went. Similarly, Bessom's black colt, one day as he was delivering groceries, mistook a bicycle bell for the fire alarm and without waiting for his driver, rushed pell mell for his place between the hose reel shafts. By the time he got there the contents of several kerosene oil cans was pretty well mixed with the other groceries.

On the other hand, a horse green at fire calls sometimes made a mistake. A mid-night fire in 1906 was nearer the fire station than it was to the stable, where the horses were kept and the firemen pulled the hook and ladder truck over by hand. In the course of time, a man from the stable brought a pair of horses and hitched them to the empty truck. He had had one drink and wanted another, so off he went. The firemen were too busy with the fire to think about horses, until the fire was out, and then suddenly realized that the truck and horses had disappeared, nobody knew where. A search was made. No horses could be found; they were not at the stable; they were not on the street. It seemed as if the horses had gone up in the smoke. Next morning, Mrs. Lowney, wife of Walter M. Lowney of chocolate fame, was startled when she looked out of the window at the Lowney Camp in the woods

THE CHIEF HAD A FIT WHEN THE TRUCK DISAPPEARED
THE DRIVER WENT HOME TIRED AFTER HE DROVE TO THE BLAZE
STEWARD TRUSSELL ON THE LOOK OUT FOR THE TRUCK
TRUCK
THE TRUCK LOST IN THE WILDS OF MANSFIELD.
SOMEBODY HOLLERED FIRE!!!
MAIN ST. SCENE

near the factory. She called to her husband to come quickly, as the house must be on fire. The fire department had arrived, she said. He came, but saw no fire department, merely two placid horses and an empty hook and ladder truck. The explanation was that one of the horses was the depot carriage horse and not accustomed to going to fires. He had mistaken his duty and had gone, as was his habit, to take Mr. Lowney to the morning train.

Beginning with 1910 the fire department began to be motorized and by 1918 the last bill for horse hire was turned in.

Herbert E. King, foreman of the Volunteer Hose Company No. 1, was a fireman in Our Town for forty years; Chief Engineer for thirty years. When he retired, in 1928, he was the third oldest active engineer in point of service in the United States.

WATER

It was the waterworks that brought about the establishment of the fire department, but the waterworks, too, had had much opposition to overcome, before the town was supplied with running water. Three men, Alfred B. Day, the secretary and treasurer of the Cooperative Bank; Alfred V. Rogerson, proprietor of a general store; and D. S. Spaulding, the jewelry manufacturer, were responsible for the initial boost. The office of Mr. Spaulding's shop, on the morning of May 20, 1886, was the gathering place for the first meeting of an official character. Percy M. Blake, a Boston civil engineer, born in Our Town to the first minister of the Congregational Church, was present. Mr. Blake had already selected in his own mind the best location for the well. A few hours after the meeting, Mr. Spaulding and Mr. Blake canvassed the influential citizens for signatures to a petition to the Legislature. Many refused to sign, but the necessary twenty-four names were secured. An employee in Spaulding's shop, Charles S. Frost, then serving in the House of Representatives, presented the petition to that body and succeeded in getting it allowed. In the Senate, it met with some objection on the part of manufacturers from Taunton, who feared their power from the watershed would be diminished, but there was not enough opposition to block the plan.

The petitioners next called a town meeting to vote on the matter. At the meeting it was pointed out that within the proposed water district there were three hundred and eighty-seven dwelling houses, sheltering four hundred and twenty-five families, fifty-nine places of business, six churches, two schools (without counting the high school, located in the Town Hall), six public halls, eighty private stables, and the railroad station and offices. It was proposed to build five miles of pipe line, at a cost of $60,000. It was also made plain that the installation of water was much needed to provide a sprinkling service to lay the irritating dust of summer.

Nothing definite came from this first meeting. A second, called for September 7, proved to be the biggest business meeting ever held, up to that time, in the Town Hall. Many from outside came to listen, but not to vote. The meeting opened, and the debate began. One man thought it was not fair to saddle a debt on the coming generation, another thought that using so much water would damage mill owners, and that they should be considered. These arguments were ably answered by Mr. Spaulding and Mr. Blake. When the vote was taken one hundred and nineteen voted for it and one hundred and six were against it. As a two-thirds vote was necessary for a bond issue, the meeting amounted to nothing.

All through the fall and winter the subject was the talk of the street and loafing places. Letters pro and con appeared in the weekly paper. Someone suggested that Mansfield and Foxboro might unite in the project and that plan was agitated, and went so far as to be presented to the Legislature, but was withdrawn before being passed upon. Spring freshets and the usual wet cellars started the opponents on a new line. They called attention to the lack of drainage on Main Street and streets off of it, and said that unless a sewerage system was installed, the condition, with running water piped into the houses, would become very much worse. One man put it, "Everybody knows that there is too much water here now."

Finally, a new bill went through the Legislature, on May 19. On August 9, another largely attended district meeting was held and when the vote was put, one hundred and forty-nine voted in favor of it and sixty-five opposed it. This was six votes over the two thirds required. The applause was deafening. Outside there was a grand jubilation. Cannon and lesser firearms were heard on Main Street.

The place unanimously agreed upon for the water supply from the first was Cate, or Kate Spring. To this day there is a disagreement as to the name. Alphonso Buck, engineer there since 1896, says it is Cate. He got the story from his mother that a man named Cate once owned the property. This man had oxen, as every farmer did, and lost them in a rather unusual way. In search of a drink, they fell into the spring and could not be hauled out. They are still there.

Another authority says that the land was never owned by a man named Cate. The man who owned it has passed into oblivion, but his old blind mare, named Kate, has a place in history. Stumbling about in her blindness, she fell into the spring, and from her mishap the spring took its name. Nobody pulled her out. She is still there.

An old resident, who lived in the vicinity of the spring and whose parents and grandparents lived there before her, says that both stories are wrong. Neither mare, nor oxen, nor a man named Cate, figure in her story. She says that nearby dwelt a woman of bad repute, named Kate. Kate found the spring a good place in which to dispose of her unwanted offspring. They are still there.

Our Town has very superior drinking water. It stands high in the chemical analysis conducted by the State. It tastes good, too. The reason for its superior quality has been explained. Long, long ago, a farmer was mowing his land, and like all farmers of his time, took his jug of rum to the meadow with him and hung it in the spring to keep cool. When he went for a drink he found that the jug had fallen in. The potency of the rum is still there.

Many may fail to believe that a horse, or an ox could fall into a spring and be lost. It is true, however. One day, Mr. Buck, the engineer, left his horse grazing about the pumping station, while he attended to the engine inside. When he chanced to look out, the horse was nowhere in sight. For an hour and a half he searched everywhere in the vicinity. No horse could he find. Just as he was about to give up in despair, he caught the glint of an eye in the water of one of the original open springs. Then he saw the almost submerged head of his horse. He had to act quickly. Fortunately, men working on a dam close by responded to his call. The horse's head was raised so that a rope could be placed around his neck. Then with blocks and tackle they began to raise him. Suddenly, one of the blocks slipped, and back the horse fell into the water, on his back, heels up. The next attempt was more successful and the horse was raised to safety. That hole is now filled, but there are springs about the grounds where the truth of the old legends may be tested.

The true spring from which the water supply is derived, has been covered ever since the town took over the property. The original cover wore out and a few years ago a new cover, built on a three-foot cement base, replaced it.

This well, or spring, has proved an unfailing source of supply. It is only twenty feet deep and thirty feet in diameter. Nobody knows how much it is capable of yielding. In 1916-17 when the railroad and all the factories were using town water, about 900,000 gallons a day were pumped from there. The greatest test was made in 1915, when the new reservoir was filled. At that time 2,000,000 gallons were pumped in twenty-two hours.

The original territory acquired by the town for the protection of its water source was around six acres. Now, the town owns one hundred and twenty-five acres, more or less.

Where does this water from the small hole in the ground really come from? Reverently it can be said that the Lord only knows. There is a story from apparently reliable sources that it comes from an underground river that takes its source in Lost River in New Hampshire. Some geologists are said to have backed that theory. Irving B. Crosby, consulting geologist of Boston, however, in an article in the May, 1933, issue of the *Journal of the New England Water Works Association*, flatly stated that there are no underground rivers in the State of Massachusetts, nor of any length in New England. He said that "the idea that underground streams flow from the White Mountains to southern New England, even to Martha's Vineyard and Nantucket, is entirely unfounded . . . . . Such streams would be obliged to flow most of the way through the dense crystalline rocks. True underground rivers exist only in limestones. In New England these subterranean streams are shorter and less important than in the limestone regions of the southern states."

CHAPTER EIGHTEEN

Military Companies

OUR AMERICAN ancestors, with Puritan and Pilgrim blood in their veins, abhorred idleness. In what might be called spare moments, the women spun, knitted, braided straw, sewed bonnets and what not; the men hammered nails, mended shoes, made baskets and did many odds and ends. Withal, they had their recreations, though not of course given so modern a name.

One of the first diversions in the nineteenth century was of necessity the militia. In fact, as far back as the seventeen-fifties, the Second Company of Norton trained here in the east part, under the command of Colonel Ephraim Leonard, he of the iron works. Just prior to the Revolutionary War, another company was formed in the west part. In Norton, at the same time, there was a flourishing Artillery Company, which came to be the oldest in the state, save the Ancient and Honorable Artillery Company of Boston. Some of our men joined the Norton outfit.

After the War the country was taking no chances. Every town in the State was required to have a part in the militia. Few of the smaller towns had a complete company, but rather, joined with other communities. In 1791 Mansfield, Attleboro, Easton and Norton were united for a cavalry company.

We can readily see that the farmers' boys would welcome the companionship of soldiering that the training in the militia offered.

During the fall, after the haying was done and the harvesting over, and before the cold of winter set in, training days came often. Leaves from an old diary tell the story.

August 24, 1788. this night Nathan put on his Regamentals and went to Rentham. (Wrentham)

Sept. 9 this Day morning I received orders from Capt. Holbrook to appear at Sim Kilber compleet in Arms at nin oclock this afternoon.

Sept. 14. this Day I went to training and trained all day.

Sept. 17. this Day the Artillery trained and the milisha Boys met at night and trained.

Sept. 30. Nothing remarkable this Day only I went to training and spent half a day.

Oct. 1. this Day was muster Day to Wrentham. I went but a very cole Day it was.

As towns grew, each was able to furnish one or more companies; a company usually consisted of a captain, lieutenant, ensign, four sergeants, four corporals, two musicians, twenty-five to thirty privates (part of them in uniform), and some unconditioned exempts. Each company was equipped with eighteen muskets (each provided with bayonet and iron ramrod), eighteen bayonet scabbards, eighteen knapsacks, thirty-six spare flints, one drum, one fife, a book of enrollment and an orderly book.

From time to time the various companies united as a battalion for a grand muster. Our boys belonged to the Bristol County Battalion of Light Infantry and Riflemen.

The first muster of the battalion was held at Taunton, October 15, 1834. By the promotion of Captain Holman, Captain Otis Skinner of Mansfield became the senior captain and the Mansfield Cadets the ranking company of the Bristol County Battalion. As a consequence, our outfit paraded on the right at the musters. Besides the muster of 1834, there was one on October 1, 1835, and one on September 28, 1836.

The lineup at the musters did not always consist of the same units. For instance, at the 1836 muster, the Attleboro Rifle Corps did not appear, but the Norton Artillery Company, in new uniform, was present and looked very fine compared to the Wellington Light Infantry of Dighton, which wore its old uniform, considerably the worse for wear. The Fall River Riflemen were in uniforms, partly old and partly new. The New Bedford Mechanics Riflemen wore elegant uniforms of gray, which they had been wearing about three years.

We have no reason to be ashamed of the way the Mansfield Cadets appeared. They wore green dress coats with yellow trimmings and green pantaloons. Their caps corresponded in part to the style called helmets and were covered with green cloth of a shade to match the coats and pantaloons. The Mansfield Cadets' buttons were not according to the State pattern, but manufactured expressly for them after a design of their own, which represented an infantry soldier, musket in hand, in the attitude of charging. There was another occasion when our town was not ashamed of its militiamen. That was in 1833, when President Andrew Jackson and Vice-President Van Buren visited New England, and the Mansfield Cadets, the Attleboro Light Infantry, and the Norton Artillery went by invitation to meet and receive the President as he crossed the line from Rhode Island into Massachusetts. Our own Ira Richardson was the Captain of the Norton Artillery.

When the presidential party reached the middle of Pawtucket Bridge the Norton Artillery was ordered to fire a salute. The gun was small and had been ridiculed by the by-standers as "Norton's popgun." Captain Richardson was on his mettle and intended that his fieldpiece should make plenty of noise. To accomplish that end he filled the gun with a double charge of powder and green hay to the muzzle. The "popgun" made a terrific noise. Moreover, the explosion broke the glass in the windows of the surrounding buildings. Storekeepers rushed out and ordered him to stop. He kept right on, for, he explained, his orders were to give the best salute he could. They threatened him and asked him if he did not see the damage that he was doing.

"Well aware, bold and fare, fire away!" he is said to have replied.

The Pawtucket storekeepers were beaten temporarily, but, so we have been told, they took their grievances to the State House and some years later were granted reimbursement by the Massachusetts Legislature for the damage.

The local companies continued until 1840, when they were disbanded by legislative enactment.

CHAPTER NINETEEN

Brass Bands

FROM MILITARY companies with musicians, it was but a step to getting together for band organization. The first band apparently came into being about the time the town militia was demobilized. Beyond the fact of its existence, little is known of that early band.

The first to make a name for itself was the Mansfield Brass Band that originated just after the Civil War closed. The young men who made up that organization were natural born musicians. Few of them had had any real musical training; some of them had developed their ability in the face of real opposition.

The band help regular practice, gave concerts, and serenaded newly married citizens, but strangely enough, it is not the band practice, the concerts, nor the serenades that are remembered by those who were here in those days. It was the Negro Minstrel Show that the band put on in Central Hall which made the lasting impression. Yet it is not strange, for that was the first minstrel show ever given in Our Town. Minstrel shows were coming into popularity in New York and Boston, but had not reached the country.

It happened in the latter 1860's and took place in Central Hall. Elbridge Cobb was the interlocutor. There were only two end men, Alson Cobb on one end, and Lorn Remmington, from out of town, on the other. Remmington was a clog dancer. One of the hits of the evening was little Gil George, then eight or nine years old. The child was dressed in ragged apparel, and, of course, with blackened face. To the merriment of the audience he sang, "I'm a Rovin' Little Darkie." Alson

Cobb's song was "The Yaller Girl that Winked at Me," with the chorus,

> As she stepped across the gutter,
> My heart was all a-flutter,
> As the yaller girl
> She winked at me.

Frank Lawton sang, "The Sweet Face at the Window, Another at the Door."

In the second part of the entertainment Elbridge Cobb, wearing knee breeches, a white wig, a long white beard, and carrying a cane, sang "Round Goes the World."

Another solo with a chorus of half a dozen voices was "The Raw Recruits," which ran something like this:

> I'm a raw recruit with a brand new suit.
> I want three hundred dollars bounty,
> I'm going down to Washingtown
> To fight for Lincoln and his bounty.

Then amid great applause they marched around the small stage.

So great was the success of the Minstrel Show in Our Town that the Band decided to repeat the performance in Norton. In one respect their plans miscarried. Jim George forbade his little son going to sing about the Rovin' Little Darkie, but the little boy, having no intention of being left behind, ran away and joined the group. Just before his skit was to be put on, father George arrived from Mansfield and dragged his wayward son out by the coat collar. Then Gil's big brother, Fred, had to don the ragged clothes and sing the song.

That band lasted until about 1871 or 1872. From its grave sprang up two bands, vigorous, full grown at the start.

Although the town had a population of less than 2,600, there seems to have been musicians to make up two good-sized bands. One was called the Mansfield Brass Band with Frank Drake as leader. The other was Cobb's Cornet Band, led by Pliny Cobb.

What a rivalry there was between those two bands! The Brass Band rehearsed in Central Hall; the Cornet Band in a little building not many rods away. Often they practiced on the same night. If one gave a concert at the north end of the town, the other chose that night to give a concert at the south end. The Congregational women cheered for the Brass Band, and the Baptist women sang the praises of the Cornet Band. If the Cornet Band serenaded an important citizen, the Brass Band found another important citizen to serenade.

Serenades were jolly occasions. If any man brought home a bride, one band or the other was soon on the spot. It was usually the custom to receive a little treat. When the bands were buying their uniforms, generous citizens helped; James Cobb, the soapmaker, gave ten dollars to the Brass Band and was serenaded; Gardner Chilson, the stove manufacturer, presented money to the Cornet Band and a musical tribute followed. Sometimes, when the band was all dressed up and wanted some place to go, they gave a series of serenades.

It was in the fall of 1872 that the Brass Band was organized, with twenty-three active members, and eighty honorary, or contributing members, who paid something every month to support the organization. The funds were also augmented by Band Sociables. Later, they gave plays: "The Last Loaf," "Among the Breakers," and "Box and Cox."

Frank Drake, the leader, played the cornet. To play a cornet successfully, one needs a full set of teeth. Mr. Drake unfortunately had lost a tooth in a conspicuous part of his mouth. To remedy this defect he had a wooden tooth, or wedge, which, when he was ready to play, he inserted in his mouth, and which by some magic, or bridge work of his own, stayed in place while he blew the cornet. The playing over, the tooth went back into his pocket. In appreciation of his leadership, when the band was about a year old, Mr. Drake was presented with a silver cornet by his band friends.

Another member of this band was "Yankee Doodle Prentiss," the cobbler. He wasn't "Yankee Doodle" when he came to town. That was the title the rival band gave him one day when he made a mistake in playing the familiar tune. The name stuck. At least once, his tormentors serenaded him by playing the air outside his door. Naughty boys annoyed him by yelling it.

Really, Mr. Prentiss was a valuable addition to the Brass Band. He had joined it, because, at the time, the Cornet Band had the ascendency and Prentiss always like to take the part of the under dog. He certainly was no tyro when he came here from Providence where he had played in the American Brass Band. Many years before that he had lived in Barre, Massachusetts, and while there played the bugle in the Unitarian Church, and on secular occasions. Of the latter the most noteworthy affair was a Fourth of July celebration, which seems to have been of a political nature. The speakers were George Bancroft for the Democrats and Daniel Webster for the Whigs. Webster was said to have been very dull that day and the reason given at the time was that the man who had personal charge of him was a real teetotaler. Mr. Prentiss, in a little book written about his own life, makes the comment that "in those days the pocket flask was not as common as now." Mr. Prentiss' "now" was 1898. The bugle that Mr. Prentiss played in the presence of Daniel Webster had been given him years before by a man for whom he worked in Sutton, and on that bugle he took his first music lessons, walking six miles alone by night to a music school in Wilkinsonville. All this prepared the young man for his position in the Providence band. That band was much in demand in Providence, Newport, at Masonic funerals, elections, and college affairs. The most exciting time for this American Brass Band of Providence was when it went to Baltimore with the Whig delegation, when Henry Clay was nominated for president of the United States. The best description of that convention is in Mr. Prentiss' own words. "That was a rum time in every sense of the word. Rum was as free as water and that was very free, as it rained. The convention was held at the Canton race track, three miles out, and down through the meadows the mud was nearly over shoes. The delegation was singing, bands were playing, and the crowds were shouting. It was a complete babel and it made dry throats."

Perhaps no musical organization in Our Town had quite the glamor of Cobb's Cornet Band. It was fully appreciated in its time; it is spoken of with fond recollection today. Someone has said that it wouldn't stand much show in competition with bands of the present day. That is not the point. Compared with bands produced by towns of less than 3,000 inhabitants, it ranked far above them. It dared to enter contests with city bands.

In 1874 or 1875 the band went to Oakland Beach, on the Providence River, to compete with twenty bands for a silver cornet and a baton. The band left Our Town in full force. There were admiring friends along, too. The band must have been a gallant looking company as they disembarked at Oakland Beach. Their uniforms were navy blue with a generous amount of gold; gold braid in a stripe down the trousers' legs, gold epaulets and rows of gold (?) buttons. They wore white belts. On their heads were pot hats, from which fluttered in the breeze magnificent white fountain plumes of ostrich. Ethan Cobb, who stood over six feet without his shoes, was a commanding drum major in his uniform and towering bear-skin busby. Pliny Cobb, the leader, like many of the others, had a fine physique, and was straight of figure.

As the Cornet Band marched down the street to the grounds

where the bands were to meet, they played a lively tune that won the admiration of the bystanders, set feminine hearts a flutter, and put fear in the breasts of their opponents. The time for the test came. There were some city bands and bands from small towns, at least half a dozen in all for the tryout. Not all the bands that had been entered came, and some of the bands that had come to play, backed out at the last moment, for said they, there was no chance for them with Cobb's Cornet Band of Mansfield in the contest. It was the Braintree Band that won the baton presented to the best band, but when Alonzo Bond of Braintree and Pliny Cobb of Our Town contended for the leader's prize, Cobb carried off the hundred and fifty dollar silver cornet. The audience called for music and Mr. Cobb played the "Last Rose of Summer," with variations, on his new instrument.

The high spots in the Cornet Band's career were the yearly trips to Martha's Vineyard. The first one seems to have been in August, 1873. The band then consisted of seventeen active members, and, as all times during the Band's existence, Pliny M. Cobb was the leader. The man responsible for the invitation to the Vineyard was Dr. H. A. Tucker. Dr. Tucker was quite a character in this vicinity. He was a native of Norton, but through his connection with the musical Cobb brothers, salesmen for "Dr. Tucker's 59," a medicine that cured everything, he was well known in Our Town. The sale of the famous nostrum brought Dr. Tucker much money and enabled him to make his summer home at Oak Bluffs one of the show places fronting Ocean Park. The presence of the band at the summer resort was to be a form of advertising. In return for their playing, Dr. Tucker gave the members of the band free entertainment that first summer. He also spread the information that the Mansfield boys were his guests and that nothing was too good for them. The young men did not make the fine appearance that they did later, for it was before they had acquired

their uniforms.   Nevertheless, they were popular and were invited to come again.

Strenuous efforts after that were then made in Our Town
to raise money to buy uniforms.   By means of band fairs, festi-
vals, concerts, and donations from generous citizens, the uniforms were bought by May, 1874.   We have already described
how they looked as the Band wore them to Oakland Beach,
therefore, we expect you to take due pride in the Cornet Band
when it started for the Vineyard, on August 17, 1874.

During the 1874 season the band was gone just eight days,
leaving on the 17th, and returning on the 25th.   They arrived
at Oak Bluffs at 12:30 and as soon as they had formed to
march, began to play as they approached Dr. Tucker's house.
That season they were lodged and fed at the Sea View house
and the expenses were divided among Dr. Tucker, H. A.
Blood (Superintendent of the Boston, Clinton, and Fitchburg
Railroad), S. D. Robinson and E. P. Carpenter, the latter two
from Foxboro.   These four men were called the "big guns"
of the island.   E. P. Carpenter owned a large tract of land on
the south shore, called Katama, some miles beyond Edgartown.   Here, he built a large summer hotel four or five miles
across the moors from Edgartown, the nearest habitation.   To
reach this new hostelry, he built a narrow gauge railway ten
miles, or so, along the shore.   The railway was completed about
the time that the Cornet Band arrived at Oak Bluffs.

We left the band marching up to Dr. Tucker's villa while
we digressed to tell about the band's hosts.   Well, they arrived
and were taken over to the Sea View Hotel for their dinner.
That evening, at 8 o'clock, they gave a band concert from the
bandstand on Ocean Park.

The next day, they serenaded H. A. Blood and S. D. Robinson, besides the evening concert.   Saturday, the day following,
they gave a concert in the afternoon in the grove opposite E. P.
Carpenter's house and the evening concert as usual from the

ICE CREAM SODA

bandstand. Sunday was a day of more than usual importance to the band. At noon they led a procession to the wharf to meet and escort J. H. Spinney of New York to the Tabernacle. That evening there was a concert at the Tabernacle and the Cornet Band played. A Mrs. Osborn and a Mr. Franklin from New York, and the band, led the audience of six thousand voices in the singing of "Nearer My God to Thee." After the concert at the Tabernacle they played at the cottage of Mr. Spinney and were served a fine supper. Monday was a red letter day. They were taken on a ninety-mile sea excursion to Gay Head, New Bedford, Woods Hole and back. On Tuesday the engine arrived over the new road from Katama and the band played to celebrate the event. That night, after the usual evening concert at the bandstand from 8 to 9:30, the band went to Dr. Tucker's for supper. The records do not tell us what they had for supper, but from what we have been told it was not very dry. Some of the band members said afterwards that they there had the best brandy they had ever tasted. Often there were concerts from the tower of "Dr. Tucker's Villa." Wednesday was another gala day. Mr. E. P. Carpenter took the band to Katama. They had the honor of being the first band to ride on the new railroad. At Katama he treated them to a clam dinner. Alas! it is years since clam dinners have been served at Katama. Long ago Old Ocean washed away the railroad. Without means to transport guests to the hotel, the house fell into disuse and a state of abandonment, and finally disappeared altogether. The band was in a very jovial mood when they returned to Oak Bluffs and that evening serenaded H. A. Blood, E. P. Carpenter and Dr. Tucker. They also played from the tower of Dr. Tucker's Villa. Next day they returned home.

Was it that time that the bass drum was so heavy? On one occasion the man who played the bass drum did a little extra work on the morning of the day they were to start home. He removed the head of his drum and filled it with sheets and blankets, which he had purloined from the clothes lines and beds. If he played the big drum on the way home it was muffled.

How many years the band took this delightful trip seems uncertain, but it must have been five or six. Sometimes they were lodged at the Sea View Hotel, sometimes at the Pawnee, or at the Fitchburg House, and sometimes they slept in tents opposite the Fitchburg House, or were lodged in cottages.

The last trip of which we have an account was that of August, 1877. That year there were twenty-two pieces and the drum major. They went a day earlier than they had at first planned, in order to be present Wednesday evening at a complimentary "hop" given to Mr. Brownell, proprietor of the Sea View Hotel ("Hops" were once quite the thing at summer hotels), and they remained over Sunday in order to take part in the entertainment at the grand illumination, which always took place on a Saturday night in mid-August. Their stay was a round of pleasure, as usual.

Shed no tears for the rival Brass Band. They, too, went places. In fact, they had their first trip a month before the Cornet Band started for Oak Bluffs the first time. They went to Belvedere Plains, a new resort at Falmouth Heights, on the invitation of Joseph Draper and Harrison Williams, jewelry manufacturers of Our Town. The boys were told before they started that there would be no expense to them after they arrived and it was even so. On their arrival they were met and conveyed to the cottages of their home-town friends, where lunch was served them at once. They played on the way, they played for an afternoon concert at Williams' Park from eight to ten, they played for a promenade concert on the Green, and at ten o'clock they played at the grand ball in the Town Hall. It was years since there had been a band concert at Falmouth and this music was much appreciated. That night fourteen slept in a haymow, two slept in small tents brought along for emergency, and the rest were quartered in homes. Early next morning they were up and off on an excursion to Oak Bluffs, where they gave a concert. When they got back to Falmouth that night, they went around serenading the people of Belvedere Plains. The next day they returned home.

Though the Brass Band did not have as many extended outings as the Cornet Band, they had day trips. The summer after they went to Falmouth they had an all-day excursion at Silver Lake, Plympton, leaving home at six o'clock in the morning to attend a musical festival of military bands. Here each band played one number alone, and all joined for one selection. The next year the Brass Band went to Charlestown to take part in the Centennial celebration of the Battle of Bunker Hill. Still another band excursion was to Lake Walden, in Concord.

The Cornet Band scored one over the Brass Band by being invited to play on the ten-day trip of the S. S. *Empire State* from Fall River to Philadelphia for the Centennial Exposition, in June, 1876. The Staples Coal Company of Taunton owned the boat, *Empire State*, and conducted excursions all that season. The boys played for dances and dinner parties en route. During the stay in Philadelphia, the boat served as hotel for the passengers, a great convenience, for the 10,000,000 people that crowded the Quaker City that season taxed the rooming capacity mightily. The boat tied up on the Camden side and the people went back and forth from there. To furnish entertainment for their guests, during their stay, the Staples Coal Company asked the Cornet Band to play for evening dances on board the boat. An orchestra was formed among the band members to play when the full band was not needed. On this particular trip of the *Empire State* there were three hundred passengers aboard, of whom thirty were people from Our Town.

In spite of the fact that the Brass Band came to birth first and was a bit stronger in numbers the first summer, its span of life was shorter.

After the Brass Band disintegrated, the Cornet Band continued, playing at every sort of social affair in winter and at outdoor concerts in summer. In summer? Once, on the balmy night of New Year's 1876, they gave a mid-winter outdoor concert.

The outdoor concerts were given from a roofless bandstand on the Common by the light of kerosene lanterns. Often small boys were hired to hold the lanterns, at ten cents an evening. Frequently, these youngsters, boy fashion, found that the easiest way to hold the lanterns was on their heads. It cost father more than ten cents to replace an oil soaked cap, which his son wore.

Another service of the band was a serenade for any notable person whose train might pause at the railroad station, a few rods from Spaulding's shop where many of the men worked. President Hayes, and also the King of the Cannibal Islands were thus honored. Likewise, if a governor, lieutenant governor, or other man of equal importance came for a political campaign meeting, or to give a dedication speech, the Cornet Band acted as escort. Usually the speaker came by train in the afternoon and was entertained at dinner by some prominent citizen. In that case the men were excused from their benches at the jewelry shop.

As the years went by it came about that most of the men composing the band worked in Spaulding's jewelry shop. That was especially true after 1886, when Pliny Cobb gave up the leadership and moved to Middleboro to open a music store. After Mr. Cobb's time the band was called the Brass Band and had many leaders. Some of the leaders worked at the bench in the shop and the band held noon rehearsals.

Just as in the earlier days, the band sometimes went to

Oak Bluffs to play, but they had little of the glamour of their predecessors. When they arrived they were just a band. They lacked the showy white fountain plumes, the gold epaulets, and the triple row of brass buttons. They wore skirted coats of wool, and padded at that. In time those skirted uniforms wore out and in 1895 the band decided they needed some new ones. They wanted some close-fitting coats of dark green, trimmed with black.

These new band suits made a lot of trouble. To begin with there was no money to pay for them. Gathering in the money was less easy than it had been in the days when there were fewer forms of entertainment. At length, two of the men, Walter Huston, who played the slide trombone, and Vernon Grover, player on one of the cornets, took the doubtful risk of lending the money to pay for the suits, and after many years got their money back. Money in hand the band sent for a man to come to take measurements. It was a sorry day for him. He developed a terrible toothache. The only relief seemed to be to go to the dentist and have the tooth out, which he did. Minus his tooth he came back to his measuring. Soon a clot of blood in the cavity of the jaw came out and a hemorrhage followed. Everybody was scared, for they thought he was going to bleed to death right there. They got him back to the dentist and fixed up. Once more he returned to his measuring and succeeded in completing his job.

The Brass Band never wore out those green uniforms. Changed customs and more ways of entertainment interferred with band practice and offered other diversions to the players. Professional bands were coming to the fore and were more popular.

With the death of the band, the uniforms were useless. Nobody wanted to be bothered with them. Once more Walter Huston came to the rescue. He was then living on Horace Street and accommodatingly gave the band remains storage room as long as he lived there. When he moved, Thomas Hibberts, who had played the small drum, took the responsibility. In time he, too, found them a burden and the possessions landed on George Clapp, one of the cornet players. This unwanted legacy had in the years diminished in size. The uniforms were no more, for a million moths had made of them a picnic ground. Somewhere to-day there rests a small trunk with some dog-eared band music and a few tarnished instruments.

CHAPTER TWENTY

Singing Schools and Choral Societies

THE MUSICAL energies of Our Town did not all go into wind instruments. We had many singers, and many who played the violin, bass-viol, and piano, and organ. To John Rogers, the owner of the straw shop and George E. Bailey, the owner of the bakeshop, belongs much credit for developing latent musical ability in our people. In the gay nineties, a piano was as much a part of the family furniture as the radio today. A part of the money earned in the shoe shop, the jewelry shop, the straw shop, and the foundry, was laid aside to give the children music lessons, which usually cost twenty-five cents, or at the most fifty cents an hour.

Singing schools had a very definite place in the social life of our people in the early days.

The same youth who recorded the military training days of 1788, told of the singing school of 1789, which began on January 20, at one o'clock in the afternoon at Captain Jesse Holbrook's. It was a snowy day and when they went home the snow was "half leg high." The school finished on another very stormy day, March 19, but the coming together to sing did not end then, for two nights later he records, "we went to Stephen Holbrook's to sing." That was Saturday, and on the following Thursday, came "our Singing Lecture beginning at Eleven o'clock and a fine one we had."

Those schools had to meet early, in the winter, in order that the singing teacher, who usually came from out of town, might get home before dark; and that the boys could get home to do the milking and chores before night came on, otherwise how could they see to milk?

Singing schools were introduced primarily to train the choir and prepare people for singing in meeting. Church music, as our ancestors knew it, was the singing of psalm tunes without the benefit of instrument or pitch pipe. Doubtless they had the *"Bay Psalm Book,"* which was in general use at that time. Some of the psalms in that book were one hundred and thirty lines long and occupied, when lined and sung, a full half-hour, the congregation standing all the while. Imagine the effect: All the singers were absolutely untrained, even if they could have read music, they had no musical notes in the book to guide them. The singing here must have been much like that recorded in Alice Morse Earle's, *"Sabbath in Puritan New England."* "No two Men in the Congregation quavered alike or together. It sounds in the Ear of a Good Judge like five hundred different Tunes roared out at the same Time, with perpetual Interfearings with one another." In some towns women were not allowed to sing in the meetinghouse, but we have no reason to think that this was true in Our Town.

About 1731, the time that the little church was built here, a new style of singing was being introduced which was called "singing by rule." The churches throughout New England were stirred by this innovation and much animosity was aroused. Some said that if they began to sing by rule they would soon be praying by rule and preaching by rule.

Rev. Samuel Danforth, the fourth minister in our neighboring church in Taunton, with two others, wrote a long essay in the form of seventeen questions and answers on the "Singing of Psalms." The essay covers fifteen printed pages and was preached upon by several ministers. It was not unlikely that our ancestors heard it, pondered over it, and discussed it. These ministers handled this moot subject with considerable skill and tact. In question IV they ask, "Do you believe that it is Lawful and Laudible for us to Change the Customary way of Singing, for a more Uniform and Regular Way of Singing of Psalms?" and they answer at length that it is. Question No. V is: "Do you believe that 'tis Lawful, and according to the Rules of God's Holy Word, that the Aged in the Churches should in their Age submit to be turned out of their Old Way of Singing of Psalms, to gratify the Younger Generation?" Note they had a "Younger Generation" with capital letters in 1723! It takes more than a page to handle this delicate question. They show that God is the author of all regularity and order, that the younger people are in the majority in numbers and have the stronger and clearer voices and they say: "To the Younger People we do in this matter of Singing not yield to You, but to God." As to whether persons of the female sex may be admitted to sing in church they decide they may. Likewise, unconverted persons and children are not ruled out. They also discuss whether fathers, forty years old and upwards, can learn to sing by rule, and they decide that it is possible.

This new system of singing by rule brought about the introduction of the singing school, which not only improved the church music, but gave the people a much needed social recreation. In those early days a singing teacher came from out of town. The first singing master in Our Town, whom we know by name, was Colonel Josiah Bird of Dedham, who came during the winter of 1835, but there were singing teachers here far earlier than that. After the schoolhouses were built, the singing school was often held in these, though they were sometimes held in private houses, as before.

Though our ancestors did not have the same amusements and conveniences that we have, their foibles were not unlike ours; they were often the victims of fads. We learn in Mrs. Earle's book of two fads introduced by the singing teachers, which were not altogether desirable. One was called "singing counter." The counter-tenor parts in European church music, she says, were written for boys' voices, but by the time it reached a small town, like Our Town, it developed into falsetto singing of the part by the men, which sometimes resulted in "a weird and apparently demented shriek which rose high over the voices of the others."

The other fad was "fugueing"—repetition of a word or syllable. At time it might have been impressive, but think with Mrs. Earle what the result would be in lines like the following:

> With reverence let the saints appear
> And bow before the Lord.

which would become "And bow-wow-wow, And bow-wow-wow," and so on until bass, treble, alto, counter, and tenor had bow-wowed for about twenty seconds.

Although there were singing schools, it is quite possible that there was no definite choir in Our Town before 1816. That year at least, it was fully recognized and the men of the parish of the center meetinghouse voted to build a pew in the front gallery for the singers, the expense to be raised by subscription. Seven years later they voted that the singers have liberty to make use of the whole of the pew ground in the front gallery. Moreover, they voted thirty dollars for the support of the singers. As the minister, Rev. Richard Briggs, was receiving but $450 a year, we may judge that they considered their choir a real asset in their worship, when they voted them thirty dollars. Money in those days was too scarce, and too hard to earn, to be spent recklessly.

Another need that arose from the new way of singing by the choir was the necessity of some means whereby they would all sing in the same key and start on the same pitch. Thus the pitch pipe or tuning fork was introduced. We have no way of knowing which was used here. Wherever these little musical aids were inaugurated it was done rather shamefacedly at first. Their use, however, soon became an established custom. The custom before long served as an entering wedge to something bigger and more revolutionary. The next step was a musical instrument, at first, a violin. As this was associated with tavern dances it was looked upon as a tool of the devil, and it was not countenanced in the meetinghouses for a long time. We read in Alice Morse Earle's, *Sabbath in Puritan New England*, of some churches where they were permitted, provided they were played wrong end up. The church people soothed their consciences by persuading themselves that thus handled they were not fiddles, but small bass viols.

Bass viols were the first instruments to be generally used. In many churches those were not accepted without a struggle. For example in Wareham, according to Mrs. Earle, there was a controversy over the question of "Bass-Viol, or No Bass-Viol," from 1794 till 1829. First, they voted that a bass viol was "expedient"; then, they voted to expel the hated abomination; the next vote was, "Leave for the Bass Viol to be brought into ye meeting house to be Played On every other Sabbath & to Play if chosen every Sabbath in the Intermission between meetings & not to Pitch the Tunes on the Sabbaths that it don't Play"; then, they tried to bribe the choir with fifty dollars not to use the "Bars-vile." When that attempt did not work, many members in open rebellion stayed away from meeting and were afterwards disciplined for the misdemeanor. The matter was finally settled by the vote that the bass viol could not be used unless Capt. Gibbs was previously notified (so that he and his family need not come to hear the hated sounds). After more than thirty years' quibbling, the bass viol was accepted without more ado. So far as we have ever heard, or read, Our Town, or any of her near neighbors, never had any such trouble over the instrument.

By 1840 musical instruments were allowed in our meeting-house, although the innovation did not meet the approval of all the members. One old man was wont to stalk down the aisle when the singing began, sit on the doorstep until the music was over, and then come back for the sermon. Most people, however, recognized the advantage of an instrument, and some were willing to pay for it. Witness the following:

Appreciating the utility of the Bassviol as an aid to church music; and whereas, its use is necessarily attended with expense, from the frequent breaking of its strings, we the undersigned, for the purpose of keeping strung our Bassviol, promise to pay the sums set against our names. Then follows twelve names. Nine subscribe fifty cents, the rest twenty-five cents.

In the days when the Congregational church orchestra consisted of two violins, two cellos, a cornet and a flute, the musicians used to practice at the noon hour between the morning and afternoon sermons. They practiced sedately and demurely, as was expected of a church orchestra in the 1840's. Intermingled with the hymn tunes they played "Yankee Doodle," but so slowly that few of the uninitiated recognized the air. Thus, no expulsion, or even reprimand, followed.

The first choir leader in Mansfield was John Rogers, already mentioned so many times. He began in the old meetinghouse, which stood on the Common. It must have been about 1833, before the church was divided, that he took up that service. It was a real service, for his training gave them a good start on a musical education. Mr. Rogers not only trained his own choir, but he conducted a singing school for all who cared to attend. When, in 1838, the Orthodox Congregational Church was about to come out from the old church, there was speculation as to which way Mr. Rogers would go. Naturally both sides wanted him. He went Orthodox Congregational and led that choir up to the time of his death, in March, 1873, forty years as choir leader.

When the choir was organized in the new Orthodox Church, in 1838, there was a little nine-year-old boy who sang alto with some other small boys, though perhaps none were quite as young as this one. Mr. Rogers was a kindly man and always much interested in anyone who showed ability and interest in music. It is easy to imagine that he gave special care to these small boys.

That littlest boy of all was George E. Bailey, and for fifty years he continued to sing in the choir. After Mr. Rogers retired, Mr. Bailey led the choir. For years before Mr. Rogers' death the two men worked together training for concerts and forming a choral society.

There was no church organ in Our Town until 1852, when the Congregational Church succeeded in raising $675 to buy one. Some years later, 1872, Mr. Rogers at his own expense, replaced that first one with a very fine organ, and at about the same time, Gardner Chilson, the owner of the foundry, gave a good organ to the Baptist Church, to replace the earlier organ, given that organization by Robert Fuller of the Newton Iron Works, whose story was told in Chapter Two.

Through the years that the singers of Our Town were meeting, somewhat aloof from the rest of the world, events that were later going to affect them, were taking place far away.

It happened in 1829 that there was a child born in Dublin, Ireland, named Patrick S. Gilmore. In time, he became a musician and landed in the United States. Eventually, he was the leader of a fine band of a Massachusetts regiment in the Civil War, stationed at New Orleans. At the close of the war he conceived the idea of a great musical festival with 10,000 school children taking part. From the success of that undertaking, and from his knowledge of the monster concert at the Crystal Palace in London in 1857, he determined to do what he could to institute a National Peace Jubilee, in Boston. He quickly had the cooperation of Eben Tourjee, the head of the New England Conservatory of Music, Oliver Ditson, musician and publisher, and Eben Jordan, patron of music.

Early in the year 1869 work was begun. Notices were sent

throughout New England. One hundred organizations responded, some of them beyond the New England states.

This is where Our Town enters into the picture. John Rogers received the word here. With his singing school as a nucleus he added others and went to work. A meeting of the singers in town was called at his house and the Mansfield Choral Society was organized. Mr. Rogers was elected president; George E. Bailey, director; Pliny M. Cobb, leader of the Cornet Band, secretary and treasurer; and Oliver Gushee, librarian.

Once a week they met at the home of Mr. Rogers. Though Mr. Bailey was the official director, Mr. Rogers often led. Mr. Rogers' daughter, Ellen, the wife of Rev. Jacob Ide, was the accompanist. The music was selected by the directors in Boston and was difficult, and the accompaniment intricate. One evening, as they were rehearsing "Inflammatus," Mrs. Ide, talented pianist though she was, had trouble with one passage. Her father corrected her. Being a rather high strung young woman, she rebelled and refused to play. Among the singers was George E. Bailey's daughter, Hattie, then sixteen or seventeen years old. She was tremendously interested. A day or two afterwards, she rushed up to her father, exclaiming, "I've got it." Sure enough, she played "Inflammatus" at the next rehearsal. From then on, the young girl was the accompanist most of the time.

While rehearsals were going on in a hundred choral societies, a great Coliseum was being built in the Back Bay in Boston. It was an immense building 500 feet long, 300 feet wide, covering nearly three and one half acres. There were four balconies and in the rear of the balcony seats, there was a promenade, which was eleven feet wide and lacked a foot of being a quarter of a mile in length. The gas required to light the Coliseum in the evening was sufficient to light a small city.

The performances began on Tuesday, June 15, 1869, and

continued for five days. Railroads offered one-half fare rates. People of Our Town, singers and audience, went back and forth, but those coming from a longer distance took rooms in Boston at a dollar or a dollar and a half a night. The tickets of admission were two dollars for a single performance. Season tickets, which were transferable and admitted three persons at every production, cost one hundred dollars.

Besides singers from many places in New England, there were four hundred from New York, fifty from Philadelphia, thirty from Chicago, and fifteen from Baltimore. Most of these groups came from places much larger than Our Town. None of the nearby towns and cities, no, not even Attleboro, nor Taunton, were represented. In all there were nearly 10,000 singers. There was an orchestra of 528 pieces, and other musicians to make the number up to 1,109 musical instruments.

Not every singer or player was present every time. If he was not able to go himself he very likely let some one have the ticket of admission to his seat; for example, one man let his nephew take his place. It caused some amusement to see a small thirteen-year-old boy sitting among the heavy basses.

Some of the great musical stars were Madame Parepa Rosa, a remarkable soprano singer, who easily took the high C in the "Star Spangled Banner"; Adelaide Phillips, another singer; and Ole Bull, the great violinist.

The second day President Grant, attended by Admiral Farragut, Mr. Thornton, the British Minister, generals and governors was present. As the President came into the Coliseum to take his seat, the great chorus, and the 1,109 musicians broke forth into "See the Conquering Hero Comes." There were 35,000 people in the audience that day. The next day there were 39,800. On Saturday there was a concert by a great number of school children. Sunday evening there was a sacred concert.

When the great Jubilee concerts were over there was a Jubilee Ball attended by 10,000.

The National Peace Jubilee closed June 20, 1869, but Our Town singers talked about it for months after. Yes, it had been a success. Though it had cost $283,000 to produce it, when all bills were paid there remained a surplus of $10,000. The cultural value to those who participated, and even to those who listened, was invaluable.

Hardly was it over when Mr. Gilmore, and the men who backed the undertaking, began to talk about another, which would be even bigger. The Franco-Russian War had ended and they suggested a World's Peace Jubilee. In the interest of this new peace celebration, Mr. Gilmore went to Europe. For several months, he went from country to country to tell the various governments about the project and secure their permission for their great military bands to come to Boston. Everywhere, he met with the utmost cordiality.

Early in 1872 the idea began to take form and was made public in this country. On February 14, a preliminary meeting was held. Enthusiasm ran high when it was announced that S. A. Starr of Camden, N. J., had already sent a check for $500 as an order for a season ticket. It was moved and voted to carry a life insurance for Mr. Gilmore for $200,000. A month later, it was voted to send Mr. Florenz Ziegfield (father of F. Ziegfield of Follies fame) to Europe to arrange for the transportation of the foreign musicians. In April, work was begun on the new Coliseum. The first one had stood about where the Copley Plaza stands today, the second one near the site of the present Mechanics Building. After the building was well started, it was demolished by a gale, on April 26. The loss was $40,000. In two days the ground was cleared and a new start made. The Coliseum of 1872 was more ornate and more substantial than that of 1869, and much larger. The new one covered eight acres and had a seating capacity of 50,000.

Small wonder with all that going on in Boston that the singers of Our Town were alert to organize and start rehearsals.

Instead of an even hundred organizations, as in 1869, there were one hundred and sixty-five to accept the invitation to participate. Our Town was No. 39 and had seventy-six singers in the group. Of course that number was far too large for John Rogers' home, where the first Choral Society met, and these rehearsals were held in the vestry of the Congregational Church.

By 1872, neighboring towns and cities had awakened an interest in the great music festival and wished to be associated with it. Taunton had a chorus of one hundred, Fall River seventy, Middleboro forty, North Middleboro twenty-five. When they were nearly ready for the final event, these, with the addition of Mansfield, Brockton, and New Bedford met in Taunton for a joint rehearsal. In the afternoon there was a private rehearsal, but in the evening the public was admitted by paid tickets. In the intervals between the afternoon and evening gatherings, the singers roamed the streets of Taunton. Each one could be spotted by the red singing book under one arm. By the time the last chords had died away in the evening, it was too late for our singers, and many of the others, to get home. Fortunately, arrangements had been made for their entertainment over night.

Finally, with all in readiness, the Great World's Peace Jubilee took place. It opened on Bunker Hill Day, June 17, and closed on the Fourth of July. Besides the great chorus consisting of 5,115 sopranos, 4,258 altos, 3,592 tenors, 4,317 basses, there were 175 leading solo singers from all parts of the country. There was also Madame Peschka Leuter, a noted soprano of Vienna, and an equally noted contralto, Madame Ermina Rudersdorff, from Russia. Aside from the Marine Band from Washington, there were eleven bands from Boston, nine other bands from Massachusetts, seven bands out of the state, a grand orchestra of 814 pieces, a regular orchestra of 1,000 instruments, the Imperial Prussian Quartette, all cornet players of the highest rank, a French band of 54 pieces, a Prussian Band of sixty men, nearly every one of them a skilled soloist; and most brilliant of all, fifty-eight men representing the English Grenadier Band. There were several composers who led their own works; as Dudley Buck and J. K. Paine, their oratorios; Franz Abt, his composition; and Johann Strauss, his "Blue Danube."

A monster organ was built in the Coliseum, the largest ever constructed up to that time. Double the size of the first Coliseum organ, it measured twenty feet deep and thirty feet wide. The loftiest pipe was forty-three feet from the base.

There was a large drum twelve feet in diameter and thirty-six feet in circumference, and required 600 feet of manila rope and seventy-eight drum ears to put the drum in proper trim for use.

One hundred anvils, weighing from 100 to 300 pounds, were imported from Birmingham, England, expressly for the Jubilee. These were arranged fifty on a side and were played upon by one hundred red-shirted firemen, also ten more firemen were requisitioned to be ready as substitutes in case any of the regulars should be sick. Outside, 200 feet from the building, were twelve cannon, attended by military men. In the Anvil Chorus, played each day, on the up beat the anvils were struck and on the down beat the cannon were fired. The cannon, though outside, were timed in perfect unison. To some of the audience, however, the sensation was not pleasant. The building shook as if by a small earthquake and sulphurous fumes from the cannon came in the windows.

While to most people these two jubilees were wonderful occasions, there were some who were not enthusiastic. John S. Wright, a music critic of the time, loathed the whole thing. He spent the entire period of the concerts in Nahant, where the "strident racket" could not reach him. We wonder if he succeeded. Mr. George P. Bailey told us he knew just what time each day the Anvil Chorus was played, and on the days when he stayed at home, he watched the clock, and by listening, could hear the detonations of the Boston cannon, twenty-six miles away.

Financially, the World's Peace Jubilee was not a success. Importing so many musicians was expensive, and the promoters were left with a large deficit. Musically, it was not the success of the National Jubilee, of 1869. The numbers were so great as to be unwieldy. No chorus of such proportions has been attempted since that time. The following year Mr. Gilmore conducted a chorus of 1,000 in Chicago for three days, then the big chorus fad died out.

Our Town, however, reaped a benefit. A taste for music had been strengthened and the Choral Society continued, under the direction of William L. Robinson.

In the spring of 1880, the Choral Society was ready with its first concert. The program consisted of fifteen numbers, most of them of a classic nature, such as "The Triumphal March," from "Naaman," "Inflammatus," and "The Anvil Chorus," with two anvils for the occasion. There were over fifty voices, with soloists from Taunton, and the instrumental music was furnished by a local orchestra. In every way the concert was a grand success. Eighty dollars, which was considered good at that time, was taken in at the door, and the musical quality was so fine that prominent citizens of Norton requested that the concert be repeated there. Accordingly, on June 16, the Choral Society traveled to Norton and gave the concert in the Unitarian Church.

Early in the fall of 1880, the Choral Society, under the direction of Mr. Robinson, began rehearsals for a second concert. That took place on Dec. 22 and proved to be as fine, if not finer, than the first. The fifty voices in the chorus were accompanied by the celebrated Germanic Orchestra, of Boston. The program, consisting of fourteen numbers, was elaborate and classical. It was feared at the time that the concert might be rather over the heads of the ordinary country audience. But Our Town proved not an ordinary country audience; instead of being bored, the audience enjoyed every number and called for encores. The most pleasing number was the "Turkish Patrol," depicting the approach and departure of the Turkish army. The whole concert was declared by many to be their ideal of music, so perfect was it in every detail. At the close of the concert, one of the singers appeared at the front of the stage with a mysterious package, which he presented to the leader as a token of appreciation from the Choral Society. What do you suppose the package contained? An elegant sealskin cap!

Eight years later Mr. Robinson was appointed organist at Berkley Temple, in Boston, and before the year was out received another gift of appreciation, but not another fur cap. It was a crayon portrait of his own small boy.

It will not do to go into detail about every rehearsal and concert, yet we must mention one or two more outstanding concerts.

On May 2 and 3, 1882, they gave "Queen Esther." It was a grand production with a chorus of seventy-one, and more than twenty-five others taking part.

The next year the Choral Society gave the cantata, "Ruth the Moabite," on two nights. As has been said, the real impetus that started a permanent Choral Society was the preparation for the first big musical festival in Taunton. That assembly of music lovers also became permanent and took the name of "South-eastern Massachusetts Musical Association." Not the entire Mansfield Choral Society, but a smaller group of Our Town people became affiliated with it. Each member paid one dollar a year, to cover the cost of the music, which was bought by the officers in Taunton and distributed from there. When the festival took place, it was a three-day affair, with rehearsals each morning, and concerts afternoon and evening. Singers of Our Town, the ladies at least, stayed through and were entertained by the Taunton people. They sang from "Stabat Mater," "The Creation," and other great oratorios. Leading soloists from larger cities assisted, as did well-known orchestras and instrumental soloists of that time.

The Choral Society flourished for at least ten years, perhaps longer. Besides cultivating a taste for good music and giving the singers excellent training, it afforded much social enjoyment.

CHAPTER TWENTY-ONE

Lectures and Entertainments

THE ENTERTAINMENTS of one hundred years ago were often held in the schoolhouses, and were rather sober affairs, taking the form of singing schools, spelling bees, writing schools, and school exhibitions, all attended by young and old. If one preferred levity, he went to husking bees and dances. There is no better way to tell about a school exhibition than giving a part of the program of one held on January 31, 1838. The program began at six o'clock in the evening and lasted through thirty-one numbers, which is just ten short of a program given at Holliston Academy, in 1842. Neither of these is exceptional.

The program of the 1838 exhibition was opened by Charles N. Hall, a nineteen-year-old youth, who gave on that midwinter night a "Salutatory Address and 4th of July Oration." This young man's seventeen-year-old brother closed the evening's entertainment with an "Oration in Commemoration of the First Settlers of New England, and Valedictory." The intervening numbers were compositions, dialogues, and declamations, as well as other orations. The classics were not neglected. There was Warren's Oration, scenes from "School for Scandal," a scene from Cato, and the address of Brutus to the Roman populace. The musical numbers were "Humble My Little Cottage," "Charming Little Valley," and "O, Say Busy Bee."

At the Holliston exhibition the salutatory was given in Latin. Declamations included "The Dying Infidel," "Rienzi's Speech to the Romans," and "The Trial of Cataline before Cicero." In an original discussion, two girls argued the question: "Is a superior knowledge of the Sciences alone, on the part of the female, productive of more good than a superior knowledge of Domestic Affairs?" The fortieth number was an original dialogue, supposed to be taking place between a fisherman, a Latin scholar and a French peddler. Some of our own boys at this school had a place on the program.

Let us skip over fifteen years. The same Charles N. Hall who gave the oration and valedictory at the school exhibition is now writing poetry for the Lyceum and has this to say of the amusements of 1853 and 1854.

> Instead of huskings now and spinning bees,
> The people have such merry times as these,
> With concerts gay, and lectures, learned and wise,
> That place the wide, wide world before your eyes.

Changes that made these new forms of entertainment possible had taken place; three public halls, Union, Temperance, and Central, had been built and made gathering places.

Union Hall got its name from the fact that the building with its store on the ground floor was built as a cooperative enterprise. Neither record nor memory can give us any accurate account of entertainments that took place there. Tradition tells us that Chandler Cobb, the cabinet maker, used to store coffins in one end of the hall and that the coffins served as seats for some of the people at the entertainments. Maybe the people of that day found pleasure sitting on their own coffins.

Temperance Hall was built by members of the Sons of Temperance, as an investment. Of the various cooperative building enterprises in town, this was the only one that was ever financially successful. At one time it paid seven per cent to the shareholders. The lower part of the building was let for a store. The upper part served as a meeting place for the Sons of Temperance and as a gathering place for lyceums, lectures and other mild entertainments.

The Sons of Temperance was a very popular temperance

organization in the eighteen-fifties and sixties. It started in 1842 and grew rapidly. In 1860 there were two hundred divisions in the state. Although its purpose was to promote temperance, it was largely a social organization. At first, ladies were admitted to the meetings simply as visitors; later, they were allowed as members; but it was not until 1863 that they were permitted to vote. Before this time there had been, starting with 1813, such temperance societies as the Massachusetts Society for the Suppression of Intemperance, The American Temperance Society, The Temperance Legislative Society, The Massachusetts Temperance Union, The Cold Water Army, and the Washingtonians. Of course not all of them had Chapters or Divisions in Our Town. At the time that men and women were joining the Sons of Temperance, their children were becoming members of the Band of Hope. Hardly had the popularity of the Sons of Temperance waned, when the Good Templars came into being and outdistanced the Sons in membership. The Good Templars was the first temperance society to do full justice to women.

In Our Town, the Sons of Temperance socials vied with the Lyceum courses and lectures. Attend a lecture with Charles Hall:

"To Temperance Hall the people all flock,
Where Tim Bigelow enters at seven o'clock.
Enough there are present the seats to o'erfill;
He rises and speaks. The room is quite still.
His voice is clear as the notes of a bird.
He spoke fast and low, yet was easily heard.
When the lecture was over they mostly went home,
Some had companions and some went alone.
A few of the gay ones remained in the rear,
Stept in at the bar a crank organ to hear.
This music enlivened their spirits so much
They wished their dear friends might have had some just such.

> So they fed the musician and started away
> And under their windows the music went gay,
> Not organ alone the whole music made,
> The sweet tamberines plied to their aid.
> These gay serenaders went the whole round."

Another of the Hall papers tells of the Mansfield Lyceum. Our information this time is contained in a little hand-written sheet called *The Mansfield Villager*, said to be published once a fortnight. The issue we have at hand is for Feb. 25, 1854. Of the Lyceum it says:

"This institution seems to be doing its share by way of entertaining and instructing the citizens of this village. The order of their meetings according to the present arrangements is to occupy a part of the time in discussing and the remainder with reading *The Mansfield Villager*, or a lecture by Dr. Palmer, the lecture and paper coming on alternate Saturday evenings."

Listed as events of the week we read that "Hon. Henry Wilson of Natick will lecture in Temperance Hall, next Tuesday evening, at seven o'clock. The subject is America, past and present. Admittance 12½ cents for those not holding tickets for the course."

"Dr. Palmer will lecture in the Lyceum room next Saturday evening on fever. Admittance free."

This Dr. Palmer who played so important a part in furnishing programs for the Mansfield Lyceum course was one of our own physicians at that time.

Among the other lectures given about this time in Temperance Hall was one by a Mr. Alvord on Russia.

Rev. Mr. Bliss of Boston gave an enlightening address in the winter of '54, in the same hall. According to Mr. Hall's notes, he attempted to explain how this country came to be ours and not other peoples', and how it came to be Protestant and not Catholic. He made use of maps. When he spoke of

Massachusetts, he said it contained more than a million inhabitants and was capable of supporting twice as many. In the whole of the United States, he said, there was room enough for 900 million people, all of whom could find employment in the various industries carried on here. The land could produce enough to feed them all. In California, there was enough gold to clothe and educate them.

A diversion in which the Sons of Temperance indulged was the holding of Tea Parties. An old diary for 1860 records several for that winter. On March seventh and eighth, such parties were held two nights in succession.

We must not forget that the women of the churches were doing their part to sustain the social life of the community. An old hand bill advertises a "Social Levee" held by the Ladies' Benevolent Society of West Mansfield on Thursday, February 14, 1856. It was held in Franklin Hall, where a few years before the coal miners and the operatives of the Williams cotton factory were wont to gather.

This levee in Franklin Hall was to begin at 6½ o'clock. All persons, "whether citizens of said Town or not," were respectfully invited to attend. The tickets cost 12½ cents.

About this same time the ladies of the Congregational Church held a "Social Tea Party at the Bonnet Rooms of Hon. J. Rogers." The entertainment consisted of "A Post Office, Various Exhibits, a Concert of Old Folkes, and an Attractive Tea Table." The tickets for this, too, were 12½ cents. That seems to have been the popular price. The money was to be used to build the fence in front of the church.

Central Hall, the third hall at the center, older than Temperance Hall, and perhaps older than Union Hall, was part of the old church. At the end of the 1830's, after the Baptist and Congregational people had left the mother church and built meetinghouses of their own, the handful of people left behind were lost in the church with its gallery. There also was

SOCIAL LEVEE!

The Ladies of the Benevolent Society in

WEST MANSFIELD,

WILL HOLD A LEVEE ON

Thursday Eve., Feb. 14th,

AT

FRANKLIN HALL,

COMMENCING AT 6 1-2 O'CLOCK

All Persons, whether Citizens of said Town or not,
are respectfully invited to attend.

(Should the weather prove unfavorable, it will be postponed to the
first fair evening.)

The object is purely benevolent, and it is hoped
this appeal will meet with a generous response.

Tickets of Admission, 12 1-2 Cents.

TICKETS TO BE HAD AT THE DOOR.

West Mansfield, Jan. 30, 1856.

Mudge & Son's Press, 21 School Street, Boston.

a financial strain on those few people. Then it was that they conceived the idea of dividing the church building horizontally. The upper part would serve well for the church auditorium, while the lower part could be made into a hall and one or two smaller rooms. The hall was really needed, since except for the old brick schoolhouse and the ballroom of the Mulberry Tavern, there was no central gathering place. Union Hall at the north end, if it was built by this time, was a mile away and not a very good hall at that. Sometime, then, about 1840, the change in the meetinghouse was made.

This hall opened directly outdoors, without vestibule or entry. Something over a hundred could be seated there. At the front was a small stage. The hall and stage would look very crude and inadequate to us today, but in 1854, when our poetical historian, Charles N. Hall, wrote, it was considered very grand.

> "But underneath is spacious Central Hall,
> Where curtains are prepared to rise and fall
> That tableaux may at various times be seen.
> Now Uncle Tom, and sweet Evangeline.
> And once the priest, and bridegroom with his bride,
> Then, decked with flowers, twin sisters side by side."

A copy of the program, when Uncle Tom appeared in tableaux, on the evening of March 13, 1854, for a "Social Gathering" has been preserved. The program consisted of two parts. Part One had six numbers, including songs and recitations. Part Two opened with an original poem read by the author and was followed by fifteen tableaux and pantomimes from "Uncle Tom's Cabin." Most pathetic scenes were chosen, such as "Uncle Tom taking leave of his family," "Little Eva taking leave of the servants before her death," "Mr. St. Clare's death," and "News of Uncle Tom's death reaches the Cabin."

These tableaux were but the forerunner of plays that were presented in the hall fifteen or twenty years later. In the 1870's plays were popular and much local talent was developed, especially by the Good Templars. One of these plays was "Down by the Sea."

"Ten Nights in the Barroom" made a great hit. The youthful Esther Dunham made up most excellently as the long-suffering drunkard's wife. Those who saw her, recall vividly how realistically she sobbed in her misery and sorrow. "Jake" Hagerdon, who was a molder at Chilson's Foundry at the time, was the drunkard.

Two lines from a song in another play suggests that all the drama was not tragedy:

> "Oh, dear, oh, dear, what have I done?
> I've married the father instead of the son."

There was a man in Our Town named William Blainey, who was excellent in Irish parts. He starred in "Handy Andy" and other Irish comedies.

All the entertainments were not by local talent. Imagine walking down street sixty or sixty-five years ago and seeing the full-length figure of a man, more than life-size, pictured on the side of the blacksmith shop, or any building that had space enough. The youngsters are calling, "Comical Brown has come to town." This happened every year, for a while. The evening that Comical Brown appeared on the little stage of Central Hall, the room was sure to be full. And what did he do? Just talked, sang, danced and made funny faces, but everything he said, or did, sent his audience into roars of laughter.

Another annual event was the Spaulding Bell Ringers entertainment. Year after year, this troupe of five or six Spauldings came to town, first to Central Hall and later to Lovell's Hall. The start of the family was Georgie Dean Spaulding.

who played with the bell ringers and also upon the harp. She was advetised as the greatest harpist in the country. The program which they gave was really very good.

Every year there were plenty of lectures scattered through the winter. Usually, the speaker was from out of town, though occasionally, a local man lectured. Tolman French, the cobbler, who had a broad knowledge of many subjects, was one of these local men. Tolie French, as he was generally called, was a California "Forty-niner," a Civil War soldier, and had traveled a bit besides. He was tall and thin and is said to have looked like Abraham Lincoln, except for his red hair. His one lecture was on "Valparaiso." In the front seat, when he delivered his lecture, was his war time comrade, Barlow Robinson. Tolie talked rapidly and his mouth grew dry. He stopped and said, "Barlow, I wish you'd get me some water." Barlow jumped up immediately. He was gone some time. When he returned he handed Mr. French the pitcher, which contained the water, and half a pint of gin, which he had procured at the drug store not far from the hall. Mr. French, a total abstinence man, poured out a glass of the water and took a sip. "Mighty man!" he exclaimed, "If I had had such water as this in California I never would have come back."

Tolie French was the central figure on one other occasion in the same hall. He became interested in politics and tried to run for representative. At town meeting he received thirty-five votes. To show his appreciation of those votes he gave an oyster supper in Central Hall to all who voted for him. Two hundred came. "Mighty man, if all these oyster eaters had voted for me, I would have been elected," was his excited comment.

We have already told of the minstrel shows given under the auspices of the Brass Band, and of the singing schools.

As there was no musical instrument in Central Hall, the music for singing and dancing was furnished by the violin.

About 1870 "Professor" Smith held a dancing school in Central Hall. The professor taught by playing the violin and dancing at the same time. The round dances, polka, waltz, and schotische, were introduced by this teacher. Dancing of this sort was highly disapproved of by all church members.

A form of entertainment sanctioned by the churches, and often conducted by them, was the Strawberry Festival, and also the Tea Party. These were well patronized and enjoyed.

Another harmless kind of amusement was attending auction. Once a year for several years, a man came with cheap crockery. He arrived in the day time and established himself in Central Hall. Two youngsters were always on hand. He gave them dinner bells and a nickel apiece and sent them out to announce the auction for that evening. Up and down the main street (few other streets existed then) they trudged.

"Auction! Auction tonight!" they shouted at the top of their lungs. You may be sure they got a crowd.

Some people would tell us that a town meeting held in Central Hall was another form of amusement. Certainly the boys sitting in the wide window seats considered it highly entertaining. Their eyes and ears took in all the fun furnished by the orators and debaters of those times; their noses caught the whiff of the coffee and huge buns that Charles Turner arranged on tables at the rear of the hall, back of the seats where the voters were sitting. Town meeting then was not an evening affair; it was an all day occasion.

All this time the town was growing; the urge for entertainment was increasing, and also need for more hall room. Temperance Hall, by the 1860's, was used chiefly by the Sons of Temperance and the Masons for their meetings in the evenings, and for private school in the day time. Central Hall was really too small to meet the new demands. More room, too, was needed for stores.

In 1870 Isaac Lovell, a storekeeper and butcher, built a

large building which included basement stores, first floor store, and two halls, the largest of which was long to be known as Lovell's Hall. Here were transferred the Lyceum lectures and entertainments, still in popular demand.

Among the noted lecturers was Dr. Dio Lewis, whose "doctor book" was a household authority in many homes. He came to Our Town several seasons, each time giving a series of lectures, and also, special talks to men and women separately. Dr. Lewis told people how to live, laying great stress on the importance of diet. He denounced rich food of all kinds. Dr. Lewis, some years later, died of indigestion. About the time that he was lecturing here, he had a sanitarium in Boston near the top of Beacon Hill. At that time there were not so many buildings, nor so tall ones, hence from the building where he was, there was an unobstructed view of the harbor in one direction, and over Medford, on toward New Hampshire, in another. On one occasion he had as a guest at the house a young woman who was studying French. She was charmed with the panorama. "Why don't you call it Belle Vue?" she exclaimed. He adopted her suggestion and it became Bellevue. The name has stuck, his building became the nucleus for the Hotel Bellevue, on Beacon Street.

Another medical lecturer was a Dr. Miller, who is said to have been a "nice" talker. His subjects were also health and hygiene.

There was also another Miller, a phrenologist, who lectured. The study of phrenology had a following in the late 1870's and the early '80's. By feeling a man's head, Mr. Miller could discover small "bumps," which indicated certain brain development and by which he could determine the individual's characteristics and along what lines of work he was most apt to succeed.

A lecturer who caused quite a sensation was Mrs. Ann Elizabeth Young, the 19th wife of Brigham Young, noted

Morman prophet. She came on January 20, 1875. Just how Our Town happened to be so lucky as to get her does not appear, for according to the newspaper of the time, she was a one hundred dollar lecturer, coming at a reduced price. She had a full house. For one hour and a quarter her audience listened attentively while she described her life with the other eighteen wives in Salt Lake City.

It almost seems as if there were more nightly "doings" in Lovell's Hall around fifty years ago than there are in the auditorium of the Town Hall today. Take for example the winter of 1876-77, in the middle of the six year depression of 1873 to 1879, which affected the whole world and was a time of bank failures and unemployment in the United States. The season began on October 19, when the hall was crowded to hear Maynard and Hatton, popular blind singers. "It was the best musical that Our Town had enjoyed for many a day." They introduced one innovation that seems a bit unusual; the audience paid to go out, rather than to come in. It is said that they received just as much, or more.

Thanksgiving week was full to overflowing. On Tuesday evening there was a Band Concert, a real eighteen piece band, led by Pliny Cobb. In addition to the band music, there were five selections by two quartets.

Two nights later, Thanksgiving night, there was an operetta for the benefit of the Reform Club. This was more largely attended, even, than the Band Concert. The *Mansfield News* the next day said that the hall "was perfectly jammed and altogether the audience must have been physically uncomfortable, whether sitting, standing, or hanging up." "All were delighted," it added. The name of the operetta was "Grandpa's Birthday."

All through the winter the people of the Methodist Church, having no building of their own, were holding their religious services in the hall and often furnishing entertainments at fifteen cents a ticket.

Sometimes during the winter there was a concert by the Alabama Jubilee Singers.

The crowning event of the season was the cantata, "The Flower Queen," the culmination of the singing school, conducted in the Orthodox Church vestry by Mr. Skinner, during the winter. The event was scheduled for March 26th. The tickets sold "like hot cakes" as soon as they were put on sale.

Every week the Reform Club was holding weekly meetings with free entertainments in Lovell's Hall.

By 1870 the popularity of the Sons of Temperance and the Good Templars had declined, and in their place, another organization came in on the wave of a new temperance reform. It grew from a Reform Club started in 1872 by some converted inebriates in Gardiner, Maine. Their motto was "Dare to do right." The next year, there were nineteen such clubs in Massachusetts. Our Town did not get into line until 1876. The neighboring town of Foxboro was ahead of us and on the evening of May 3rd came with a delegation to help us organize.

The speaker of the evening was Major A. D. Welch of the New England Reform Club of Providence. He was followed by J. E. Carpenter, president of the Foxboro Club. John Dill, also of Foxboro, told the story of his release from rum and said that before his reform he had come to Our Town hundreds of times and always got all he wanted. Others told reform stories, both amusing, and sad; Mr. Ide of the Congregational Church made remarks, both serious and witty. Father Blain, who had formerly preached in the Baptist Church, said that he had made his first temperance speech fifty years before. Feelingly, with tears running down his cheeks, he told of having stood at death beds and over open coffins where widows or orphans wept over the remains of drunkards. The music was furnished by a chorus of the best singers in town, supported by a several piece orchestra. Lustily they sang temperance parodies on "When Johnnie Comes Marching Home," "Rally, O Ye Friends of Temperance," and "The Battle Cry of Freedom." Before the meeting closed, pledges were circulated. One hundred signed. The Foxboro delegation was of great assistance in soliciting the signatures and obtained many from their old barroom associates.

On the next Friday evening the second meeting was held. Lovell's Hall was crowded in every part. At this meeting there was a delegation from Stoughton. The president and several members of the Stoughton club spoke. Mr. Mills of Stoughton said that he had drunk rum for twenty years, but had now reformed. He described his home town as having been the banner town in the state for rum. Seventy-five new names were added. A larger proportion than before were names of men who had been addicted to drink.

By the third meeting there were four hundred and fifty members. At the end of two months the Club had over six hundred members.

Something unusual happened at the third meeting. A woman spoke! The news of a woman speaking in meeting must have reached Foxboro, for the following week at the meeting of the Reform Club of Foxboro someone had the temerity to suggest that he would like to hear from some of the women present. The President was on his feet in an instant with objections. In expressing his disapproval, he said it savored of women's rights. Thereupon, the women were displeased and many left the hall. Some of the men championed the women and President Carpenter resigned. It began to look as if the Foxboro Temperance Reform Club would become a Suffrage Reform Club. The executive committee refused to accept the president's resignation. The matter was finally straightened out, probably the women promised to be good, and all went smoothly on. In Our Town the women continued to have part in the meetings and also had a temperance club of their own. That was called the Amaranth Temperance Club.

After the men's Reform Club became well launched, local orators were developed and many dramatic tales were told. One of the orators was Dennis Lovett, who told his life story as a drinking man, and as a teetotaler, when he enjoyed a "level head." From then on, Dennis became a star member of the club. He was made one of the vice-presidents and always sat on the platform and spoke in the meetings. Dennis said that he had been a drunkard for thirty years and that no one until then had advised him to stop drinking. That was hardly true, if we can believe all we hear. It is said that his wife advised him many times, even at times adding physical persuasion to the advice. They lived at the far north end of the town. On one day in particular, Dennis had been forbidden to go down town. That was one of the days when he had a level head. He went out in the yard and tied one of his wife's hens by its leg to a high limb of a tree. The squawking hen attracted her attention. With a ladder, she went to rescue it. As she stepped from the ladder to the limb, Dennis removed the ladder. With his wife and the hen high up in the tree, he made his get-away and trotted down town to get his drink. That, of course, was before he was reformed.

Another man to sit on the platform, but one who never spoke, was Gov. Walsh of Kansas. This man held no public office, nor did he live far away. He was one of our men living in that part of the town that for no reason at all was called Kansas. Gov. Walsh attained his title by his clothes, chiefly his up-standing collar, the points of which reached nearly to his ears, and his general dignified bearing. Governor Walsh was a drinking man for sixty years, but through the efforts of the Reform Club he reformed, and, unlike Dennis Lovett, he stayed reformed. Poor Gov. Walsh! They tell us that he met his death by falling down stairs and breaking his neck, when perfectly sober.

While the Club could point with pride to the reform of Gov. Walsh, there were many who caused discouragement. More than once the president had to speak words of reproof to those who had broken their pledges.

The weekly meetings continued, sometimes with outside speakers and sometimes with local entertainment. One speaker who came here for a Saturday night and two Sunday meetings was Dr. Reynolds. He had been a drinking man for twenty years, had squandered $30,000, had had delirium tremens; then reformed.

For several years the Club remained strong, then, as such things do, the attendance dropped off and finally the organization disbanded. To the glory of the Club be it said that there were many hard-drinking men who, through the influence of the club, gave up rum forever.

CHAPTER TWENTY-TWO

Dances and Indoor Athletics

NEVER think that all our young people were satisfied with singing schools and lectures, or hearing reformed drunkards tell of their inebriate days. Many liked to dance.

Every tavern catered to that desire, and the ballroom was as important at the supper table. Often for the young men, it was a choice between going to singing school to practice

> Heaven has confirmed the dread degree,
>> That Adam's race must die:
> One general ruin sweeps them down—
>> And low in dust they lie.
>
> Ye living men, the tomb survey,
>> Where you must shortly dwell;
> Hark! how the awful summons sounds,
>> In every funeral knell!

or hanging around the tavern to hear the fiddler sing "Begone Dull Care," beginning,

> "My wife shall dance and I will sing,
>> And merrily pass the day."

A bowl of egg pop, or milk punch, or a sling made of rum, sugar and nutmeg, enlivened the evening.

Before the days of the railroad, the taverns in Our Town were built on the main roads to catch the travel between Taunton and Worcester, or Taunton and Boston. The Mulberry Tavern especially got a good deal of patronage from sailors going from New Bedford to Boston. These guests were frequently boisterous and hilarious.

Quite naturally as the more fastidious young people shunned the taverns, kitchen dances became popular.

The opening of Central Hall was a boon to dance lovers and when Lovell's Hall was built that became a rival dancing place. One of the opening events of the latter was a Calico Ball.

The halls were very nice for winter, but rather close and stuffy in summer. Then came dance boards. The first one was built about 1870, in Clark's Grove beside the blacksmith shop where Simeon Clark repaired broken rails for the railroad, and was conducted by Cobb's Cornet Band.

A little later a similar board was built at Happy Hollow, near where McMoran and Robinson had built their knife shop on the site of the old Williams cotton factory. Robinson was running the knife shop at that time and the dance board was set close by his house on the water's edge. In fact, a part of it was actually built over the water. Delightfully cool it must have been. To these dances came people from Attleboro, Mansfield Center, as well as from West Mansfield, and perhaps from Foxboro. Kite Sherman played the fiddle for the dances. From what we have heard he could easily have been the whole show. It has been said that he could dance, play the fiddle, and call off, all at the same time. Two of his favorite tunes were "The Girl I Left Behind Me" and "Pop Goes the Weasel." He could make the weasel pop, too. Dances were never slow when he was around. He kept the dancers stepping lively. When he yelled, "Swing your partners," they *swung* their partners. Now it chanced that one couple swung so vigorously that they bumped into the none too substantial railing. Splash! Splash! The railing had given away and the couple were in the water. There was no chance for a heroic rescue, for the water was shallow.

There were, in time, several other dance boards around town, but the most popular was the one in Sodom, run by the people of the Swedenborgian Church, near the pond by

Fisher's basket shop. The board was built in a clump of trees and not near enough the water to be dangerous to rapidly swinging partners.

Dancing everywhere was threatened in popularity, about 1880, by roller skating. Mr. S. C. Lovell realized what was going on in other towns and quickly put his hall in condition to be used as a rink. Skates were procured and all was soon in readiness. Mrs. Lovell abetted her husband in this enterprise. She not only encouraged him, but she had her own skates and in secret went over to practice so that she might be a proficient enough skater to aid beginners. The hall was open every evening from seven until ten o'clock. Admission to the floor was ten cents for those who owned their own skates. To any who wished to hire skates, fifteen cents additional was charged. All skates left in the anteroom were kept oiled and in good condition. Now and then there was a fancy dress party that was a real event and called forth a good deal of ingenuity in costuming. One of the first of these, if not the first, was on April 23, 1881. Aside from advertising in the *Mansfield News,* cards were given out. These cards were about the size of a postal and showed a colored picture of a gay scene. On it was printed the notice of the "Fancy Dress Roller Skating Party in Lovell's Hall." (Such advertising cards were frequently used in the eighties, and children attracted by their bright colors made a hobby of collecting them.) For this particular party the hall was gayly trimmed with paper festoons, and we suspect that Mrs. Lovell had something to do with that. We know that she interested herself in planning and helping about the costumes, even going into Boston to pick out costumes for those who wished to hire. Some paid as much as ten dollars for the rental of their garments. The night came and the hall was filled. Mr. Lovell appeared as King Charles, resplendent in red velvet. Mrs. Lovell made a spritely gypsy girl.

The skating parties were conducted as at a dance, couples skated together and all went in the same direction. To these parties came everybody; rich and poor, high and low. There was no class distinction. Everything was orderly and no disturbance ever occurred, though sometimes amusing things happened, as when dignified Mrs. Hastings, dressed in a handsome black silk dress, slipped and slid across the floor. There was music, of course, for these parties and Cobb's Band rendered lively tunes. Sometimes the couples sang as they skated. One favorite song was:

> Where was Moses when the light went out?
> Where was Moses? What was he about?
> Now my little man, tell me if you can,
> Where was Moses when the light went out?

Just how long the fad continued to be popular we are unable to say.

There have always been fads in amusements. Before roller skating became the rage, the young men took up velocipede riding in Central Hall. Do not picture any sort of vehicle such as children ride to-day. Those velocipedes had two large, iron-tired, wooden wheels; the front one as large as a cart wheel, while the rear one was slightly smaller. Nor were these creations in any way like the bicycles which appeared years later on the street. The seat of this kind of velocipede was over the front part of the rear wheel; the handle-bar was a straight piece of wood; there was no gearing. This sport was introduced by the versatile Cobb brothers, Elbridge and Alson. They brought four velocipedes, three large and one small, to the hall to be let by the hour. The riding, enlivened by the Cobbs' music, was a nightly performance and drew quite an audience.

Jave Lawson did some specialty stunts. Charlie Shepardson, even more of an entertainer, rode around the hall with three or four small boys on his shoulders, or hanging on wherever they could.

The fad might have lasted indefinitely had not the trustees of the hall realized how fast the floor was wearing away under the iron tires and refused to let the hall for velocipede riding.

Another amusement craze was the walking match. Walking matches were not indigenous to Our Town. They, like the endurance tests of more recent years, had a boom all over the country. There were all-day walking matches, seven-day walking matches, songs about walking one thousand miles in one thousand hours, and indoor walking matches.

These indoor meets in Our Town were held in Lovell's Hall. In the center of the main room sat the audience; the path for the walkers was around the outside. Round and round they went, two, three, four, even at times five men. On and on they traveled, until they had covered ten miles. A timekeeper sat at one side and announced their progress as they crossed the line. The band was playing all the while. A champion could walk ten miles in one hour and forty minutes. There was a prize, or prizes, offered, and plenty of excitement.

The winning contestants, accompanied by walking match fans, often went to other towns and cities, particularly Providence, to compete.

CHAPTER TWENTY-THREE

Horse Racing

WHILE THE young men enjoyed indoor velocipede riding and walking matches, the older men gratified their sporting instincts by racing horses.

The first race track was Main Street. That course, starting at a big elm by the Common and measuring a mile, served very well for a time, then some of the horsemen wanted a real racing track. Consequently, in 1869, a meeting was called in Central Hall to talk it over. Enthusiasm ran high; upon the spot they organized the Mansfield Trotting Association. One of the members of the new organization called attention to just the piece of land they wanted. With true sporting spirit, and no haggling as to whether they could afford it, they bought the area, which on the east side of the land had a fine spring; hence, the name they chose: Mineral Spring Trotting Park.

The course they laid out was half a mile. The men gave their services to make the track, a poor track maybe, but their own.

After a few years the association sold out to John Holmes. John Holmes was a sporting character of his day, a large man, weighing some two hundred and fifty pounds, of fine physique. For several years he had run the Eagle Hotel, conducted turkey raffles, and a pool room. After he bought the Park he continued his hotel, and his son, John, Jr., went to the race course to live. Mr. Holmes improved the track and built eight or ten horse sheds near the entrance, back to the road. He owned six or eight horses, among them one of the best known was Light Foot. Races were held there all through the summer, perhaps once a week. The men who had formed the association earlier continued their interest. Holmes sometimes offered prizes, never in cash, but usually in oats, twenty or thirty bushels.

The love of horses in the Holmes family was not confined to the men. Mrs. Holmes was a good horsewoman and sat well in the saddle. Florence Holmes, the daughter-in-law, rode equally well, and now and then took part at the race track. Sometimes she was the only woman riding; sometimes she raced with Annie Twitchell of Framingham.

A speed race was common; to vary the program a slow race was sometimes introduced. Alden Fuller's Old Molly never liked to hurry and when she was entered in the slow race she poked along at her usual gait, and won.

Old Molly lost one race, or was it some other horse of Alden Fuller's? That race was unscheduled, nor did it have the distinction of the race track, but it furnished fun for the spectators. The idea started at the Mulberry Tavern. Somebody bet that Charles Williams' bull could beat Alden Fuller's horse. Thereupon, Charles Williams said it could. Alden Fuller took him up. The owner of the animal that won was to have a free dinner at the Tavern. The race took place on Main Street; traffic was held up; everybody watched. The bull won. Charles Williams ate the dinner with relish.

Mr. Williams was satisfied with one winning; he never entered the bull at the Trotting Park.

Eventually, John Holmes decided the city was more to his taste. He sold out his tavern, left the Trotting Park and buildings without a tenant, and went to Boston, there to run a hotel and bar on Tremont Street. After Holmes left the track, the buildings became a resort for tramps. Finally, the building burned and nobody was greatly stirred. Neither Holmes, nor anyone else, saw fit to rebuild. In the course of the time the place was offered for mortgage sale.

There was an ambitious young man of twenty taking care of horses in Foxboro and just waiting for such an opportunity. For $500 he bought the fifty acres. Some years later, after he had built it up, he refused $15,000 for it. All his life this young man, Frank Brawn, had lived with horses and knew the ways of horses and horsemen. His father worked at the Goodwin Stock Farm in Wolfsboro, New Hampshire, and when but a lad, Frank was sent with two horses from the New Hampshire farm to Dan Mace's Flashing Stud Farm, Long Island. Brawn remained for a time and while there, Mace offered a prize to the boy who would keep his horses and stalls neatest. Frank Brawn won and was awarded a good suit of clothes.

With just that attitude toward his work, Mr. Brawn built up the Mineral Spring Trotting Park. He built a large barn, also shed stalls on the opposite side of the track. On the outside and the inside of the track, which he graded, he built a fence. Later, when he married, he built a fine house.

He started with three horses of his own, then increased the number. He boarded and trained horses for other people. Frequently he had fifteen to twenty horses in training. At one time there were twenty horses in the stalls and twenty-one in the pasture.

Races, with an admission fee of twenty-five cents, were held at the Trotting Park on holidays and usually on Saturday afternoons, and often attracted two or three hundred people.

After Mr. Walter M. Lowney came to Our Town to conduct his chocolate factory, he became much interested in the races and sometimes served as one of the judges.

Mr. Brawn owned the Mineral Spring Trotting Park from 1882 until 1912, when his health began to break and he sold the property.

Just beyond Brawn's Trotting Park was John W. Cobb's horse farm.

It is a question whether Mr. Cobb enjoyed most the owning of a speedy horse, the raising of a likely colt, or the entering into a good horse trade. Certain it is that he got a great deal of pleasure out of all three. His most famous horse was J. W. C. and his most famous horse trade was the J. W. C. episode.

Raising horses was the avocation of Mr. Cobb's later life. He had acquired his fortune in the real estate business in Melrose and Malden. Before returning to his native town he bought a foundry in Taunton. At the foundry, one day, a man appeared to him and wanted to swap a horse for one hundred and fifteen dollars' worth of cheap stoves. Mr. Cobb, a good judge of horses, thought that while the horse was good enough looking, it was only a plodder, yet worth the stoves, and he took up the offer. Later, he returned to Our Town to live on the old Cobb place in Sodom and used the new horse in the express wagon to drive back and forth from Sodom to a farm he had bought. One day he remarked to his nephew, James R. Cobb, who was working with him, that he would like to know if there was any speed in the horse and asked Jim if he could ride. Whereupon Jim jumped on the horse, bareback, and started for the Four Corners. Nothing happened until he turned the horse to go back to the farm, then, a liberal use of the whip brought Jim to the farm as fast as he cared to travel bareback. There was speed! From that time, the horse became J. W. C., a pacer, and was promoted from the express wagon to the race track, receiving his training, first, at Mason's farm in Taunton, and later, on Brawn's track. Ultimately, J. W. C. was in the 2:23 class and won many prizes. Every time that J. W. C. won a prize, the men at the farm knew it, for Mr. Cobb always bought the horse a new harness or a new blanket.

Though Mr. Cobb sometimes had as many as ten horses and colts (never a cow) at his farm, he coveted any horse that would go faster than his own. Frank Bessom, his niece's husband, had a beautiful horse named Gray Eagle that could beat any Cobb horse and Mr. Cobb wanted it. Gray Eagle had a history. He began his racing career in Canada under the name of Billy A. His next home was East Boston, where as a ringer he was given the name of Gray Eagle. It was there that Mr. Bessom found him and for him traded in a colt that had been slightly injured.   Next, Mr. Bessom, owner of a grocery store at the time, traded Gray Eagle to E. E. Ellis of New Bedford for $275, twenty barrels of molasses, twenty cases of canned beets, a large quantity of B. L. tobacco, and some other things. Ellis failed after he bought Gray Eagle and Mr. Bessom bought the horse back for $110.   It was then that John Cobb wanted the horse.   The trade was made.   John Cobb gave up two house lots, and another horse for Gray Eagle.

There was never a time when Mr. Cobb lacked for horse interest.   On one side was Frank Brawn, his race track and training ground; and on the other, A. A. Austin, a writer for the *American Horse Breeder*, and owner of fast horses.   One colt in particular won Mr. Austin a lot of money in prizes and was finally sold for $1,600.

There were many good horses about town.   In winter, at least in the gay nineties, one did not have to go to the Trotting Park to see them race.   Main Street after a fall of snow made a perfect speedway.   What fun those men had!   After the first good snow storm they prepared their race track.   They sometimes used a wooden horse drawn roller.   That, however, balled up, if the snow was wet, and they found that heavy planks drawn over the snow were more effective.   The distance they raced was about a third of a mile.   There were spectators along the way, but the greatest gathering was at Lovell's corner, which was considered "under the wire."

Unforeseen events in connection with these races sometimes occurred.   Usually precaution was taken to hold up traffic during the races, especially at Lovell's corner.   One day, however, nobody was on the job and two girls came driving through from West Street into East Street.   Just then, Jesse Smith, driving Hardroad, raced his opponent down the street. Hardroad was a hard drinker.   Before each race he had to have a pint of whiskey, which he loved.   On this particular day the horse was "loaded" as usual.   At Lovell's corner he struck the girls' sleigh. What saved the girls nobody knows; a heavy fur cap with ear laps is said to have saved Jesse Smith from death. The girls' horse received an injury that laid him up for the rest of the winter. Hardroad was a "hit and run" horse. He stopped for nothing until he turned in at the stable back of the hotel a few rods further on. There, they found him, leaning up against the building.

This form of sport extended over a number of years and was given up only when the electric car line to Taunton was put in. An electric car on the race course was more than even Jesse Smith's Hardroad could buck up against.

To-day, a bus takes the place of the trolley car. There is a traffic light at Lovell's corner. The Mineral Spring Trotting Park is an airport.

CHAPTER TWENTY-FOUR

Torchlight Parades

OUR GRANDEST torchlight parades were in the fall of 1880, the year of the Garfield and Arthur campaign. The first one came on Saturday night, October 16, and was started by the North End Republican Club. The club was less than a week old and had begun with the supposedly unlucky number of thirteen members. Perhaps General Grant, passing through the town the day after they organized, took away the curse of the numeral. Anyhow, the membership quickly increased and plans for a parade were put through with alacrity and energy.

The opening feature was to be a parade, rally, and flag raising. It was the first time that Our Town had ever tried to do anything just like this. Nevertheless, they planned to make it a grand affair. Not content with getting out the whole town, they invited Attleboro and Foxboro. It was a dash of cold water when the day before the event Attleboro sent word that they could not come. It was a slap in the face when the night before they heard that Foxboro could not, or would not, come because two of the men on the Foxboro campaign committee had not been formally invited. The local committee, discouraged, but undaunted, started for Boston Saturday morning. At three o'clock in the afternoon they had one hundred uniforms and one hundred men to fill the uniforms. Hopes began to rise. Two men drove to Foxboro to issue an official invitation to the two Foxboro men whose dignity had been offended. The Foxboro men graciously accepted in spite of the lateness of the formal invitation. The Attleboro men, at the last moment, decided that they could come.

At 7:10 the "Tin Kettle" train from Providence pulled in, bringing the Attleboro Battalion under the command of

Major Horton. The procession formed at once. The escort was the North End Republican Club under Captain John H. Howe. The chief marshal of the parade was T. S. Pratt, the editor of the *Mansfield News*. In line was Cobb's Band, Foxboro Drum Corps, Foxboro Torchlight Club, Attleboro Battalion, composed of Company A, the "Boys in Blue," Company B, "Young Republicans," and Company C, the "Garfield Guards." The North End Club carried transparencies with their name on the sides, and "Garfield and Arthur" on the ends. The Foxboro men bore American flags. The Attleboro transparencies were in the form of canal boats. The whole route of a mile and a half was brilliantly illuminated. This was before the days of street lights and to assist in making the transparencies and house lighting more effective, the moon hid itself behind a cloud. One of our marching torchbearers was Captain Charles Day, then eighty-five years old, a veteran of the war of 1812, yet sprightly on his feet. It was a wonderful parade; said to have been the largest in the country, except in the cities.

Upon arrival at the Lovell Building, the flag was flung out from the Hall on a line to the Methodist Church across the street. The band played "Hail Columbia" and three cheers were given for the flag and the names it bore. Addresses were given by Judge Reed and Rev. Jacob Ide, the most brilliant minister in town, from the balcony at Lovell's Hall.

After the speeches, a collation was served at the Depot Restaurant, with plenty for all invited guests. The Attleboro people, especially, expressed themselves as much pleased with their reception. The campaign was well launched.

Every Republican was filled with ardor for the cause. Even the stork was aroused to activity and that night left twin boys in a Republican cradle. Next morning the proud father announced their arrival and promised that if Garfield and Arthur were elected he would name the twins for them. After the election the babes were named James Garfield Bryant and Chester Arthur Bryant.

On Oct. 26, two companies of Our Town men, numbering 120 in all, accompanied by Cobb's Band, went by special train to Taunton to join in their torchlight parade. Attleboro sent four companies and Norton one. In all there were 1,400 in line at Taunton. It was a year of big parades. In Boston they had a procession longer than the route laid out.

On Oct. 29, the Mansfield Garfield Guards took part in the celebration in Foxboro. Nov. 1, two companies of Garfield Guards, ninety strong, took a special train for Attleboro. A thousand men marched that night.

The next day, Nov. 2, was election day. The polls were open from 10:10 A.M. until 2:10 P.M. Our Town, with a population of 2,765, which of course, included men, women and children, had a small number of voters. Three hundred and thirteen votes were cast for the Republican ticket.

By no means did the red hot Republicans settle down as soon as the election was over. At once they planned a Victory Parade to be held the following night. While the women of that day were not voters, neither were they drones. They came forward with the offer of a complimentary supper in Central Hall.

The Town outdid itself in brilliancy on the night of this parade. Many had feared that the half-moon would dull the effect of their illumination, but that romantic luminary accommodatingly drew a veil over its face.

At seven o'clock, sharp, the two companies of the Mansfield Guards, Cobb's Band, and the Clean Sweep Battalion, began to arrive on Central Street where the procession formed. At 7:45, they were under way, headed by the marshal, T. S. Pratt. The torchbearers formed the advance guard. Then came Cobb's Band of twenty pieces, followed by Company A, the Boy Battalion, each boy carrying a broom and a transparency,

"A Clean Sweep"; Company B was next, and lastly citizens in carriages. There were fully two hundred in line. It took a long while to complete the march, for at every lighted house they stopped and gave three cheers, and most of the houses were specially lighted.

To be sure, there were some Democratic houses in total darkness. Red fire was burned in many a yard, Chinese lanterns and transparencies floated from wires strung from houses to trees, red railroad lanterns were given a new use, candles were set in windows. People not on the line of march gathered by the roadside, some of them in fantastic garb and bearing transparencies, "Hold the Fort." On balconies and in yards were tableaux. In the Judge Reed yard were numberless flags and his young daughter posed there with an immense rooster in her arms. John Rogers, the owner of the straw shop, decorated his yard with stuffed birds, stuffed animals, swaying lanterns and unfurled flags. This parade, as planned, extended over a longer route than the first one. By request they marched an extra mile and a half to pay their respects to Ira Richardson, that irrepressible captain, who in 1833, had fired the salute at Pawtucket Bridge when President Jackson and Vice-President Van Buren came into Massachusetts.

An hour or so later, the line filed into Central Hall and the men enjoyed the good supper the women had prepared for them.

After supper the men rose and gave three cheers for the women. The women tried to give three cheers for the men. Then they all gave three cheers for Garfield and Arthur.

Thus ends the tale of a plain people and a romantic age. Perhaps Mansfield of the twentieth century will also have a quaint appearance in retrospect. If so, the curious narrator will have such subjects as cleats and spikes for the shoes of athletes, taps and dies for automobiles and airplanes, flowers for the city florists, sweet and coating chocolate, and foundry fixtures for the modernistic fireplace.

These, and the way they fit into the complex twentieth century, will be a patchwork quilt of a different pattern.

THE END

Sources

My father's love for his native town, and the old desk which he had filled with three generations of original documents and account books, provided the initial impulse to write this book.

A large part of my material has come by word of mouth from scores of elderly people, many of whom have not lived to see this book.

Old files of *The Mansfield News*, the *Taunton Independent Gazette*, and the *Foxboro Reporter* have yielded many items.

To check up the local sources much time has been spent in the Bristol County Registry of Deeds, and the Registry of Probate in Taunton, and also in examining the records of the Court of Common Pleas in the same city. Books have been consulted in the Boston Public Library, the State Library, the Baker Library at the Harvard Business School, the library and the museum of Railway and Locomotive Historical Society, located in the above mentioned Baker Library building, and the library of the Old Colony Historical Society in Taunton. Original documents have been examined in the State Archives and the archives of the Baker Library. The various persons from whom I have sought aid in these institutions have been most courteous and helpful. Especially I wish to thank Mr. Charles E. Fisher, president of the Railway and Locomotive Historical Society.

Bibliography

GENERAL

Early History of Factory Legislation in Massachusetts. (From 1825 to the passage of the 10-hour law in 1874.) By Charles Edward Persons. Boston, 1911. Found at the State Library in *Labor Laws and Their Enforcement*, pages 1-129.

Economic and Social History of New England. 1620-1789. 2 vols. By William Babcock Weeden. Boston. Houghton, Mifflin and Company. 1890.

Historical address of Hon. Edmund H. Bennett, pages 29-77 of *Quarter Millennial Celebration of the City of Taunton, Massachusetts*. Published by the City Government, Taunton, 1889.

Historical address of Hon. E. P. Carpenter. 29 pp. In *Foxborough's Official Centennial Record*. Published by the Authority of the Town Centennial Committee. 1879.

History of Massachusetts Industries, their inception, growth and sources. By Orra Laville Stone. Boston. The S. J. Clarke Publishing Company, 1930.

History of American Manufactories from 1608 to 1860. 3 volumes. By John Leander Bishop. Philadelphia. E. Young. 1867-8.

History of Manufacturing in the United States. 1667-1860. By Victor Sheldon Clark. Washington. Carnegie Institution Publications. No. 215 B. 1916.

History of Taunton, Massachusetts, from its settlement to the present time. By Samuel Hopkins Emery. Syracuse, N. Y. Mason and Company. 1893.

History of the Town of Norton, Bristol County, Massachusetts, from 1669 to 1859. By George Faber Clark. Boston. Crosby, Nichols and Company. 1859.

Industrial Evolution of the United States. By Carrol D. Wright. New York, Flood and Vincent. 1895.

Industrial History of the United States. By Katherine Coman. New York. The Macmillan Company. 1933.

The Industrial Worker. 1840-1860. By Norman J. Ware. Boston. Houghton, Mifflin Company. 1924.

Industries of American Manufacturing. By Robert Malcolm Keir. New York. Ronald Press. 1928.

Industries of Massachusetts. Published by the Associated Industries of Massachusetts.

Laws of the General Court of the Commonwealth of Massachusetts.

Private and Special Statutes of the Commonwealth of Massachusetts.

Resolves of the Commonwealth of Massachusetts.

New England Historical Genealogical Register.

Statistics of the condition and products of certain branches of industry in Massachusetts for the year ending April 1, 1845. Prepared by John G. Palfry, Secretary of the Commonwealth. Boston. State printer. 1846.

Statistical information relating to certain branches of industries in Massachusetts from the year ending June 1, 1855. Prepared from official returns, by Francis Dewitt, Secretary of the Commonwealth. Boston. W. White, State printer. 1856.

Statistical information relating to certain branches of industry in Massachusetts for the year ending May 1, 1865. Prepared by Oliver Warner, Secretary of the Commonwealth. Boston. Wright and Potter, State printer. 1866.

COTTON

Brief History of the Conditions of Women in Various Ages and Nations. By Mrs. Lydia Maria Childs. (For wages of women in the cotton mills.) New York. C. S. Francis and Company. 1854.

Economic History of the United States. By Ernest Ludlow. Bogart. 1912.

Introduction and Early Progress of the Cotton Manufacture. By Samuel Batchelder. Boston. Little, Brown and Company. 1863.

RAILROADS

Boston and Providence Railroad Corporation. General Court; Committee on Railroads, 1839. Report and Bill concerning the Seekonk Branch Railroad Company and the Boston and Providence Railroad Corporation. State Senate Document. No. 49. 1839.

Boston and Providence Railroad Corporation. Report of Leonard M. Parker, Esq. made to the Legislature of Massachusetts on the subject of Railroads from Boston to Providence. 1828.

Boston and Providence Railroad Corporation. By a freeman of Massachusetts. (John Daggett, Attleboro.) Pamphlet. Boston. Printed by Light and Horton. 1834.

History of the Railways of Massachusetts. By Hon. Edward Appleton, Railway Commissioner. In the Official Topographical Atlas of Massachusetts. Boston. Stedman, Brown and Lyons. 1871.

Report of Board of Directors of Internal Improvements of the State of Massachusetts on the practicability and expedience of a Railroad from Boston to the Hudson River and from Boston to Providence. Submitted to the General Court, January 16, 1829.

BAKERY

Bakers and Baking in Massachusetts from 1620 to 1909. By Arthur W. Brayley. By authority of Master Baker's Association of Massachusetts. 1909.

COAL MINES

Final Report on the Geology of Massachusetts. Maps and 55 plates. By Professor Edward Hitchcock, State Geologist. 1841.

Massachusetts Geological Survey. 1837-44. By Professor Edward Hitchcock.

Report on Coal and Ancient Glaciers. By Professor Edward Hitchcock. 1853.

The three references on coal mines are to be found in the State Library, State House, Boston.

BOG IRON

Manufacture of Iron in New England. By James W. Swank. Vol. 1. Philadelphia. Published by the Author. 1884.

History of the Manufacture of Iron in All Ages, and Particularly in the United States. 1585-1885. By James M. Swank. 1885.

Ancient Iron Works in Taunton. By John Williams Dean Hall. Old Colony Historical Society Collection. No. 3. pp. 131-162. Taunton. 1885.

TAPS AND DIES

History of the Bolt and Nut Industry. By W. R. Wilbur.
Greenfield Tap and Die Corporation. Pamphlet. Greenfield, Mass.

YANKEE PEDDLERS

Hawkers and Walkers of Early America. By Richard Little Wright. Philadelphia. J. B. Lippincott. 1927.

STRAW BONNETS

Essay on the Manufacture of Straw Bonnets. Author unknown. Providence. 1825.

LAND BANK

Financial History of Massachusetts. Vol. 1. No. 4. By Charles Douglas.

Calendar of Land Bank Papers. Vol. IV. Colonial Society of Massachusetts. Massachusetts Archives. State House. Boston.

PEACE JUBILEES

History of the National Peace Jubilee and Great Musical Festival. Boston. June 1869. Boston. Lee and S. 1871.

National Peace Jubilee and Musical Reporter. May 15, June 17, June 27, July 24, 1869. Boston. Usher. 1869.

World Peace Jubilee. Pamphlet. All the references on the Jubilees to be found in the Boston Public Library.

TEMPERANCE SOCIETIES

History of the Temperance Reform in Massachusetts. 1813-1883. By George Faber Clark. Boston. Clark and Carruth. 1888.

CHURCH MUSIC

The Sabbath in Puritan New England. By Alice Morse Earle. New York. Charles Scribner's Sons. 1893.

"An Essay Preached by Several Ministers of the Gospel for the Satisfaction of Their Pious and Conscientious Brethren, as to Sundry Questions and Cases of Conscience, Concerning the Singing of Psalms. Boston. Printed by S. Kneeland and S. Gerrish, and sold at his shop in Corn Hill. 1723", in volume I of *The Ministry of Taunton*, by Samuel Hopkins Emery. Boston. John P. Jewett & Co. 1853.

MANSFIELD HISTORY

For purely local history see *Mansfield in Other Days*, Nos. 250— by Jennie F. Copeland, in the *Mansfield News.* Published by the Mansfield Press.

Index